Education Policy in Britain

CONTEMPORARY POLITICAL STUDIES SERIES

Series Editor: John Benyon, *University of Leicester*

Published

DAVID BROUGHTON
Public Opinion and Political Polling in Britain

JANE BURNHAM and ROBERT PYPER
Britain's Modernised Civil Service

CLYDE CHITTY
Education Policy in Britain: 2nd edn

MICHAEL CONNOLLY
Politics and Policy Making in Northern Ireland

DAVID DENVER
Elections and Voters in Britain: 2nd edn

JUSTIN FISHER
British Political Parties

ROBERT GARNER
Environmental Politics: Britain, Europe and the Global Environment: 2nd edn

ANDREW GEDDES
The European Union and British Politics

WYN GRANT
Economic Policy in Britain

WYN GRANT
Pressure Groups and British Politics

DEREK HEATER and GEOFFREY BERRIDGE
Introduction to International Politics

DILYS M. HILL
Urban Policy and Politics in Britain

RAYMOND KUHN
Politics and the Media in Britain

ROBERT LEACH
Political Ideology in Britain: 2nd edn

ROBERT LEACH and JANIE PERCY-SMITH
Local Governance in Britain

PETER MADGWICK
British Government: The Central Executive Territory

ANDREW MASSEY and ROBERT PYPER
Public Management and Modernisation in Britain

PHILIP NORTON
Parliament and British Politics

MALCOLM PUNNETT
Selecting the Party Leader

ROBERT PYPER
The British Civil Service

Forthcoming

CHARLIE JEFFREY
Devolution and UK Politics

Contemporary Political Studies Series
Series Standing Order ISBN 978-0-230-54350-8 hardback
Series Standing Order ISBN 978-0-230-54351-5 paperback
(outside North America only)

You can receive future titles in this series as they are published by placing a standing order. Please contact your bookseller or, in case of difficulty, write to us at the address below with your name and address, the title of the series and one of the ISBNs quoted above.

Customer Services Department, Macmillan Distribution Ltd
Houndmills, Basingstoke, Hampshire RG21 6XS, England

Education Policy in Britain

Second Edition

Clyde Chitty

palgrave
macmillan

First edition 2004
Second edition 2009

PALGRAVE MACMILLAN

Palgrave Macmillan in the UK is an imprint of Macmillan Publishers Limited, registered in England, company number 785998, of Houndmills, Basingstoke, Hampshire RG21 6XS.

Palgrave Macmillan in the US is a division of St Martin's Press LLC, 175 Fifth Avenue, New York, NY 10010.

Palgrave Macmillan is the global academic imprint of the above companies and has companies and representatives throughout the world.

Palgrave® and Macmillan® are registered trademarks in the United States, the United Kingdom, Europe and other countries.

ISBN-13: 978–0–230–22277–9 hardback
ISBN-10: 0–230–22277–3   hardback
ISBN-13: 978–0–230–22278–6 paperback
ISBN-10: 0–230–22278–1   paperback

This book is printed on paper suitable for recycling and made from fully managed and sustained forest sources. Logging, pulping and manufacturing processes are expected to conform to the environmental regulations of the country of origin.

A catalogue record for this book is available from the British Library.

A catalog record for this book is available from the Library of Congress.

10 9 8 7 6 5 4 3 2 1
18 17 16 15 14 13 12 11 10 09

Printed and bound in China

Contents

List of Boxes and Tables

Boxes

Tables

List of Abbreviations

AEAs	Advanced Extension Awards
ALL	Association of Language Learners
ATL	Association of Teachers and Lecturers
CASE	Campaign for the Advancement of, or Campaign for, State Education
CATs	Colleges of Advanced Technology
CBI	Confederation of British Industry
CCCS	Centre for Contemporary Cultural Studies
CNAA	Council for National Academic Awards
CPG	Conservative Philosophy Group
CPRS	Central Policy Review Staff
CPS	Centre for Policy Studies
CSE	Certificate of Secondary Education
CTCs	City Technology Colleges
DCSF	Department of Children, Schools and Families
DES	Department of Education and Science
DfE	Department for Education
DfEE	Department for Education and Employment
DfES	Department for Education and Skills
EAZs	Education Action Zones
ECM	Every Child Matters
ETS	Educational Testing Services
EYFS	Early Years Foundation Stage
FE	Further Education
FEVER	Friends of the Education Voucher Experiment in Representative Regions
GCE	General Certificate of Education
GCSE	General Certificate of Secondary Education
GNVQ	General National Vocational Qualification
HE	Higher Education
HEFC	Higher Education Funding Council

HMI	Her Majesty's Inspector, or Her Majesty's Inspectorate
HMSO	Her Majesty's Stationery Office
ICT	Information and Communications Technology
IEA	Institute of Economic Affairs
ILEA	Inner London Education Authority
IQ	Intelligence Quotient
LCC	London County Council
LEA	Local Education Authority
LSC	Learning and Skills Council
MSC	Manpower Services Commission
NAA	National Assessment Agency
NASUWT	National Association of Schoolmasters/Union of Women Teachers
NCC	National Curriculum Council
NCPTA	National Confederation of Parent Teacher Associations
NCVQ	National Council for Vocational Qualifications
NEETs	Those not in Education, Employment or Training
NFER	National Foundation for Educational Research
NUS	National Union of Students
NUT	National Union of Teachers
NVQ	National Vocational Qualification
NYEC	National Youth Employment Council
OECD	Organisation for Economic Co-operation and Development
Ofsted	Office for Standards in Education
OPEC	Organization of Petroleum-Exporting Countries
PFI	Private Finance Initiative
PISA	Programme for International Student Assessment
PSE	Personal and Social Education
PSHE	Personal, Social and Health Education
QCA	Qualifications and Curriculum Authority
ROSLA	Raising of the School-Leaving Age
SATs	Standard Assessment Tasks or Tests
SCAA	School Curriculum and Assessment Authority
SEAC	School Examinations and Assessment Council
SED	Scottish Education Department
SHA	Secondary Heads Association
TGAT	Task Group on Assessment and Testing
TSO	The Stationery Office
TUC	Trades Union Congress
TVEI	Technical and Vocational Education Initiative

Acknowledgements

My thanks are due to all my students at Goldsmiths College, past and present, who have never been reluctant to challenge many of the views expressed in this book and to provide alternative perspectives of their own. Above all, I owe a special debt of gratitude to Margaret Brittain, who has played such a major role in preparing my manuscript for publication.

CLYDE CHITTY

Introduction

This is the second edition of a book which was first published in 2004. It is a source of some frustration that the process of writing contemporary history can never have a full stop and that all judgements have to be transitory. Andrew Gamble, who has spent many years analysing post-war British politics, has written that 'there are few things more difficult than trying to make sense of contemporary political events and the direction in which they are moving' (Gamble, 1988: x). It is, of course, true that the confident assertions one is tempted to make can so easily be nullified by unforeseen happenings. Historian Eric Hobsbawm has gone so far as to suggest that contemporary issues are not really a proper subject for the historian. In an essay on the formation of British working-class culture, written in 1979, he argued that: 'like Britain itself, anchored in the nineteenth century, the British working class is in danger of losing its bearings. But its present situation and prospects are a subject for the reporter and the sociologist. They are not yet a subject for the historian' (Hobsbawm, 1984: 193). That said, this historian is grateful for the opportunity to bring the story of educational policy-making in Britain down to the Summer of 2008 and to repair some of the deficiencies and shortcomings of the earlier edition.

Traditionally, it has been customary to write about policy formulation in England and Wales (and it usually *has* been England and Wales, rather than Britain as a whole), treating these two countries as if they constituted a single entity. But this book has had to take account of some of the most important developments for centuries in terms of devolved power in the UK, with the establishment in 1999 of a Scottish Parliament, together with a separate Assembly for Wales, thereby signifying a major reduction in the power and influence of the Department for Education and Skills (more recently the Department for Children, Schools and Families), based in London.

England, Wales and Scotland share in many aspects a common educational history, but, as Ken Jones has pointed out, they are countries whose educational patterns have never been identical and 'whose trajectories seem now to be divergent' (Jones, 2003: 3). The social and political experience of Wales and Scotland in the period before 1939 provided a powerful impetus to the creation of the British Welfare State in the 1940s. And all three countries appeared to be in favour of the comprehensive reform of the 1960s. But in the last three decades, England has been pursuing educational policies, both radical and divisive, which have found little favour in Wales or Scotland. Certainly Scotland now prides itself on running a system that is more inclusive, more socially cohesive and less privatized than anything envisaged at Westminster. And this is a point to which we shall be returning in Chapter 4.

In all the chapters that follow, emphasis is laid upon the importance of the *historical* approach and upon the need to avoid seeing history as a succession of chance events or as just one thing after another. The argument propounded is that policy-making is always influenced by what has happened in past decades and that the historical account must always be presented within a coherent explanatory framework stressing the key themes underpinning political and social change.

Chapter 1 argues that, although all the main political parties talk in terms of the need to 'raise educational standards', particularly in state primary and secondary schools, there is less agreement about what this actually means *in practice* and how best to set about achieving it. It is pointed out that if we adopt a broad historical perspective, we find that raising educational standards for *all* children – indeed, the very idea of providing something that deserves to be labelled 'education' for *all* children – is a fairly recent concept for members of Britain's political establishment.

Chapter 2 argues that for around 30 years after the Allied victory in the Second World War, most of the establishment shared a tacit governing philosophy which embraced a three-fold commitment: to the necessity for full adult employment; to the co-existence of public and private sectors in the economy; and to the idea of a fully resourced Welfare State. Where education was concerned, the post-war consensus survived the local political battles over comprehensive schooling in the 1950s and 1960s, but began to break down in the mid-1970s, when economic recession fundamentally altered the map of British politics.

Chapter 3 follows on chronologically from Chapter 2, taking the story of education policy to the end of 18 years of Conservative government in 1997. It was after the mid-1970s that the post-war period of partnership and consensus was followed by two decades of reconstruction and conflict when even the well-established concept of 'a national education system, locally administered' came under sustained attack. Certainly legislation passed during the third Thatcher administration (1987–90) constituted a very real threat to the power and status of local education authorities.

The Labour Party gained a landslide victory in the General Election of May 1997 with a pledge to make education its top priority in government. Yet, as Chapter 4 shows, there was to be no real departure from the education agenda of the Thatcher and Major administrations. Where England is concerned, the New Labour modernizing project has meant marginalizing local education authorities and continuing with a divided system, particularly at the secondary level. All governments since 1979 have deemed it expedient to move away from the comprehensive ideal.

A relatively new feature of education in England is the steady growth of privatizing initiatives, and this is the subject of Chapter 5. Any history of privatization in education would have to take account of the intellectual and political influence of Keith Joseph, but Joseph failed to introduce the education voucher when he was Education Secretary and it is only in the last 20 years that we have seen privatization make major inroads into the education service. Chapter 5 devotes much space to the Private Finance Initiative, City Technology Colleges and Academies.

Chapter 6 goes *beyond* policy description and analysis to ask *how* specific policies and strategies come to be formulated. The argument is advanced that since the mid-1970s, political advisers and members of 'think-tanks' have usurped one of the key functions of the Education Department's bureaucracy. This means that key policies have often been devised by young idealists in the Downing Street Policy Unit which has recently been merged with the Prime Minister's Private Office to create the 'Policy Directorate' and is now in an even stronger position to further the process of moving away from *collective* to *presidential* government. This chapter also looks at the current situation in Scotland and Wales where there appears to be little inclination to emulate many of the policies on school organization, curriculum and assessment that have caused such anxiety and controversy in England.

The National Curriculum and its related testing arrangements have undergone a number of important changes since their introduction at the end of the 1980s. Many of the problems have been associated with the issue of excessive overload at Key Stage Four and these are discussed in Chapter 8; while Chapter 7 concentrates on the changes affecting Key Stages One, Two and Three. Both chapters recognize the importance of the 1993 Dearing Review (SCAA, 1993), which recommended a number of measures for 'slimming down' the Curriculum. Chapter 7 looks at the current controversy over what many see as England's rigid, centralized approach to teaching at the primary stage; and Chapter 8 ends by focussing on the debate about the future of GCSEs and A Levels and the possibility of replacing them with an English Baccalaureate (or series of Diplomas) designed to assess a broader range of academic and vocational subjects.

Chapter 9 is devoted to higher education which has been transformed since the middle of the last century from an *elite* to a *mass* system, the overall participation rate in England having increased from just 3 per cent in 1950 to just over 40 per cent today. The chapter looks at questions of equity and access in the light of the new fees structure laid down in the 2004 Higher Education Act; and once again it is emphasized that England is pursuing policy options not favoured by Scotland and Wales.

Chapter 10 brings together a number of separate issues: pre-school provision and childcare strategies and the concept of lifelong learning. It can be argued that New Labour has shown more interest in Early Years than has any other government in recent times; but the Early Years Foundation Stage (EYFS) curriculum framework, to be launched in the autumn of 2008, has provoked stiff opposition from a powerful lobby of leading authors and educationists. A belief in early intervention to improve the health, well-being and educational attainment of 'disadvantaged' children has led to a series of initiatives, from Sure Start to Children's Centres. And the *Every Child Matters* agenda can be seen as the Government's response to the death of Victoria Climbié in 2000. Having discussed these issues, the last section of the chapter looks at differing concepts of a learning society.

Chapter 11 examines a number of the topics which together represent a general broadening of the school curriculum and which also add considerably to the pastoral role of the teacher. Issues of equity and social justice are now expected to be on the agenda of every school in the country; and there is broad agreement that citizenship should form an important part of the school curriculum. It has become fashionable to talk in terms of the 'inclusive curriculum', although it is not always clear what this means in practice. What does seem beyond dispute is that there is no place in any school for practices that lead to unfair treatment and discrimination.

The Conclusion brings together some of the topics of the previous chapters and places them in an international context. It needs to be emphasized that the dominant themes of current government policy – the privatizing agenda, the concern to promote differentiation at the secondary level and the emphasis on teacher accountability – apply to England, but hardly at all to Wales and Scotland. It is still too early to assess the full impact of New Labour's education programme, but it can at least be argued that there has been no real attempt to depart from the policies of previous Conservative administrations and that the agenda set in the late 1980s is still alive and flourishing (albeit with modifications) in the early years of the twenty-first century.

1

Why Education Matters

This chapter deals with a number of related issues: the current concern with the raising of educational standards; the campaign for a state system of education and its fairly recent origins; and the whole question of what schooling is for.

All the major political parties vying for voters' support in Britain today would seek to assure the electorate that one of the primary objectives of their education policies is the raising of standards in all the country's institutions providing education for the young. Indeed, it is hard to see how they could hope to ally themselves with the wishes of parents (and, indeed, of all voters) if they said anything different since, according to the famous dictum of the great Socialist historian and political thinker R. H. Tawney, to be found in his 1931 classic work *Equality*: 'What a wise parent would desire for his [*sic*] own children, so a nation, in so far as it is wise, must desire for *all* children' (Tawney, 1931: 146). Naturally, all our political parties would wish to see 'wisdom' as one of their most significant and enduring contributions to political and educational discourse.

Before he was first elected Prime Minister in May 1997, Tony Blair was proud to announce (several times) that 'education, education, education' would be the top three priorities of a New Labour administration. The DfEE White Paper, *Excellence in Schools,* published in July 1997 just 67 days after the General Election, declared its 'core commitment' to achieving 'high standards for all', argued forcibly that all schools would be expected to 'take responsibility for raising their own standards' and pledged that 'standards of performance in all schools' would indeed be 'higher by the year 2002' (DfEE, 1997: 3, 13, 14). The emphasis throughout this first White Paper was on the key principle that 'standards matter more than structures', an oft-repeated mantra that first saw the light of day in a highly influential 1996 book co-authored by Peter Mandelson and Roger Liddle with the title, *The Blair Revolution: Can New Labour Deliver?* There it was argued that 'the first priority of

a new government must be to raise general educational standards . . .
New Labour believes that, throughout schooling, standards are more
important than structures . . . Under a New Labour government, there
will be zero tolerance of failure' (Mandelson and Liddle, 1996: 92).

The Labour Party Manifesto for the June 2001 General Election,
Ambitions for Britain, listed as one of the Party's *ten* goals for the year
2010: 'Expanded higher education as we raise standards in our
secondary schools'. The Manifesto went on to argue that, since 1997,
rising standards had already been achieved – particularly in the primary
sector – through 'major new investment and significant reforms'; but
there was still much more to be done. The 'dramatic advances at primary
level' meant that pupils would increasingly arrive at secondary school
'demanding the best'. A second Labour administration would
'modernise the whole secondary curriculum to promote higher standards
and better progression from school and college to university or work-
based training' (Labour Party, 2001: 3, 18). In a comparatively brief
section on education, the Conservative Party's 2001 Election Manifesto,
Time for Common Sense, announced that: 'Our objective is to give
parents choice and headteachers freedom . . .These reforms will lead to
schools of the sort parents want – schools with higher standards, schools
which have their own traditions, a distinct ethos and where children
wear their school uniform with pride' (Conservative Party, 2001: 8). In
the view of the Liberal Democrat 2001 Manifesto, *Freedom, Justice,
Honesty*, the whole purpose of government intervention in education
matters was to raise standards; and a sine qua non of improved standards
was the proper funding of schools and colleges with the appointment of
more teachers 'to make a real difference to class sizes' (Liberal
Democrats, 2001: 4).

The DfEE Green Paper, *Schools: Building on Success*, published in
February 2001, boasted the sub-title *Raising Standards, Promoting
Diversity, Achieving Results*, thereby conveying the clear message that
all these processes were *synonymous* and were to be pursued simultaneously. The Green Paper reiterated the Labour Government's theme of
building on the progress already made in primary and early years provision by launching a new 'standards drive' in the early secondary years
with 'ambitious new targets for performance in tests for 14-year-olds in
English, mathematics, science and ICT [information and communications technology]' (DfEE, 2001: 7). Then the third chapter of the newly
re-elected Blair administration's first education White Paper, *Schools
Achieving Success*, published in September 2001, had the title,
Achieving High Standards for All – Supporting Teaching and Learning.

Here it was argued right at the outset that the Labour Government's education agenda was driven by 'a belief in the need to raise standards'. The key to 'raising standards' was said to be 'the quality of teaching and learning in the classroom'; but this was by no means the whole story. The Government wanted to ensure high national standards throughout the system which were 'capable of being interpreted flexibly to meet the needs of all pupils'. The need for 'flexibility' was indeed one of the key themes of the 2001 White Paper, along with the taken-for-granted desirability of choice, innovation and diversity, particularly in the secondary sector. Chapter 5 ('Excellence, Innovation and Diversity') argued that high standards could be achieved only by the creation of a flexible and diverse system in which every school was excellent and was encouraged to play to its strengths; where schools learned from one another, were free to innovate, and where the best schools led the system. In the words of the document itself: 'At the heart of our vision for transforming secondary education is the ambition for every school to create or develop its distinct mission and ethos, including a mission to raise standards and enlarge opportunities for all its pupils' (DfES, 2001: 17, 37, 38).

So a pledge to raise standards is clearly prominent among all the confident assurances to be found in election manifestos and government Green and White Papers. Yet having noted the widespread use of this key phrase in all the above documents, we can also see that the area where there is, in fact, little agreement and consensus – even allowing for the facile and oppositional nature of much party political rhetoric – centres on the vital questions of what the concept of 'raising standards' actually means and how best to set about achieving it. Indeed, we could go even further and say that there is little real agreement about what education is for and why it matters so much.

The threat of mass education

If we take a broad historical perspective, we find that raising educational standards for *all* pupils – indeed the very idea of providing something that could be called 'education' for *all* children – is a fairly new aspiration for Britain's political leaders and that, over the centuries, there has been a strong view within the 'political establishment' that a policy of universal high-quality education would lead inevitably to widespread disaffection and possibly even popular insurrection.

We know from Christopher's Hill's studies of sixteenth- and seventeenth-century England (see, for example, Hill, 1993) that the upper classes in that revolutionary period were terrified of the use that could be made of the translated Bible as a handbook for the radical transformation of England. The emphasis here is on the word 'translated', for it was, of course, central to the Protestant Project of 'the priesthood of all believers' that the individual Christian should have direct access to the Word of God, and that meant translating the Bible from Catholic Latin into the appropriate vernacular. One of the results of the availability of the translated Bible was a decline in the respect for traditional authority, *secular* as well as *religious*. Teaching the masses to read was seen by the ruling order as a foolhardy and possibly even dangerous enterprise if it gave the ordinary people access to liberating ideas; consequently, there were demands that something must be done to curtail the Bible's potential for subversion. An Act of Parliament passed in 1543 attempted to prevent women (apart from noblewomen and gentlewomen), artisans, husbandmen, labourers and servants from reading or discussing the Bible; but Henry VIII's prohibition was found to be unworkable, and first the government of Edward VI and then that of Elizabeth was forced to allow free access to the scriptures in English. Over the next hundred years, both biblical texts and the commentaries that usually accompanied them were used as powerful weapons in the Puritan–radical struggle against monarchy, popery and even the established social order.

Eighteenth-century proponents of liberal political economy objected to all forms of education for the poor – and particularly charity schools – as dangerous and misconceived prototypes of benevolence. They took seriously the view that too much education or schooling would simply make the working poor discontented with their lot, a proposition put forward by Bernard Mandeville in *The Fable of the Bees*. This eighteenth-century *cause célèbre* and notorious piece of social satire by a native of Rotterdam in Holland who spent most of his adult life in London was published in its final form in 1742; and its author's views on the education of the poor were to be found in a late addition to the work called 'An Essay on Charity and Charity Schools':

> The Welfare and Felicity . . . of every State and Kingdom require that the Knowledge of the Working Poor should be confined within the Verge of their Occupations, and never extended (as to things visible) beyond what relates to their Calling. The more a Shepherd, a Plowman or any other Peasant knows of the World and of the things that are Foreign to his Labour or Employment, the less fit he'll be to go through the Fatigues and Hardships of it with Cheerfulness and Content . . . Reading, Writing and Arithmetic are very necessary to those whose Business require such Qualifications, but where

Peoples Livelihood has no dependence on these Arts, they are very perni-
cious to the Poor, who are forc'd to get their Daily Bread by their Daily
Labour. Few Children make any progress at School, but, at the same time,
they are capable of being employ'd in some Business or other, so that every
Hour those poor People spend at their Books is so much time lost to the
Society. Going to School in comparison to Working is Idleness, and the
longer Boys continue in this easy sort of Life, the more unfit they'll be when
grown up for downright Labour, both as to Strength and as to Inclination.
Men who are to remain and to end their Days in a Laborious, Tiresome and
Painful Station of Life, the sooner they are put upon it first, the more
patiently they'll submit to it for ever after. (Mandeville, 1970: 294–5)

The campaign for national education in the first decades of the nineteenth century, spearheaded by the 'radical wing' of the middle class,
was repeatedly thwarted by aristocratic members of Parliament using
arguments very similar to those deployed by Bernard Mandeville. The
essential ingredients of the Tory opposition case can be gauged from the
following extract from Davies Giddy's famous speech attacking the
Parochial Schools Bill, a bill for the establishment of parish schools
introduced into the House of Commons by Samuel Whitbread, the
liberal-Whig Leader, in 1807:

However specious in theory the project might be of giving education to the
labouring classes of the poor, it would, in effect, be found to be prejudicial to
their morals and happiness; it would teach them to despise their lot in life,
instead of making them good servants in agriculture and other laborious
employments to which their rank in society had destined them; instead of
teaching them the virtue of subordination, it would render them factious and
refractory, as is evident in the manufacturing counties; it would enable them
to read seditious pamphlets, vicious books and publications against
Christianity; it would render them insolent to their superiors; and, in a few
years, the result would be that the legislature would find it necessary to direct
the strong arm of power towards them and to furnish the executive magis-
trates with more vigorous powers than are now in force. Besides, if this Bill
were to pass into law, it would go to burthen the country with a most enormous and incalculable expense, and to load the industrious orders with still
heavier imposts. (*Hansard*, House of Commons, Vol. 9, 13 July 1807, quoted
in Simon, 1960: 132; see also Green, 1990: 262)

So strongly were views like these held among the upper classes that
even Hannah More, a leading philanthropist and author of a number of
influential religious tracts whose loyalty to Church, monarchy and the
established order was never in doubt, had experienced sharp criticism for
setting up her Sunday Schools in the Mendips mining area in the late
1790s. These schools, as far as she was concerned, had the clear political

purpose of inculcating a state of resignation and obedience in the labouring classes. In defending her Schools against the charges levelled at
them, she was anxious to clarify her limited view of the purpose of
education for the poor:

> My plan of instruction is indeed extremely simple and limited. They learn, on
> weekdays, such coarse works as may fit them for servants. I allow of no writ-
> ing for the poor. My object is not to make them fanatics, but to train up the
> lower classes in habits of industry and piety. (Johnson, 1925: 183)

Even after 1870, when the Forster Education Act laid the first foundations of a *national* system of education, there were many influential
writers and politicians who questioned the principle of 'universality' in
the provision of elementary schooling. The legislative reforms of the last
decades of the nineteenth century – introducing compulsory school
attendance in 1880 and making most elementary education free in 1891
– were viewed with alarm by the ardent disciples of classical market
liberalism. On the one hand, or so it was believed, mass education would
inevitably create aspirations that society could not match; while, at the
same time, the reforms clearly represented an unnecessary and costly
diversion from the true path that legislators should be following, leaving
education as a matter of purely *private* concern. As recently as the
1980s, the late Keith Joseph, who was Margaret Thatcher's Secretary of
State for Education from 1981 to 1986, was arguing that Parliament had
made a big mistake back in 1870; and that the fundamental problem with
the state education system they had inaugurated lay in the very fact that
it was a *state* system:

> We have a bloody state system; I wish we hadn't got one. I wish we'd taken
> a different route in 1870. We got the ruddy state involved. I don't want it. I
> don't think we know how to do it. I certainly don't think Secretaries of State
> know anything about it. But we are landed with it. If we could move back to
> 1870, I would take a different route. We've got compulsory education, which
> is a responsibility of hideous importance; and we tyrannise children to do that
> which they don't want, and we don't produce results. (Quoted in Chitty,
> 1997a: 80)

The 1944 Education Act sought to extend educational opportunity by
introducing the principle of 'free secondary education for all'; but
patronizing attitudes towards the sort of education thought 'appropriate'
for working-class children persisted in the type of curriculum provided
for the majority of the pupils attending the new secondary modern
schools. In a debate in the House of Commons in January 1965, the late

Conservative politician, Quintin Hogg, articulated a commonly held view about the low aspirations and capabilities of secondary modern pupils when he launched an attack on Labour MPs for supporting comprehensive reorganization:

> I can assure Hon. Members opposite that if they would go to study what is now being done in good secondary modern schools, they would not find a lot of pupils biting their nails in frustration because they had failed the eleven-plus. The pleasant noise of banging metal and sawing wood would greet their ears, and a smell of cooking with rather expensive equipment would come out of the front door to greet them. They would find that these boys and girls were getting an education tailor-made to their desires, their bents and their requirements . . . I am not prepared to admit that the Party opposite has done a good service to education, or to the children of this country, by attacking that form of school, or seeking to denigrate it. (*Hansard,* House of Commons, Vol. 705, Cols 423-4,21 January 1965)

Some of the recent contributions to the ongoing debate about the desirability or otherwise of mass education have returned to the themes that have preoccupied leading philosophers and political thinkers over the last 400 years. In his influential book *The Meaning of Conservatism,* first published in 1980, Professor Roger Scruton of Birkbeck College, London, later to become a prominent member of the right-wing education think-tank the Hillgate Group, argued forcibly that it was 'absurd' to embrace the aim of 'equality of opportunity'.

> Such a thing seems to be neither possible nor desirable. For what opportunity does an *unintelligent* child have to partake of the advantages conferred by an institution which demands *intelligence?* His case is no different from that of a plain girl competing with a pretty girl for a position as a model. The attempt to provide equality of opportunity, unless it is to involve massive compulsory surgery of an unthinkable kind, is simply a confused stumble in the dark. (Scruton, 1980: 157)

Professor Scruton went on to echo one of the key points made by Bernard Mandeville in *The Fable of the Bees*:

> It is simply not possible to provide universal education. Nor indeed, is it desirable. For the appetite for learning points people only in a certain direction; it siphons them away from those places where they might have been contented . . . It is important for a society that it contain as many 'walks of life' as the satisfaction of its members may require . . . and that it does not seek to sustain institutions which merely siphon away people to the point where they no longer wish to do what in fact they might otherwise have done willingly and well. (Scruton, 1980)

At the time when *The Meaning of Conservatism* was first published there were, in fact, widespread fears that educational reform would bring with it social unrest and a discontented workforce. This was, after all, the period (the early 1980s) when, for reasons that were not strictly 'educational' and had much to do with racial tension and mounting unemployment, there were localized but serious outbursts of rebellion among young people in (among other places) Brixton in South London, Moss Side in Manchester and the Toxteth district of Liverpool (see Young, 1989: 233–4, 237–8). In interviews conducted at this time with senior Department of Education and Science (DES) officials and policy advisers, Stewart Ranson of Birmingham University was made acutely aware of very real DES fears about the additional dangers and threats arising from 'overeducation' in a contracting labour market. In a famous paper first published in 1984, more than one DES official was shown to be quite open about the need to restrict educational opportunities for the sake of social harmony and a compliant workforce:

> To offer young people advanced education but not thereafter the work opportunities to match their career aspirations is to offer them a false prospectus.
>   There has to be selection because we are beginning to create aspirations which increasingly society just cannot match. In some ways, this points to the recent success of education in contrast to the public mythology which has been created. When young people drop off the education production line and cannot find work at all, or work which meets their abilities or expectations, then we are only creating frustrations with perhaps disturbing social consequences. We have to select: to ration the *educational* opportunities to meet the *job* opportunities, so that society can cope with the output of education.
>   We are in a period of considerable social change. There may be social unrest, but we can cope with the Toxteths. But if we have a highly educated and idle population, we may possibly anticipate more serious social conflict. People must be educated once more to know their place. (Ranson, 1984: 241)

All the above statements, by three different individuals, emphasize the dangers of an 'overeducated' society and tell us a great deal about the thinking at the very heart of government. Taken in conjunction with the comments of Professor Scruton, a leading adviser to Margaret Thatcher on education matters, they articulate the twin related fears that large numbers of 'well-educated' youngsters will find it impossible to find work that matches their qualifications, and the jobs they do manage to find will make them feel cheated and alienated. As we shall see in a later section, such fears and reservations have been matched in recent years by the arguments of leading employers and industrialists that for large numbers of young people, education – and particularly secondary education – should be far more practical and vocational.

What is education for?

Much of the previous section has concentrated on the arguments marshalled over the centuries to undermine the extension of educational opportunities to the children of the working classes. If we now accept the idea that access to education is a human right, we still have to ask (and answer) some fundamental questions about the form which that education should take and about the basic objectives it should set itself.

Professor Richard Aldrich has pointed out that 'education is the most important shared experience in our lives'. In his view, 'it is so important and so all-pervasive that it is almost impossible to define' (Aldrich, 1996: 1). Obviously, it cannot be confined to what takes place in schools and colleges and universities; but the work of these places will, somewhat inevitably, constitute the main preoccupation of the majority of the chapters that follow in this book. The justification for this very precise focus is that these institutions represent the most immediately visible expression of our contemporary commitment to education. Since the raising of the school leaving age to 16 in 1972–3, all pupils have been entitled to at least 11 years of compulsory schooling; and, currently, just around 43 per cent of young people pursue full-time education beyond the age of 18. Clearly, we have a duty as educators and citizens to prove the late Keith Joseph wrong and ensure that we do not 'tyrannise children to do that which they don't want' while, at the same time, failing to produce results. To quote Richard Aldrich again: 'Education will not supply all the answers to the problems that beset us, either as individuals or as a nation, but if we set about it the right way, it is the best single means of promoting intellectual, moral, physical and economic well-being' (1996).

Since the end of the Second World War – and particularly since the 1970s – politicians have tended to see the aims of education or schooling in terms of individual personal fulfilment and the acquisition of the skills and attitudes thought necessary for the pursuit of a successful working life. The Foreword by Secretary of State for Education and Skills, Estelle Morris, to the September 2001 White Paper, *Schools Achieving Success,* argues for an education that 'teaches us the joy of learning and gives us the qualifications for employment, that builds confidence and self-esteem and gives us the skills and values to meet the demands of a fast-changing world'; such, according to Ms Morris, is 'the education we are seeking for all of our children' (DfES, 2001: 3).

A utilitarian perspective

The idea of education as 'personal fulfilment' may be a somewhat bland and unproblematic concept; the idea of schooling, and especially secondary schooling, as essentially preparation for 'the world of work' carries with it more worrying connotations.

It was in the mid-1970s, as Britain faced economic dislocation following the collapse of fixed exchange rates in 1971–2 and the quadrupling of the price of oil in 1973, that a mood of defeatism and despair gripped the nation; and schools and teachers became convenient scapegoats for the failure of successive governments to cope with the economic down-turn.

The Labour Government of James Callaghan (1976–9) was particularly influenced by the views of leading employers and industrialists (a point to which we will return in Chapter 3). It was their argument that there were large numbers of young people for whom *vocational training* was the most appropriate form of schooling beyond the age of 14. In their opinion, too many secondary schools were showing a marked reluctance to train their pupils to meet the needs of wealth-producing industry and could therefore be held largely responsible for the rising rate of youth unemployment. Indeed, it was a version of the employers' critique that the Prime Minister was anxious to publicize in the famous speech he delivered at Ruskin College, Oxford, in October 1976. He was proud to acknowledge that Labour had always shown recognition of the need to cater for a child's personality and 'to let it flower in the fullest possible way'; but he went on to stress that 'there is no virtue in producing socially well-adjusted members of society who are unemployed because they do not have the necessary skills' (quoted in Chitty, 1989a: 171).

This *economic* function of education was later reiterated in the 1985 DES White Paper *Better Schools*: 'it is vital that schools should always remember that preparation for working life is one of their principal functions' (DES, 1985b: para. 46). At the time, this viewpoint may have seemed commonplace; but it could, of course, have divisive implications for the organization of the secondary-school curriculum. The new vocationalism, which became such an important element in government policy between 1976 and 1988, was based on some pretty atavistic assumptions about the sort of 'education' deemed to be 'suitable' for the vast majority of working-class pupils. As Dan Finn, at that time Research Officer at the Unemployment Unit based in London, observed in a book published in 1987:

> The guiding philosophy behind educational policy became the creation of appropriate curricula for different groups of pupils, to be derived mainly from their assumed destination in the division of labour. It was not that schools were simply expected to prepare their pupils to get jobs; they were also now required to make them cognitively and attitudinally better potential employees. (Finn, 1987: 168)

For many young people, the *instrumental* view of schooling enshrined in many official documents was to mean little more than the acquisition of a number of low-level transferable skills. And for all those being prepared for 'working life', there was a clear emphasis (hinted at in the above quotation) on the need to become willing members of an adaptive, flexible and compliant workforce. Indeed, this was the message still being highlighted in 1996 by Gillian Shephard, Conservative Secretary of State for Education and Employment between 1994 and 1997, in her Foreword to the DfEE consultative document, *Equipping Young People for Working Life*:

> The Government has carried through major reform over the last few years to bring our educational system in line with the needs of a modern competitive economy. Our vision is of a prosperous Britain in the 21st century with a strong economy in which the skills of each individual are developed through education and deployed to the full. Thus, we must do all we can to help . . . our young people to acquire the skills, knowledge and understanding they will need to be part of a highly adaptive workforce. (DfEE, 1996a: 1)

The social function of schooling

The crucial factor missing from all the positions so far outlined is the *social* dimension of education. Many would subscribe to the view that all education systems have social functions and consequences; but these 'consequences' have often been framed in very simplistic and narrow terms. It has often been claimed, for example, that educational reform on a large scale can have social effects which are discernible *within a relatively short timespan*.

In the mid-1960s, when the new comprehensive school became national policy, it was widely believed by academics and social reformers that secondary reorganization would be a major step on the road to achieving greater equality: greater equality in the sense that it would now be possible for large numbers of working-class children to move into 'white-collar' occupations or proceed to higher education. The leading Oxford sociologist A.H. Halsey could begin an article on 'Education and Equality' in *New Society* in June 1965 with the ringing declaration: 'Some people, and I am one, want to use education as an instrument in pursuit of an egalitarian society. We tend to favour comprehensive schools, to be against public schools, and to support the expansion of higher education' (Halsey, 1965: 13).

Other supporters of the Labour Government's policy simply believed in the theory of the 'social mix' which looked forward to the *amelioration* of social class differences through the pupils' experience of 'social mixing' in a common secondary school. Comprehensive reorganization – or so the theory went – would produce a degree of social harmony without seriously disturbing the basic class structure of society. The 'social mix' concept even found expression in Circular 10/65, the device used by the Government in July 1965 for requesting local education authorities to prepare plans for reorganizing the secondary schools under their control: 'A comprehensive school aims to establish a school community in which pupils over the whole ability range and with differing interests and backgrounds can be encouraged to mix with each other, gaining stimulus from the contacts and learning tolerance and understanding in the process' (DES, 1965: 18).

As we have already noted, the general mood of optimism and hope that characterized the 1960s gave way to one of cynicism and defeatism in the following decade (particularly after the economic crisis of 1973) and it was a change that affected both politicians and academics. It was now widely believed among a group of influential sociologists that schools could do little or nothing to improve the life-chances of working-class youngsters, and that education's chief function was to ensure the reproduction of the existing social structure. Even the creation of a degree of social harmony was seen as an illusory aspiration. According to what was basically a form of neo-Marxism, the organization of schooling and the assumptions of classroom teachers meant that various forms of inequality were perpetuated from one generation to the next. One version of the theory, popular in France, argued that in modern times the education system had taken the place of the Church as the chief means by which the dominant ideology of a class society was sustained. Teachers and other workers within the field of education were inevitably recruited as 'agents' of ideological domination, and nothing they could do could have any significant effect on the nature of society.

Another powerful contribution to 'social reproduction' theory, by the American neo-Marxists Samuel Bowles and Herbert Gintis, became highly influential in Britain when their book, *Schooling in Capitalist America,* first published in 1976, was adopted by the Open University as a set reading text. This American analysis of 'educational reform and the contradictions of economic life' came to be known as the 'correspondence theory', with its argument that the modern educational structure and ethos 'corresponded' to the structure and ethos of the major institutions of monopoly capitalism: the factory and the modern corporation. Just as schools were invariably hierarchical organizations with dominant teachers exercising control over subordinate pupils, so also were industrial and commercial organizations with dominant managers expecting obedience from subordinate workers. There was therefore a close 'parallel' or 'correspondence' between the social relations of schooling and those in the 'world of work'. At the same time, young people were not simply slotted into the occupational structure in a random or haphazard manner. The school system, though making claims to be 'fair' and 'meritocratic', actually worked to ensure that some pupils (predominantly middle-class) moved into occupations of 'dominance', while others (mainly working-class) moved into positions of 'subordination'. In this way, the education system helped to ensure that the class structure was maintained and 'reproduced' from generation to generation. In the words of Bowles and Gintis:

> The educational system operates to perpetuate the social relationships of economic life not so much through the conscious intentions of teachers and administrators in their day-to-day activities, but through a close correspondence between the social relationships which govern personal interaction in the work place and the social relationships of the educational system. Specifically, the relationships of authority and control between teachers and students . . . replicate the hierarchical division of labour which dominates the work place. (Bowles and Gintis, 1976: 11–12)

Pupils who were destined for the world of higher education and then for professional and managerial roles enjoyed social relations with their teachers which emphasized freedom, autonomy, independence and personal creativity. Those who were earmarked for various low-level manual occupations were subjected to more formal regimes which emphasized obedience to rules and passivity: they had to be 'trained' to become compliant members of a docile workforce:

The educational system, through the pattern of status distinctions it fosters, reinforces the stratified consciousness on which the fragmentation of subordinate economic classes is based . . . To reproduce the social relations of production, the educational system must try to teach people to be properly subordinate and render them sufficiently fragmented in consciousness to preclude their getting together to shape their own material existence. (Bowles and Gintis, 1976: 130)

Social reconstructionism: an ideology for the future?

All the views outlined in the previous section have attracted powerful support, if only for limited periods of time; but they could all be said to represent fairly narrow and superficial interpretations of the social functions of schooling. Mostly, they reduce the debate about education and social change to a simplistic and ultimately futile discussion as to whether or not educational reform can promote equality and social justice with almost immediate effect.

A more dynamic and sophisticated view of the relationship between education and society can be found in the educational ideology often referred to as 'social reconstructionism'. To describe this perspective as 'society-centred' is somewhat misleading since an important aspect of 'reconstructionism' is to see individuals and society as harmoniously integrated, with the development and empowerment of individuals going hand-in-hand with the improvement of society. Schools are seen as having the task of preparing their students both to function effectively within society *and* to use their various abilities and talents to change that society in the light of changing circumstances and developing aspirations. What is *not* part of the philosophy is to expect education systems embedded in societies with sharp class divisions to act directly and immediately to transform that society in any particular direction.

In the USA, social reconstructionism has often been associated with the writings of John Dewey, for whom democracy was not simply a particular form of government but a way of life which provided maximum opportunities for individual growth. Education for all was a desirable aspect of a democratic society, as well as a means of achieving an even better democracy. Education provided opportunities for individual growth, thereby ensuring an improving quality of life for individuals, as well as improving the quality of society itself. For Dewey, it was particularly important that society should view change as a positive virtue: in his 1916 book, *Democracy and Education,* he argued that a society committed to change would have an education system that reflected that commitment: 'It is, of course, true that a society which not only changes, but which has the ideal of such change as will improve it, will have different and better standards and methods of education from one which aims simply at the perpetuation of its own customs' (Dewey, 1916: 94). For Professor Denis Lawton, a version of social reconstructionism would be the most appropriate template for planning a national curriculum. Such a curriculum would lay stress upon social values and experiences appropriate for developing citizenship and social co-operation. Knowledge would not be ignored or downgraded; but knowledge *for its own sake* would be questionable. Knowledge would be justified in terms of social needs: 'not in terms of custom, nor cultural heritage *per se*' Lawton, 1989: 6).

No one can pretend that the relationship between education and society is straightforward or uncontroversial. We may want to be held together by a set of common beliefs and patterns of behaviour; but we no longer live in the post-war world of 'taken-for-granted' assumptions about class, culture and morality. If we reject the idea of a society which aims simply at 'the perpetuation of its own customs', we must promote a form of education which is similarly open to new ideas and prepared to challenge past orthodoxies. Above all, it must surely be one of the social functions of schooling to tackle issues of equity and social justice and help create a truly inclusive society in which all forms of diversity – cultural, racial, religious and sexual – are celebrated and endorsed.

2

The Rise and Fall of the Post-War Consensus

In this chapter, we follow the development of the education system in Britain from the end of the Second World War in 1945 to the economic recession of 1971–3 and the breakdown of the post-war political consensus in the mid-1970s.

It surprised many leading politicians in Britain and also in the Allied countries, especially America, when the Labour Party won a landslide victory in the General Election held in early July 1945, two months after the end of the war with Germany. The sense of amazement was quite genuine, even among Labour politicians, for the victory was indeed massive, representing the greatest electoral 'turnabout' since the famous Liberal victory in the election of January 1906. In statistical terms, the Labour Party obtained a total of 393 seats compared to 213 for the Conservatives and their allies and a mere 12 for the Liberals. Two Communists and a total of 20 Independents were also elected. The results meant that around 48 per cent of the total vote went to Labour, just under 40 per cent (39.8) to the Conservatives and 9 per cent to the Liberals.

This decisive Labour victory seemed, at a superficial level of analysis, to represent a marked display of sheer ingratitude for all that Winston Churchill had done to guide Britain through arguably the most difficult period in its history; but, in reality, it was an expression of a widespread conviction that Britain now needed a government committed to a detailed programme of social reform and reconstruction.

In his assessment of the 1945 Labour victory, the Oxford historian Kenneth Morgan has argued that 'Labour was uniquely identified with a sweeping change of mood during the war years, and with the new social agenda that emerged'. It was noted by contemporary commentators how large a part the housing shortage played in the 1945 election; so, too, did the need for drastic economic policies to prevent a return to the mass unemployment of the 1930s. In Dr Morgan's view, 'a variety of factors enabled Labour to exploit the vogue for planning and egalitarianism during the war, and to turn them to electoral advantage in a way that was impossible for the Conservative members of the late Coalition'. With the Liberals falling victim to seemingly irreversible forces of social, religious and political change, 'Labour alone seemed to understand and project the new mood'. It reinforced it by 'bringing its own traditional supporters out to vote in unprecedented numbers', and by 'breaking down old parochial or ethnic barriers in cities such as Birmingham, Liverpool, Cardiff and Leeds which had long held back the Labour cause'. It was indeed a remarkable victory for which the Party had well prepared and organized in the latter stages of the war; yet 'it was also a victory which left its leading figures stunned and for a moment almost overwhelmed' (Morgan, 1984: 44). When the House of Commons assembled for the first time after the election, it reverberated to the enthusiastic singing by nearly 400 Labour MPs of the traditional Socialist anthem, 'The Red Flag'. To many, it seemed as if a new era had truly begun.

It would, however, be wrong to give the impression that *only* Labour politicians appreciated the need for an extensive post-war programme of social and economic reconstruction. David Marquand has argued that in the post-war period, most of Britain's political class actually shared a tacit governing philosophy which might be called 'Keynesian social democracy' and which embraced the need for social reform. It did not cover the whole spectrum of political opinion, and neither did it prevent the frequent outbreak of vigorous party conflict. The Labour and Conservative Parties often differed fiercely about the specific details of policy; on a deeper level, their conceptions of political authority and social justice differed even more. They differed, however, within a structure of generally-accepted values and assumptions. In Professor Marquand's words:

> For most of the post-war period, most frontbenchers in the House of Commons, most senior civil servants, most of the leaders of the most powerful trade unions, most nationalised industry chairmen, most heads of large private-sector companies and most commentators in the quality press shared a common experience and a broadly similar set of aspirations. They were determined to banish the hardships of the pre-war years, and to make sure that the conflicts which those hardships had caused did not return. Thus, both front benches accepted a three-fold commitment: to full employment, to the Welfare State and to the co-existence of large public and private sectors in the economy – in short, to the Settlement which had brought the inter-war conflicts to an end. (Marquand, 1988: 3)

The 1944 Education Act

It was the Labour Government of Clement Attlee (1945–51: see Box 2.1) which had the task of implementing the provisions of the 1944 Education Act, regarded by many political commentators and historians as the single most important piece of legislation to be passed between 1939 and 1945.

The Act can be said to have owed much to a growing appreciation among policy-makers, administrators and teachers of the importance of state education to economic advance and social welfare; and, in the course of its administration by both Labour and Conservative education ministers, it established itself as a cornerstone of the post-war Welfare State. It was the product of around three years of *genuine* consultation with a number of interested bodies; and it was piloted through the Houses of Parliament by a wartime coalition government that was beginning to comprehend, in the words of historian Brian Simon (1991: 35), that 'it was impossible, if Britain defeated Germany, to go back to the stagnant, class-ridden depressing society of the 1930s'. In his book of memoirs, *The Art of the Possible,* published in 1971, the leading Conservative politician R.A. (Rab) Butler, whose name is often associated with the 1944 Act and who had become President of the Board of Education in the summer of 1941, talked of his excitement at being given by Churchill the

	Box 2.1 Post-war administrations, 1945–76	
Party	**Date formed**	**Prime Minister**
Labour	July 1945	Clement Attlee
Labour	February 1950	Clement Attlee
Conservative	October 1951	Winston Churchill
Conservative	May 1955	Sir Anthony Eden
Conservative	January 1957	Harold Macmillan
Conservative	October 1959	Harold Macmillan
Conservative	October 1963	Sir Alec Douglas-Home
Labour	October 1964	Harold Wilson
Labour	March 1966	Harold Wilson
Conservative	June 1970	Edward Heath
Labour	February 1974	Harold Wilson
Labour	October 1974	Harold Wilson

opportunity to 'harness to the educational system the wartime urge for social reform and greater equality' (Butler, 1971: 86).

The 1944 Act certainly made great changes in the structure of the education system. Secondary education for *all* children was now established as an integral part of that system which was to be seen as a continuous process, ranging from the primary sector to further or higher education. Despite all the anomalies, which will be discussed later, the new approach, involving the recognition of a clear distinction between *primary* and *secondary* education, marked a genuine improvement on what had gone before. In the period before the Second World War, the vast majority of the nation's children (88 per cent in 1938) had been educated (if that is the right word) in the elementary schools within the maintained system (often in 'all-age' elementary schools); and of these youngsters, most had left school at the age of 14 (the minimum school-leaving age at that time) to enter the labour market. Only a small minority of elementary-school pupils (just over 14 per cent in 1938) had been given the opportunity to transfer to secondary schools at the age of 10 or 11. So it can be argued that the idea of 'secondary education for all' accompanied by the proposed elimination of the elementary sector and the phasing-out of fees for secondary schooling, represented something of a triumph for the reform movement.

Section 35 of the Act gave added meaning to the concept of secondary education by making provision for the raising of the school-leaving age to 15 (which actually happened in 1947), and by stipulating that this could be extended to 16 once the Minister was satisfied that it had become a 'practicable' proposition (though this was, in fact, to be postponed for a whole generation, until 1972–3).

Despite its remarkable longevity and a reputation for being, in the words of the Conservative MP, Timothy Raison, 'a Rolls-Royce among statutes' (Raison, 1976: 76), the 1944 Act still had a number of serious ambiguities and shortcomings which were to bedevil the smooth running of the education system for the next 45 years.

For one thing, the Act provided no guidance as to the *content* of primary or secondary education. The word 'curriculum' does appear in the Act (on p. 20), but only in passing, and at the end of a section (Section 23) giving responsibility for secular instruction in state schools (though not in voluntary-aided secondary schools) to local education authorities. We shall return to this curious but telling omission in Chapter 7.

At the same time, the Act was remarkably vague on issues relating to the actual structure of the proposed new secondary sector. The wording of the legislation, and of the 1943 White Paper, *Educational Reconstruction* (Board of Education, 1943), which preceded it, appeared to legitimize a *tripartite* structure of secondary schools (comprising grammar, technical and secondary modern schools), but the Act did not specifically *proscribe* experiments with multilateral or comprehensive schools. Here the key part of the legislation is Section 8 which stipulates that:

> The secondary schools available for an area shall not be deemed to be sufficient unless they are sufficient in number, character and equipment to afford for all pupils opportunities for education, offering such variety of instruction and training as may be desirable in view of their different ages, abilities and aptitudes, and of the different periods for which they may be expected to remain at school, including practical instruction and training appropriate to their respective needs. (Ministry of Education, 1944: 5)

One interpretation of this Section effectively ensured that secondary reform of a far-reaching nature was deferred for many years. Yet it is also true that the ambiguity in the drafting of the Section meant that when the pressure for reform became almost irresistible in the mid-1960s, it could be addressed by simply *reinterpreting* the formula without the necessity for further legislation. In fact, attention was drawn to the possibility of having just one secondary school serving a given area or neighbourhood (even while the Bill was under discussion in Parliament) by an experienced educational administrator, J. Chuter Ede, the Labour Parliamentary Secretary to the old Board of Education:

> I do not know where people get the idea about *three* types of school, because I have gone through the Bill with a small toothcomb, and I can find only one school for senior pupils – and that is a secondary school. What you like to make of it will depend on the way you serve the precise needs of the individual area in the country. (Speech reported in *The Times*, 14 April 1944)

In fact, of course, there was very rarely just *one* type of school for senior pupils in the post-war period. After all the discussion and legislative arguments, the country emerged with a rigid and essentially hierarchical educational structure almost exactly as planned and developed in the mid-nineteenth century. This comprised five (or more strictly six) grades or levels serving different classes or groups within society:

- the so-called public schools, established as a system in the period 1860–1900, at the top of the hierarchy
- the direct grant grammar schools, which received a grant direct from

central government in return for offering a number of free places to
local children, in addition to charging fees
- the grammar schools, representing the elite group within the maintained sector and taking, by 1950, roughly 20 per cent of the relevant
age group
- a small group of technical, 'central' and other types of 'trade' schools;
- the new 'secondary modern' schools, taking the vast majority of
working-class children at the age of 11
- the old, unreorganized 'all-age' elementary schools which were abolished in the 1944 Act but which took another 20 years to disappear
completely.

There was the added complication of the position with regard to *religious schools*. Here the system established in 1944 was largely the result
of negotiations between R.A. Butler and Archbishop William Temple in
the period from 1942 to 1944. The Act created a unified framework
which brought Church schools under state control, but left them with
varying degrees of independence according to how much financial
support the Church continued to provide. Those schools owned and run
by the local authorities were named 'county' schools; those owned by
the churches and run in partnership with the local authority became
'voluntary' schools. Of the latter category, there were to be two main
types: 'aided' and 'controlled'. Voluntary aided schools were set up by
voluntary bodies or trusts, mainly the churches. They provided their own
premises and met some of the maintenance costs in exchange for a
degree of control, which included control over the curriculum. Voluntary
controlled schools were set up by voluntary foundations, usually the
Church of England or the Roman Catholic Church, but sometimes a
non-denominational privately supported body. They provided their own
premises, but all the running costs were met by the local education
authority and the governing bodies had control only over the religious
education in the curriculum.

A national system, locally administered

If we now turn to the actual system of policy making established in
1944, it needs to be stressed that it was seen at the time as a peculiarly
British response to the dangers inherent in the centralizing tendencies so
obvious in other parts of Europe.

Some of the unique elements of that post-war system will be discussed in detail in Chapter 5. Suffice it to say at this stage that the idea of a 'national system, locally administered', in which post-war ministers invested so much pride, involved the continuing operation of a benign partnership between central government, local government and individual schools and colleges.

The 1950 Report of the Ministry of Education (which was actually published in 1951) was intended to celebrate the 50-year history of a unified central department as a consequence of the 1899 Board of Education Act, and it began with a joint introduction by Minister of Education, George Tomlinson (see Box 2.2), and his Permanent Secretary Sir John Maud which emphasized that the post-war system was building on a structure which had already made a significant contribution to the democratic life of the nation:

Box 2.2
Ministers of Education, 1945–64

Ellen Wilkinson	July 1945–February 1947
George Tomlinson	February 1947–November 1951
Florence Horsburgh	November 1951–October 1954
Sir David Eccles	October 1954–January 1957
Viscount Hailsham	January 1957–September 1957
Geoffrey Lloyd	September 1957–October 1959
Sir David Eccles	October 1959–July 1962
Sir Edward Boyle	July 1962–March 1964

In 1964, the Education Minister became known as the Secretary of State for Education and Science, when the Ministry of Education was reorganized as the Department of Education and Science.

Secretaries of State, 1964–75

Quintin Hogg	April 1964–October 1964
Michael Stewart	October 1964–January 1965
Anthony Crosland	January 1965–August 1967
Patrick Gordon-Walker	August 1967–April 1968
Edward Short	April 1968–June 1970
Margaret Thatcher	June 1970–March 1974
Reginald Prentice	March 1974–June 1975

This is the story of a progressive partnership between the central department, the local education authorities and the teachers. To build a single, but not uniform, system out of many diverse elements; to widen educational opportunity and, at the same time, to raise standards; to knit the educational system more closely into the life of an increasingly democratic and industrialised community: these are among the main ideas which, despite two major wars, have moved legislators and administrators alike. (Ministry of Education, 1951: 1)

An important part of the post-war consensus as far as education was concerned involved leaving considerable powers in the hands of schools and teachers, and this was particularly true in the case of matters relating to the school curriculum. The 1951 Ministry of Education Report, cited above, was certainly anxious to stress the Government's policy of non-intervention in curriculum matters:

If this Report comes into the hands of readers from overseas, as we hope it will, they may be expected to look first for a substantial chapter on educational method and the curriculum of the schools. They will not find it. This does not, of course, mean that the schools have made no response to the new knowledge about the nature and needs of children or to the changing conceptions of the function of education in a democratic community. The reason is that the Ministry has traditionally valued the life of institutions more highly than systems and has been jealous for the freedom of schools and teachers. (Ministry of Education, 1951: 1)

Section 23 of the 1944 Education Act stipulated that dates of terms, length of the school day and secular instruction, in all except voluntary-aided secondary schools, were to become the responsibility of the local education authority, unless otherwise provided for in the school articles of government:

In every county school and, subject to the provisions hereinafter contained as to religious education, in every voluntary school except an aided secondary school, the secular instruction to be given to the pupils shall, save in so far as may be otherwise provided by the rules of management or articles of government for the school, be under the control of the local education authority. (Ministry of Education, 1944: 19)

In most schools, however, the actual decisions about curriculum content and teaching methods were to be taken by the headteacher and his or her staff, under the general, if somewhat perfunctory, oversight of the school governing body; this state of affairs existed until at least the late 1970s.

For all the cosy post-war rhetoric, there were, of course, occasions when the 'partnership' model broke down, and particularly where it

applied to the relationship between central government and local authorities. In 1954, for example, the Conservative Minister of Education,
Florence Horsburgh, intervened to prevent the then London County
Council (LCC) shutting down Eltham Hill Girls' Grammar School and
transferring these 'selected' pupils to the new Kidbrooke School, the
LCC's first *purpose-built* comprehensive. Her successor, Sir David
Eccles, shortly after taking office late in 1954, was anxious to reassure
the grammar school lobby that comprehensive reorganization was not
acceptable to the Conservative Party. In setting the pattern of secondary
education, he said:

> One has to choose between justice and equality, for it is impossible to apply
> both principles at once. Those who support comprehensive schools prefer
> equality. Her Majesty's present Government prefer justice. My colleagues
> and I will never allow local authorities to assassinate the grammar schools.
> (Quoted in *The Schoolmaster*, 7 January 1955)

Nevertheless, as flaws in the tripartite system became increasingly
apparent in the late 1950s and early 1960s, it was not only Labour politicians who argued the case for some degree of secondary reorganization.
Although the Conservative Governments of the 1950s were generally
hostile to local experiments in comprehensive schooling, there is much
to be said for Roger Dale's view (1983: 234) that from 1954, when Sir
David Eccles became Minister for Education, until the General Election
of October 1964, when the Conservatives under Alec Douglas-Home
were narrowly defeated by Harold Wilson's Labour Party, education
policy at a national level was becoming increasingly 'non-partisan', and
even (when Sir Edward Boyle was Conservative Minister of Education
from 1962 to 1964) almost 'bi-partisan'.

Flaws in the 'tripartite' system

The post-war 'tripartite' system of secondary schools was based on the
widely held belief that it was possible to say, from the results of tests
administered at the age of 10 or 11, what a child's future accomplish-
ments would be. This was itself based on the view that every child was
born with a given quota of 'intelligence' which remained constant
throughout his or her life, and that this key quality was a direct product
of genetic endowment and therefore not susceptible to any educational
influence.

In fact, despite reference in the 1943 Norwood Report to 'three types of mind', concerned respectively with 'academic', 'technical' and 'practical' pursuits (Secondary Schools Examinations Council, 1943: 4), the post-war secondary system never really was a *tripartite* structure in practice. After 1945, priority was given to establishing the new system of secondary modern schools; while the majority of local authorities were reluctant to spend the money needed to develop new secondary technical schools. The reasons for this caution were not clear-cut: it may have resulted from a certain amount of confusion as to the precise function of these schools, or it may have been due to the cost of the equipment required. Whatever the truth, as late as 1958, secondary technical schools still accounted for the education of less than 4 per cent of the secondary age group. The structure that emerged was, in reality, a *bipartite* system comprising grammar schools on the one hand and secondary modern schools on the other, with the former taking, in the 1950s, around one in five of all children at the age of 11. In most parts of the country, an 11-plus selection examination, consisting of tests of intelligence and tests of attainment in English and arithmetic was employed as the principal means of allocating children to the different types of secondary school.

Probably the chief begetter of the theory and practice of intelligence testing and of the 11-plus examination in which IQ (intelligence quotient) played such a prominent part was the famous (now notorious) educational psychologist, Cyril Burt, who had been appointed to the LCC in 1912 (the first educational psychologist to be appointed to a local authority in Britain), and then, as Professor of Psychology at University College, London from 1932, provided theoretical justification for the divided system of education being recommended in official reports.

From his earliest work, not long after the turn of the century, Burt was concerned to uphold *three* (interrelated) principles, namely:

- that 'intelligence' was the most important factor of the mind
- that it was largely (or even wholly) innate or inherited, and not therefore capable of being affected by particular educational approaches
- that its distribution among the population conformed to the 'normal' (or bell-shaped) curve.

In the course of a long and active career, which ended only with his death in 1971 at the age of 88, Burt also set out to prove that human intelligence related closely to social class, with the highest social (or occupational) groupings possessing the highest intelligence scores (or IQs). We now know that much of Burt's research (particularly his later work) was based on fraudulent data (see Kamin, 1974; Hearnshaw, 1979); but in the 1930s and 1940s his findings were taken very seriously indeed.

As a leading eugenicist (accepting completely the need to find methods of improving the 'quality' of the human race), Burt's initial concerns had been centred on the provision of 'suitable' educational experiences for 'backward children', 'delinquent children' and 'the feeble-minded'. In an article for *The Eugenics Review,* published in 1913, he had made clear that his growing interest in the data to be obtained from intelligence testing derived largely from his concern with the problem of mental deficiency, emphasizing, at the same time that refined statistical techniques were necessary in order to identify those 'problem children' who were simply not capable, by reason of mental defect, of benefiting from the instruction given in an ordinary elementary school. Arguing that there was no such thing as 'manufactured feeblemindedness', his conclusion was simple and dogmatic: 'The fact of mental inheritance can no longer be contested: its importance scarcely over-estimated . . . There assuredly could be no problem upon which experimentalist, statistician and psychologist could so fruitfully concentrate their wisdom as the problem of heredity and its influence upon the mind' (Burt, 1913: 4).

Burt's own definition of 'human intelligence' was clearly stated in *How the Mind Works,* a book for popular consumption based on a series of broadcast talks delivered by Burt in 1933:

> By the term 'intelligence', the psychologist understands *inborn, all-round intellectual ability.* It is inherited, or at least innate, not due to teaching or training; it is intellectual, not emotional or moral, and remains uninfluenced by industry or zeal; it is general, not specific, i.e. it is not limited to any particular kind of work, but enters into all we do or say or think. Of all our mental qualities, it is the most far-reaching. Fortunately, it can be measured with accuracy and ease. (Burt, 1933: 28–9)

The implications of such a theory for the structuring of the post-war education system were both clear-cut and profound, as Burt himself acknowledged in a talk broadcast in November 1950:

> Obviously, in an ideal community, our aim should be to discover what ration of intelligence nature has given to each individual child at birth, then to provide him [sic] with the appropriate education, and finally to guide him into the career for which he seems to have been marked out. (Reprinted in *The Listener,* 16 November 1950)

Such views, expressed with uncompromising zeal, encouraged a fatalistic attitude among many classroom teachers who were clearly being led to believe that the level of 'intelligence' or 'intellectual ability' any child could reach was already determined by biological mechanisms. In other words, each child was born with *all that he or she could become*. As the American Professor of Philosophy, James Lawler, has pointed out, theories of the innate intellectual inferiority of certain classes of children mean that 'schools cannot be thought of as providing an enriching and creative environment, but should simply be adjusted to the function of sorting out and selecting the "bright" from the "dull", as determined by nature, and as basically reflected in the existing social hierarchy' (Lawler, 1978:3).

Yet, somewhat paradoxically, it was the development of the divided system itself in the period after 1945 that served to challenge and undermine the cast-iron convictions of Cyril Burt and his fellow psychometrists. In particular, the successes secured by many secondary modern school candidates in the new GCE (General Certificate of Education) Ordinary Level (O Level) examination introduced in 1951 had the unforeseen effect of exposing the fallibility of the 11-plus selection process. It was now becoming increasingly difficult to sustain the argument that a child's intellectual capacity was *wholly* or *mainly* due to something as fixed as genetic endowment.

One secondary modern school for girls serving a working-class area in a large industrial city, which took in only those children who had failed to gain a place at either a grammar or a selective central school, entered a number of pupils for the O Level examination in 1954. Of those who secured five or more passes, one had had an IQ of 97 on entry to the school in 1949, and another an IQ of 85. This was at a time when an IQ of 115 or over was generally considered to be essential in order to profit from examination courses. Indeed, other secondary modern schools were soon in a position to tell similar success stories, so that the psychometrists' standpoint did seem to have serious weaknesses (see Simon, 1955: 64–6).

Many suspected that 11-plus results were always *manipulated,* or at least the pass marks *adjusted,* to fit the number of grammar-school places available in any given area, and this certainly worked to disadvantage girls. In 1954, a front-page story appeared in *The Hunts Post,* the county paper for Huntingdonshire, under the bold headline 'Girls Brainier than Boys'. Too many girls had apparently been 'passing' the 11-plus and the education authority, ignoring the formal protests of teachers, had decided to limit their numbers. 'As a result', said *The Post,* 'some boys will be admitted to the grammar school, although their educational performance may be inferior to that of some of the girls who are excluded' (quoted in Grant, 1994: 37). Such stories did nothing to instil public confidence in a system which subjected children at the age of 11 to the very real strain of a fiercely competitive examination on which not only their future schooling, but also their future careers clearly depended.

In *The Comprehensive School,* first published in 1963, Robin Pedley gave voice to a number of popular concerns about 11-plus selection when he pointed out that none of the tests conceived and tried over the course of 60 years could satisfactorily distinguish 'natural talent' from 'what had been learned'. In his view, 'heredity' and 'environment' were too closely entangled to be clearly identified. This meant that children from 'literate homes', with 'interested and helpful parents', had a distinct advantage over 'children from culturally poor homes', where books were unknown and conversation was 'either limited or unprintable' (Pedley, 1963: 16-17).

Of even greater significance, the first chapter of the 1963 Newsom Report, *Half Our Future,* a report concerned with the education of 13–16 year-old students of 'average or less than average ability', contained the famous unequivocal statement: 'Intellectual talent is not a *fixed* quantity with which we have to work, but a variable that can be modified by social policy and educational approaches . . . The kind of intelligence which is measured by the tests so far applied is largely an *acquired* characteristic' (Ministry of Education, 1963a: 6). In his Foreword to the Report, the Conservative Education Minister, Edward Boyle, implicitly rejected the psychometrists' arguments by stating that the essential point we have to grasp is that 'all children should have an equal opportunity of acquiring intelligence, and of developing their talents and abilities to the full' (Ministry of Education, 1963a: iv).

Such thinking appeared to support the introduction of the comprehensive reform which is the theme of the next section. Even *Black Paper Two: The Crisis in Education,* published in 1969 and one of a series of right-wing documents attacking the associated concepts of comprehensive education, egalitarianism and 'progressive' teaching methods, contained an article by Dr Rhodes Boyson, the then Headteacher of Highbury Grove School in London, conceding, albeit in cautious terms, that the 11-plus selection system was flawed: 'There is no doubt that the eleven-plus test made considerable mistakes, that very many secondary modern school pupils can undertake academic work and that the arrangements for transfer within the tripartite system were unsatisfactory' (Boyson, 1969: 57).

Circular 10/65

By 1960, the number of pupils being educated in comprehensive schools in Britain amounted to less than 5 per cent of the secondary school population, but, between 1960 and 1964, one-quarter of all local education authorities made major changes in their selection procedures. This was the period when a social movement of considerable significance was clearly taking place. Indeed, looking back on this defining moment in post-war educational history in an article published in 1972, Edward Boyle recalled that when he became Education Minister in July 1962, it was clear to him that 'support for the development of secondary education along comprehensive lines was gaining considerable momentum' (Boyle, 1972: 32).

Harold Wilson's Labour Party was returned to power in the October 1964 General Election with a slight majority of just four over the other political parties. The new Secretary of State (in a reorganized Department of Education and Science) was Michael Stewart, who announced early in the new Parliament that it was the Government's policy to reorganize secondary education along comprehensive lines.

Under Stewart's successor, Anthony Crosland, it was decided (that implementation of the new policy in England and Wales would take the form of a Circular to be issued to all 163 local education authorities. We know that there was a fierce debate *within* the DES as to whether the Circular should *require* or *request* local authorities to prepare plans for reorganization, and this is a theme to which we will return in Chapter 5.

In its final form, Circular 10/65 began by declaring the Government's intention 'to end selection at eleven plus and to eliminate separatism in secondary education'. Local authorities were *requested* to submit, *within a year,* 'plans for reorganising secondary education in their areas on comprehensive lines'. No single pattern of comprehensive organization was laid down; instead, the Circular outlined the 'six main forms' that had so far emerged from 'experience and discussion'. Two of these would be acceptable only as 'interim solutions'; while the most favoured type was the 'all-through' 11–18 comprehensive school as pioneered in London, Coventry and elsewhere.

The two patterns regarded as 'acceptable' only as 'interim solutions' involved the use of separate schools for pupils over the age of 13 or 14 and the continuance of some form of selection. In one, for example, older pupils had to choose between a senior school catering for those who expected to stay at school well beyond the compulsory age and a senior school catering for those who did not.

The four patterns accepted as 'fully comprehensive' were:

- the orthodox comprehensive school for pupils aged 11–18
- a two-tier system whereby *all* pupils transferred automatically at 13 or 14, *without any form of selection,* to a senior comprehensive or upper school
- a two-tier system comprising schools for the 11–16 age range, combined with sixth form colleges for those over 16
- a two-tier system comprising new 'middle schools' for pupils aged 8–12 or 9–13, followed by 'upper schools' with an age range of 12 or 13 to 18.

It was accepted that the most appropriate system would depend on 'local circumstances' and that an authority might well decide to adopt 'more than one form of organisation' in a single area. It was made clear that the Government was not seeking to impose 'destructive or precipitate change on existing schools' and that 'the evolution of separate schools into a comprehensive system must be a constructive process requiring careful planning by local education authorities in consultation with all those concerned' (DES, 1965: 1,2,11).

In the event, and despite its conciliatory tone, the Circular was to prove unpopular with *both* the champions *and* the opponents of the comprehensive reform. For one thing, it stated that no extra money would be available to assist the process of reorganization before 1967/68, which meant that many of the new comprehensive schools would have to begin life in buildings designed for use as *separate* schools. Then again, the range of patterns which would be considered 'acceptable' as comprehensive schemes – even if only on a *temporary* basis – was so great as to create the well-founded suspicion that the resulting national system would resemble a patchwork quilt of uneven quality. The decision to rule out compulsion *might* have worked if government policy had not involved the phasing-out of a number of prestigious selective schools; but in the years following 1965, a number of local authorities, mainly Conservative-controlled, were able to make eye-catching headlines in the right-wing press with decisions that were clearly designed to flout the spirit of the Circular. Proponents of comprehensive reorganization would certainly have welcomed something more *dirigiste,* particularly after the March 1966 General Election which gave the Labour Party a Commons majority over the other political parties of nearly 100, with the clear prospect of a full five-year term ahead.

The end of consensus

It was at the end of the 1960s that the post-war consensus on a number of welfare issues first began to disintegrate, and this was particularly true in the case of education. For one thing, there was growing evidence of the exposed nature of Boyle's position on the 'liberal' wing of the Conservative Party, which became increasingly untenable as large groups of right-wing backbenchers and constituency activists mobilized against the beleaguered Shadow Education Minister (see Knight, 1990: 22–60). Matters came to a head at the 1968 Conservative Party Conference, where Boyle was challenged to acknowledge that the Party was irredeemably split on such major issues as comprehensive reorganization and the future of the grammar schools, and where he was forced to make a passionate plea on behalf of moderation and consensus: 'I will join with you willingly and wholeheartedly in the fight against Socialist dogmatism wherever it rears its head. But do not ask me to oppose it with an equal and opposite Conservative dogmatism, because in education, it is dogmatism itself which is wrong' (quoted in Corbett, 1969: 785).

By the end of the 1960s, it was obvious that Boyle's 'non-partisan' (or even 'bi-partisan') approach to key educational issues had lost the support of many grass-roots activists in the Party. But when he relinquished the post of Shadow Education Minister in 1969, the views of his vociferous critics still did not add up to what could be called a truly coherent 'rival philosophy'. Above all, there was a very real division on the far right of the Party between the so-called 'Preservationists', who wanted to maintain the grammar schools and some form of 11-plus selection, and the so-called 'Voucher Men', who were keen to experiment with new and untried ways of organizing education, principally the notion that all parents should be issued with a free basic coupon, fixed at the average cost of schools in their area, to be 'cashed in' at the school of their choice.

With the post-war consensus already beginning to fall apart, it was the economic recession of 1971–3 (already referred to in Chapter 2) that fundamentally altered the map of British politics. The oil crisis precipitated by the Organization of Petroleum Exporting Countries (OPEC) exposed all the underlying weaknesses of Keynesian social democracy; and the governments of Edward Heath (1970–4), Harold Wilson (1974–6) and James Callaghan (1976–9) were all unable to breathe new life into the old system. The post-war 'welfare capitalist consensus' relied on an increasing prosperity for any success it might have had in

creating a semblance of social unity; and, when that prosperity disinte-
grated, so, too, did the consensus, together with the false consciousness
it generated. As David Marquand has argued, the Keynesian approach to
the management of capitalism, with its tacit rejection of the reality of
class conflict, simply could not cope with the economic shocks and
adjustment problems of the mid-1970s:

> The post-war consensus finally collapsed under the Wilson–Callaghan
> Government of 1974–79, amid mounting inflation, swelling balance of
> payments deficits, unprecedented currency depreciation, rising unemploy-
> ment, bitter industrial conflicts and what seemed to many to be ebbing
> governability. The Conservative Leadership turned towards a new version of
> the classical market liberalism of the nineteenth century. Though the Labour
> leadership stuck to the tacit 'revisionism' of the 1950s and 1960s, large
> sections of the rank and file turned towards a more inchoate mixture of neo-
> Marxism and the 'fundamentalist' Socialism of the 1920s and 1930s.
> (Marquand, 1988: 3)

In Professor Marquand's view, both these opposing 'successor-
doctrines' were no better suited to the world of the late 1970s and 1980s
than was the Keynesian social democracy of the immediate post-war
period. 'At the centre of the neo-Liberals' moral universe lies the
idealised Market of the rising manufacturers of the first Industrial
Revolution. At the centre of the neo-Socialists' lies the epic struggle
between expropriators and expropriated, whose most compelling
hymnodist was Karl Marx' (Marquand, 1988).

It is, of course, important to point out that while both major political
parties contained groups with radical proposals for the future direction
of society, it was only in the Conservative Party – at least after the defeat
of Edward Heath as Leader and his replacement by Margaret Thatcher
in February 1975 – that such groups enjoyed easy access to the leadership. Indeed, it has been suggested by Mrs Thatcher's biographer, Hugo
Young (1993), that the economic crisis of the mid-1970s 'put paid to an
entire tradition of British Conservatism'.

3

From Callaghan to Major, 1976–97

This chapter carries on the story begun in Chapter 2 and covers the years from the Callaghan administration of 1976–9 to the dramatic fall of the Major Government in 1997.

A book published in 1984 examining education as social policy in the 35-year period from the passing of the 1944 Education Act to the end of the 1970s and the defeat of the Callaghan administration (Finch, 1984) was in the remarkable position of being able to summarize the major educational and social changes of that period in a table that contained only *three* Education Acts for the years from 1944 to 1976: the 1944 Education Act itself; the 1971 Education (Milk) Act passed during Margaret Thatcher's period as Education Secretary and removing the entitlement of free school milk for all children; and the 1976 Act requiring that, in future, admission to all state secondary schools should be non-selective. To be strictly accurate, there *were* other pieces of educational legislation passed in the 1950s and 1960s (specifying the responsibilities of local education authorities and schools, setting up middle schools, and establishing teacher negotiating procedures), but these were obviously not considered sufficiently important to be included in Janet Finch's table.

By contrast, the 20-year period from 1979 to 2000, which occupies our attention for most of this chapter, saw the passing of over 30 separate Education Acts, together with large numbers of accompanying circulars, regulations and statutory instruments. As part of the lengthy implementation of the 1988 Education Reform Act, described by education correspondents Ngaio Crequer and Peter Wilby in *The Independent* (28 July 1988) as 'a Gothic monstrosity of legislation', schools found themselves inundated with hundreds of curriculum documents, working group reports and explanatory circulars. Towards the end of this period, successive Secretaries of State tried to earn the goodwill of the teaching profession by promising a reduction in the volume of paperwork to be handled by headteachers and governing bodies; but, in practice, the amount of documentation continued to grow, with the pace of reform being especially frenetic after the victory of New Labour in 1997 (to be discussed more fully in Chapter 4).

Accountability and control under James Callaghan

The growth in legislative activity was accompanied by, or perhaps more accurately precipitated by, a breakdown in trust between central government, local government and teachers, but it would be wrong to see the Conservative electoral victory of May 1979 as marking the end of the post-war 'welfare capitalist consensus'; as we saw in the last chapter, that consensus had already fallen apart during the Wilson-Callaghan administration of 1974–9 (see Box 3.1). In addition to the economic crisis of 1971–3, which sent shock waves through the political establishment, there were a number of new and significant factors which together accounted for the general mood of pessimism and reappraisal which had set in by the middle of the 1970s.

For one thing, the state education system, in particular aspects of the secondary sector, was proving an easy target for a number of leading employers and industrialists. A major survey of employers' attitudes to young workers carried out by the National Youth Employment Council (NYEC) in 1974 reported that the majority of those questioned were becoming increasingly disillusioned with the output from the schools. They complained of a marked deterioration in the behaviour of young workers who were now 'more questioning', 'less likely to respect authority' and 'more likely to resent guidance about their general appearance' (NYEC, 1974: 74). Then, in January 1976, *The Times*

Box 3.1　Administrations, 1976–97

Party	Date formed	Prime Minister
Labour	April 1976	James Callaghan
Conservative	May 1979	Margaret Thatcher
Conservative	June 1983	Margaret Thatcher
Conservative	June 1987	Margaret Thatcher
Conservative	November 1990	John Major
Conservative	April 1992	John Major

Educational Supplement published a challenging article by Sir Arnold Weinstock, Managing Director of the General Electric Company, which stressed the *economic* function of schooling (already touched upon in Chapter 1). Entitled 'I blame the teachers', it argued that the shortage of both skilled and adaptable workers could be attributed to the failings of the education system. Moreover, the failure of schools to prepare their students for entry into the world of work raised important questions about the whole issue of the accountability of schools and teachers to the wider community. In Sir Arnold's view, teachers invariably lacked any direct experience of industry and in some cases were overtly hostile to the capitalist ethic and anxious to impose their views on their impressionable students:

> Teachers fulfil an essential function in the community but, having themselves chosen *not* to go into industry, they often deliberately, or perhaps unconsciously, instil in their pupils a similar bias. In so doing, they are obviously not serving the democratic will. And this is quite apart from the strong though unquantifiable impression an outsider receives that the teaching profession has more than its fair share of people who are actively politically committed to the overthrow of liberal institutions, democratic will or no democratic will . . . Educationists in schools, and in the teacher-training colleges, should recognise that they do no service to our children if they prepare them for life in a society which does not exist and which economic reality will never allow to come into existence, unless at a terrible price in individual liberty and freedom of choice. (*The Times Educational Supplement,* 23 January 1976)

Other industrialists were happy to endorse these views, notably John Methven, Director General of the Confederation of British Industry, who contributed his own article to *The Times Educational Supplement* entitled 'What industry needs' in October 1976. Here it was argued that educational standards were so low that many young people left school ill-equipped for almost any kind of employment and dreadfully ignorant about the basic workings of the British capitalist system:

> The question of standards rightly dominates much of our thinking about education today, particularly at the schools level. Employers have contributed to this debate because there has, over recent years, been growing dissatisfaction among them at the standards of achievement in the basic skills reached by many school leavers, particularly those leaving at the official age . . . It is a sad fact that, after one of the longest periods of compulsory education in Europe, many young people seem ill-equipped for almost any kind of employment and woefully ignorant about the basic economic facts of life in Britain.

According to John Methven, it was now time for employers to help secondary schools with the planning of their vocational programmes for students of 'average' and 'below-average' ability:

> Not until recently has industry been admitted even to peer into what has been called 'the secret garden of the curriculum'. Although it understands and respects the reason for this, it does now call for a rather new dimension in employers' thinking and, in our decentralist education system, something of an excursion into unknown territory. Employers generally have supported longer periods of schooling in their own and young people's interests. But they are now convinced that further advances in mass education must be concentrated on improving its quality; and they are ready and willing to help the schools in whatever ways seem appropriate and practicable . . . They certainly believe that shortcomings in the vocational preparation of young people are basically an educational problem which cannot be passed on to employers under the guise of training and induction. It is for this reason that they welcome the development of vocationally biased or relevant studies which has taken place in some secondary schools, and would now wish to see this extended. (*The Times Educational Supplement,* 29 October 1976)

To give added force to the employers' critique, important sections of the media were happy to publicize a picture of unscrupulous, unaccountable teachers delivering an increasingly irrelevant curriculum to large numbers of bored teenagers totally disenchanted with the business of learning and incapable of getting a proper job after 11 years of compulsory schooling. The five Black Papers published between 1969 and 1977 (Cox and Dyson, 1969a, 1969b, 1970; Cox and Boyson, 1975, 1977) were given a warm reception in the right-wing press which applauded their sustained attack on the associated concepts of comprehensive education, egalitarianism and 'progressive' teaching methods. There was much concentration on the problems of discipline (or, rather, the lack of it), with the oft-repeated accusation that unruly pupils in 'all-ability' comprehensive schools prevented hardworking 'academic' students from getting on with their studies and securing good examination results.

It was held by many that all the problems besetting state education began in the primary school and here much of the blame for a supposed decline in standards was laid at the door of the report of the committee examining primary education, chaired by Lady Plowden, which had been published in 1967 (DES, 1967). While initially welcomed for its warm humanity ('at the heart of the educational process lies the child'), the Plowden Report soon came to be attacked for its promotion of 'child-centred' learning and for its rejection of the traditional didactic teaching methods associated with the preparation of primary-school children for the old 11-plus selection examination. Evidence that the didactic teaching of the 1940s and 1950s produced much failure and demotivation and that many primary-school teachers were never particularly innovative in their teaching methods even after 1967 (see Simon, 1991: 379–82) did not trouble those who were anxious to demonize the 1960s as a decade when 'progressive education' destroyed the life-chances of thousands of children.

Along with the appearance of a number of hard-hitting articles calling for the vocationalization of the secondary-school curriculum for 'less able' students, 1976 also saw the publication of *Teaching Styles and Pupil Progress,* the report of the research findings of the controversial Lancaster Study into primary-school teaching methods undertaken by Neville Bennett. The main conclusion of Bennett's research was that pupils taught using so-called 'formal' methods (whole classes taught together often in silence, with regular testing and a good deal of healthy competition) were, on average, four months ahead of those taught using 'informal' methods; this conclusion was based on the results of tests in the basic skills in English and mathematics. There were other groups of classroom teachers who employed so-called 'mixed' styles, but their 'achievements' were generally too difficult to evaluate from the available data (Bennett, 1976). Although this study was heavily criticized for defects in research design and the use of oversimplified categorizations to represent teaching methods (see, for example, Gray and Satterly, 1976; Wragg, 1976; Galton, Simon and Croll, 1980), it was represented in the media as a full-scale scientific study of 'progressive' teaching methods which proved that they simply did not work. It is interesting to note that Bennett's book achieved unprecedented national publicity, and that the objections of the critics were largely ignored.

Even more damaging for the advocates of 'informal' or 'progressive' teaching methods in the primary school was the so-called William Tyndale Affair which occupied several column inches in the London and national press in the mid-1970s. Put simply, William Tyndale Junior School in Islington in North London was beset with troubles and conflicts between late 1973 and the autumn of 1975 which had a devastating effect on its standing in the local community. A group of teachers (including the Head) found themselves in conflict with parents, managers and eventually the Inner London Education Authority (ILEA) for operating a progressive curriculum which apparently ignored – or at least down-played – proficiency in reading, writing and arithmetic. The ILEA set up an inquiry into the running of the School; and the Auld

Report published in 1976 found that a group of extremist primary-school teachers had indeed been allowed to continue for far too long in what could be described as gross mismanagement of the curriculum (Auld, 1976). In the eyes of the media, the William Tyndale Affair was conclusive proof that enormous harm could be done by a group of 'progressive' teachers in a state school when parents were kept out of school decision-making and when managers and inspectors were clearly guilty of failing to fulfil their statutory duties. What was true of one badly managed primary school in North London might well apply to large numbers of primary and secondary schools in other parts of the country. Newspaper accounts offered the unedifying spectacle of unaccountable teachers who were at best sincere but misguided and at worst dangerous and politically motivated. In October 1976, a leading article in *The Times* went so far as to equate 'the wild men of the classroom' with trade union 'disruptors' and 'wreckers', arguing that they must be 'brought to heel' for the sake of the children (quoted in Simon, 1981: 7). In the more measured tones of *The Guardian,* some rearrangement in the patterns of accountability and control was now clearly necessary:

> Only the naive now believe that teachers can be left to teach, administrators to administer and managers to manage. Anyone who still believes this should be led gently to the Report of the William Tyndale Inquiry, which demonstrates the great difficulties of drawing clear boundaries of accountability in education. (*The Guardian,* 13 October 1976)

Between 1975 and 1977, a number of prominent national newspapers were instrumental in creating the idea that schooling in Britain was undergoing some sort of crisis, with teachers unable or unwilling to uphold standards, and managers, governors and inspectors incapable of tackling the malaise. There were confident assertions that 'parents throughout the country are becoming increasingly frustrated by the lack of discipline and the low standards of state schools' (*The Daily Mail,* 18 January 1975); that 'literacy in Britain is marching backwards' (*The Daily Mirror,* 7 February 1975); and that 'millions of parents are desperately worried about the education their children are receiving' (*The Daily Mail,* 27 April 1976). Parents were reported as blaming trendy, progressive teachers and child-centred pedagogy for the rising rate of youth employment and a breakdown in law and order. In the words of a history of schooling and social democracy in England from 1944 to 1980, published by the Centre for Contemporary Cultural Studies (CCCS) at the University of Birmingham in 1981: 'The reforms of the 1960s, especially the introduction of progressive methods and of comprehensive schools, were held responsible for an alleged decline in general standards and basic skills, for a lack of social discipline and the growing incongruence between the world of school and the world of work' (CCCS, 1981: 212). Parents now wanted to see a greater control of schooling by 'non-teachers', a return of formal teaching methods in the primary school and the re-introduction of selection at the secondary level. Labour politicians, in particular, were attacked for doing very little to respond to popular concerns.

The Conservative Party was naturally prepared to exploit the sense of 'crisis' surrounding the state education system although, as we saw in Chapter 2, there were clear divisions within the Party between, on the one hand, those who simply wanted to protect the remaining grammar schools and hankered for the return to some form of 11-plus selection and, on the other, those who were anxious to make the case for the education voucher as a means of strengthening parental choice and undermining the powers of local education authorities. In July 1975, Norman St John-Stevas, the Chief Opposition Spokesperson on Education from 1974 to 1978, joined forces with Leon Brittan, Chairperson of the Legal Sub-Committee of the Conservative Parliamentary Education Committee and later to become a leading member of various Thatcher Cabinets, to produce a short, highly legalistic, Conservative Political Centre pamphlet called *How to Save Your Schools*. This was, in effect, a brief handbook for Conservative local government activists, giving guidance on how to 'save the existing grammar schools' by 'utilising every possible legalistic procedure' (Brittan and St John-Stevas, 1975; see also Knight, 1990: 107; Simon, 1991: 443–4). In the same year, right-wing contributors to the fourth Black Paper, *Black Paper 1975: The Fight for Education* (Cox and Boyson, 1975) joined the ranks of those who blamed Labour ministers for a seemingly irreversible decline in educational standards and for rejecting the whole idea of 'excellence' in education. Amid the general climate of suspicion and recrimination, it was hardly surprising that by the time Harold Wilson resigned as Labour Prime Minister in March 1976, the Labour Party had been thrown on the defensive by the sheer ferocity and scale of the right-wing attack on its education and social policies. There did indeed appear to be much justification for the triumphant claim made by Dr Rhodes Boyson, a former headteacher of Highbury Grove School in London, co-editor of the 1975 and 1977 Black Papers and by the mid-1970s a prominent right-wing Conservative MP, at a well-attended meeting organized by the National Council for Educational Standards (NCES) in May 1976 that: 'the forces of the Right in education are on the offensive. The blood is flowing from the other side now' (reported in *The Times Educational Supplement,* 21 May 1976).

Shortly after succeeding Harold Wilson as Prime Minister in April 1976, James Callaghan received an important memorandum from Bernard Donoughue, Head of the newly created Downing Street Policy Unit, suggesting, among other things, that it would be politically expedient, given the widespread interest in the subject, for the new occupant of Number Ten to make educational standards a central feature of his new administration. (A discussion of the key role played by Donoughue and the Policy Unit in educational policy-making between 1976 and 1979 will be found in Chapter 5.) According to Donoughue's book of memoirs, published in 1987, education was felt to be a key area where the new Prime Minister would be able to reveal his personal concern and commitment:

> I suggested to Mr Callaghan that although it was undesirable for a Prime Minister to meddle in every department's affairs, it would be no bad thing if he were to identify a few areas of policy of genuine interest to himself where he could try to make an impact; and I put forward education as a leading candidate. (Donoughue, 1987: 111)

The Prime Minister's response to Donoughue's memorandum was certainly positive, and he opted for the chance to deliver a major speech on education at the earliest opportunity. In the event, this proved to be a foundation stone-laying ceremony at Ruskin College, Oxford, in the middle of October. Donoughue spent part of the summer of 1976 working on the proposed speech with Elizabeth Arnott, the education specialist in the Policy Unit, and the first draft was ready in the early autumn. Donoughue and Arnott also wrote the section on education which the Prime Minister included in his Address to the 1976 Labour Party Conference held at the end of September and which served as a 'curtain-raiser' to the Ruskin College speech delivered three weeks later. Both of these speeches were viewed by members of the Downing Street Policy Unit as opportunities to launch a Great Debate on Education and wrest the populist mantle from the Conservatives.

In the meantime, the Prime Minister decided to interview leading members of the Cabinet using briefing papers prepared by Donoughue; and his reasons for doing this were outlined in his own book of memoirs published in 1987:

> It had been my experience that ministers usually asked to see the Prime Minister only when they had a personal problem or had run into a difficulty;

and I decided to reverse this trend. So during the early months after I took office, and in pursuit of my intention not to become over-immersed in the Chancellor's economic problems, I invited other ministers to come to see me individually, and without their officials or civil servants, to tell me about their work. We sat informally in the study at Number Ten, and I put to all of them two basic and fundamental questions. What were they aiming to do in their Department? What was stopping them? I prepared for these informal chats by asking Bernard Donoughue and his Policy Unit, in conjunction with my Private Office, to prepare an overview of each Department's activities before I saw the Minister, and Bernard would also suggest certain areas for me to probe. I was told later that preparations for these occasions used to cause a flurry of activity in the Department. Officials and civil servants were naturally anxious to put the best possible face on their work, and the fact that their Minister would be accounting *à deux* to the Prime Minister, who might ask awkward questions if he were well enough informed, added spice and a touch of danger to the meeting. Moreover, it gave ministers the opportunity to bend my ear and create a favourable climate for their activities. I learned a lot, and I believe it made busy ministers immersed in never-ending departmental activities pause and think. (Callaghan, 1987: 408)

One of the first ministers to be interviewed was Fred Mulley who had been a pretty 'low-profile' Secretary of State for Education and Science since June 1975 (see Box 3.2); and when the 'informal chat' took place in May, Callaghan raised with him four of the major areas of concern that were to preoccupy his administration over the coming three years.

- Was the Department satisfied with the basic teaching of the three Rs?
- Was the curriculum sufficiently relevant and penetrating for older children in comprehensive schools, especially in the teaching of science and mathematics?

Box 3.2   Secretaries of State, 1975–97

Fred Mulley	June 1975–September 1976
Shirley Williams	September 1976–May 1979
Mark Carlisle	May 1979–September 1981
Sir Keith Joseph	September 1981–May 1986
Kenneth Baker	May 1986–July 1989
John MacGregor	July 1989–November 1990
Kenneth Clarke	November 1990–April 1992
John Patten	April 1992–July 1994
Gillian Shephard	July 1994–May 1997

- How did the examination system shape up as a test of achievement?
- What was available for the further education of 16-19 year olds?

At the end of the meeting, Mulley undertook to prepare a lengthy memo-randum on the state of the education system: the so-called Yellow Book was on the Prime Minister's desk two months later.

This Yellow Book, dated July 1976, which has never appeared in the public domain in its entirety, was in fact a 63-page confidential docu-ment compiled by DES civil servants which addressed many of the issues that concerned James Callaghan and his political advisers. It began by referring to the widespread nature of press and media criticism of the performance of state schools, and was prepared to accept that much of this criticism was justified. In the first place, it was very uneasy about the 'child-centred' approach to primary-school teaching which had been endorsed by the influential Plowden Report published in 1967. In the view of the DES, this new approach *could* have positive results in the hands of gifted teachers; but all too often it was applied uncritically, with a consequent undermining of standards of performance in the three Rs. At the same time, the memorandum was highly critical of 'experi-mentation' in the secondary school which had led to teachers becoming too easy-going and demanding too little work from their pupils and inad-equate standards of performance in all the important core disciplines.

What, then, could be done to restore public confidence in the state education system? Of the various proposals put forward in the Yellow Book, *three* were guaranteed to gain the approval of James Callaghan and Bernard Donoughue (DES, 1976: 11, 14, 25):

- The need to restore rigour to the teaching of the three Rs in primary schools and to establish generally accepted principles for the compo-sition of a 'core curriculum' for pupils in secondary schools.
- The need to make suitable provision for vocational elements within school education for those combining 'average' and 'below-average' ability with practical interests.
- The need to make politicians and the teachers' unions realize that an essential prerequisite for effective change along lines approved of by the Government was a general assault on the principle that 'no one except teachers has any right to any say in what goes on in schools'.

The Yellow Book ended by stating that it would be good to get on record from ministers and, in particular, from the Prime Minister 'an authoritative pronouncement on the division of responsibility for what goes on in schools, suggesting that the Department should give a firmer lead' (DES, 1976: 25). At the same time, the document was anxious to emphasize that the DES did not seek enhanced opportunity to exercise influence over curriculum and teaching methods *for its own sake*. It needed control in order to promote changes in schools, at both the primary and secondary levels, which would restore public confidence in the state system. The civil servants of the Department felt that they had a legitimate right to be concerned about standards and the efficiency of the system because they were accountable to politicians and parents who had a right to demand 'value for money'. A new core curriculum and an emphasis on vocational courses for those who would benefit from them would do much to allay the misgivings of parents and employers.

The general tone of the Yellow Book fitted so well with the message that Callaghan was hoping to get across in his Ruskin College speech that it was considered 'appropriate' to 'leak' key sections of it to *The Guardian* and *The Times Educational Supplement* in the middle of October 1976 as a means of 'testing the water' prior to the Prime Minister's visit to Oxford (see Chitty, 1989: 81–6). *The Guardian* carried a front-page article on the Yellow Book on 13 October under the bold headline 'State must step into schools'; this was followed two days later by a major three-page report on the document in *The Times Educational Supplement.*

Both James Callaghan and Bernard Donoughue had clear ideas about the purposes that the Ruskin speech was meant to serve. According to the Prime Minister:

> My general guidance for the Speech was that it should begin a debate about existing educational trends and should ask some controversial questions. It should avoid blandness and bring out some of the criticisms I had heard in my travels around the country, whilst explaining the value of teachers' work and the need for parents to be more closely associated with their children's schools. It should ask why industry's status was so low in young people's choice of careers, and the reasons for the shortage of mathematics and science teachers. (Callaghan, 1987: 410)

For Bernard Donoughue, it was particularly important that the speech should concern itself with the improvement of standards and the relatively new concept of teacher accountability:

> In the Speech, I made sure that I included all the feelings which I shared with the Prime Minister on the need for more rigorous educational standards, for greater monitoring and accountability of teachers, for greater concentration

on the basic skills of literacy and numeracy, and for giving greater priority to technical, vocational and practical education. (Donoughue, 1987: 111)

The speech itself, delivered on 18 October 1976, argued that, first and foremost, there was the need to make effective use of the money – roughly £6 billion a year – that the Government was now spending on education. In recent years there had been a massive injection of resources into education, mainly to cope with increased pupil numbers and partly to raise standards. Now the challenge was to raise standards still further by the skilful use of existing resources:

> With the increasing complexity of modern life, we cannot be satisfied with simply maintaining existing standards, let alone observe any decline. We must aim for something better . . . But in the present circumstances, there can be little expectation of further increased resources being made available, at any rate for the time being . . . and a challenge in education is to examine its priorities and to secure as high efficiency as possible by the skilful use of the £6 billion of existing resources.

At the same time, teachers had to accept that where educational standards were concerned, theirs was not the only voice with a right to be heard:

> I take it that no one claims exclusive rights in this field. Public interest is strong and legitimate and will be satisfied . . . To all the teachers I would say that you must satisfy the parents and industry that what you are doing meets their requirements and the needs of our children. For if the public is not convinced, then the profession will be laying up trouble for itself in the future. (Quoted in Chitty, 1989: 94)

According to the Prime Minister, there were six areas of concern that required further investigation and study as a matter of priority (Chitty, 1989):

- The methods and aims of 'informal instruction'.
- The case for a so-called 'core curriculum' of basic knowledge.
- The means by which the use of resources might be monitored in order to maintain a proper national standard of performance.
- The role of the Inspectorate in relation to national standards.
- The relationship between industry and education.
- The future structure of public examinations.

As I have argued elsewhere (1989: 95), James Callaghan's much-publicized Ruskin College speech can be viewed and assessed on a number of different levels, all of them interrelated. Essentially, it marked the end of the period of educational expansion which had been largely promoted by the Labour Party, though it is fair to point out that, as Education Secretary, Margaret Thatcher had issued a White Paper in 1972 with the title *Education: A Framework for Expansion* (DES, 1972). That period was clearly over; there had to be a public re-definition of educational objectives involving the more skilful use of limited resources. To a large extent, the timing of the speech was a considered response to immediate events: the economic crisis of the first half of the 1970s, escalating youth unemployment and a declining birth rate. It also owed much to the need to wrest the populist mantle from the Conservative Opposition and show an awareness of perceived public disquiet at the alleged decline in educational standards. Sections of the national press had played a major role in undermining public confidence in the comprehensive system; and popular reservations about 'progressive' or informal teaching styles appeared to be justified by the William Tyndale Affair and by the Bennett study of primary teaching methods. The Labour Government was anxious to demonstrate that it shared the concerns of ordinary parents. Then again, the speech marked a clear shift on the part of the Labour leadership towards policies which would facilitate greater control of the education system. This 'control' was obviously necessary if new government ideas on the curriculum were to be implemented throughout the country. For, above all, the speech can be viewed as a clear attempt to construct a new educational consensus around a more direct subordination of education to what were perceived to be the needs of the economy. This was the consensus underpinning the so-called Great Debate of 1976–7 which culminated in the publication in July 1977 of the Green Paper, *Education in Schools: A Consultative Document* (DES, 1977a) reaffirming a strictly utilitarian view of education and training.

The first two Thatcher administrations, 1979–87

Much was expected of the new Thatcher administration elected in May 1979 as far as radical social and educational policies were concerned. Since being elected to replace Edward Heath as Leader of the Conservative Party in February 1975, Margaret Thatcher had, after all, been particularly anxious to encourage the development of ideas and policies which challenged all the 'taken-for-granted' assumptions of the post-war welfare consensus.

There was certainly no shortage of groups and individuals prepared to 'think the unthinkable'. Contributors to the last two Black Papers, published in 1975 and 1977, included those who wished to move *beyond* the cautious conservatism of the first three documents, and this involved advocating voucher schemes based on the beguilingly simple principle that all parents should be issued with a free basic coupon, fixed at the average cost of schools in the local authority area. The editors of the 1975 Paper urged the introduction of the education voucher in at least two trial areas (Cox and Boyson, 1975: 4); and support for the voucher was then reiterated in the Editorial Introduction to *Black Paper 1977* which took the form of a 'Letter to Members of Parliament': 'The possibilities for parental choice of secondary (and also primary) schools should be improved via the introduction of the education voucher or some other method. Schools that few wish to attend should then be closed and their staff dispersed' (Cox and Boyson, 1977: 9). The new emphasis was clearly on choice and competition and parental control of schools. Even the very concept of a 'national system, locally administered' was being called into question as part of the attempt to make a clean break with the past (this will be discussed more fully in Chapter 5).

The new ideas put forward in the last two Black Papers were very much in line with the thinking of a vast array of right-wing think tanks and pressure groups which had acquired great power and influence by the time of the Conservatives' 1979 election victory, guided by a clear determination to have a real say in the future direction of government policy-making. Mrs Thatcher had herself played a major role, with Sir Keith Joseph and Alfred Sherman, in the establishment in August 1974 of the Centre for Policy Studies (CPS), a think tank intended to be more daring and radical than the essentially moderate Conservative Research Department headed by Chris Patten (see Knight, 1990: 90). It soon spawned a variety of study groups, among them the Education Research Group whose brief was to devise innovative solutions to existing problems. In the same year, Marjorie Seldon presented a motion in favour of experimental education vouchers at the Annual Conference of the National Council for Women, which led directly to the setting up in December 1974 of a group called FEVER (Friends of the Education Voucher Experiment in Representative Regions). The spring of 1975 saw the formation of the Conservative Philosophy Group (CPG) by Roger Scruton and John Casey, then two academics at Peterhouse College, Cambridge; and Roger Scruton went on to become a founder member of the Salisbury Group established in 1977 (and later Editor of *The Salisbury Review,* 'a quarterly magazine of conservative thought' which began life in 1982 and published a number of articles on education). While all the above pressure groups were very much *recent* creations at the time of Mrs Thatcher's first election victory, a further body, the Institute of Economic Affairs (IEA), had been in existence for nearly 25 years. Described by the historian, Clive Griggs, as the institution which probably deserves the greatest credit for moving the political debate to the right in the 1970s (Griggs, 1989: 101), the IEA had been set up as a research and educational trust in 1955. It had begun disseminating its ideas in 1957 with the first of a series of specialized studies of markets and pricing systems as technical devices for registering preferences and apportioning resources. The Hobart Paperbacks, begun in 1971, were designed to analyse the circumstances in which IEA proposals emerging from economic analysis were likely to be adopted as official government policy; the introduction of education vouchers was one of the Institute's pet projects. Throughout the 1970s, the IEA worked tirelessly to persuade the Conservative Party to abandon the post-war welfare consensus and embrace social and educational policies based on nineteenth-century free-market anti-statism.

All these think tanks and study groups, with their impressive titles and interlocking memberships – and pressure of space has permitted discussion of only a select group of them – constituted what is commonly referred to as the New Right. This encompassed a wide range of groups and ideas and there were many internal divisions and conflicts; but what made it special and important was a unique combination of a liberal defence of the free economy with a traditional conservative defence of state authority. The New Right was, in reality, a broad coalition of neo-liberals, interested chiefly in competition, free markets and tight control of public spending, and neo-conservatives, interested primarily in upholding nineteenth-century notions of tradition, hierarchy and social order. We shall see later how, where education was concerned, the two groups could not reach agreement on the desirability or otherwise of introducing a compulsory national curriculum.

Yet, having recorded all this intellectual activity and preparation, it comes as something of a surprise that the first two Thatcher administrations were, in fact, notable for a remarkable degree of caution in the actual *implementation* of radical or innovative social policies. As Mrs Thatcher herself conceded in her memoirs (Thatcher, 1993), education was not a priority of the Government in 1979. The initial objectives were two-fold: to bring down the rate of inflation (even at the risk of sustaining very high levels of unemployment) and to curb the power and influence of such troublesome extra-Parliamentary institutions as the big trade unions. Much of the Welfare State was left intact; and there was little evidence of pioneering reappraisals in the areas of housing, health and education.

Educational issues were accorded comparatively little space in the 1979 Conservative Election Manifesto; and plans to maintain and improve standards were included as part of a larger section with the broad title 'Helping the Family'. In this part of the Manifesto, the Conservatives' chief proposals included (Conservative Party, 1979: 24–6):

• the repeal of those sections of the Labour Government's 1976 Education Act that had *required* recalcitrant local education authorities to proceed with comprehensive reorganization
• more effective use of Her Majesty's Inspectorate (HMI) and of the Assessment of Performance Unit (APU) which had been set up in 1974 to 'promote the development of methods of assessing and monitoring the achievement of children at school'
• the introduction of a new Parents' Charter
• the introduction of an Assisted Places Scheme.

Designed, in the words of the Manifesto, to enable 'less well-off parents to claim part or all of the fees at certain independent schools from a special government fund', the Assisted Places Scheme was the one truly radical measure introduced by Margaret Thatcher's first Education Secretary, the moderate and essentially pragmatic Mark Carlisle (1979–81). To some extent, it can be seen as an attempt to revive the principle of the 154 direct grant grammar schools abolished by the previous Labour Government in March 1975. It was broadly conceived as a sort of 'scholarship ladder' that would benefit 'able' children from 'poor homes' who would otherwise be 'inadequately stretched' at their local 'underachieving' comprehensive school. According to Carlisle himself, the purpose behind the Scheme was 'to give certain children a greater opportunity to pursue a particular form of academic education that was regrettably not otherwise, particularly in the cities, available to them' (quoted in Griggs, 1985: 89). As far as Labour critics were concerned, the Scheme simply reinforced the view that comprehensive state education was unable to offer all children a decent education and was thereby bolstering the image of the private sector. It was described by Labour peer Lord Alexander during a fierce debate in the House of Lords in September 1982, as 'an offensive public declaration by a government that the national system of state education is incapable of providing for our most able children' (reported in *The Times Educational Supplement,* 19 September 1982). Subsequent research showed that the Scheme did not, in fact, achieve very much for those for whom it was supposedly intended, and that the majority of children who took 'assisted places' came from homes with 'educationally advantaged' parents (Edwards, Fitz and Whitty, 1989). The Labour Party pledged to abolish the Scheme (and this actually happened in 1997).

If much of a radical nature was expected from the DES during Margaret Thatcher's period as Prime Minister, this was especially true when Sir Keith Joseph replaced Mark Carlisle as Education Secretary in September 1981. Sir Keith had, after all, been a co-founder of the Centre for Policy Studies in 1974, and had played a leading role in encouraging Mrs Thatcher's disillusionment with the corporatist and collectivist nature of the Heath Government's social and economic programme. In an important speech to the Oxford Union delivered in December 1975, he had argued that the Conservative Party had become obsessed with occupying 'the middle ground of politics'. Since it possessed no coherent philosophical position of its own, the Party had been forced to make humiliating concessions to the left-dominated consensus. In the cynical and ultimately futile pursuit of votes, politicians of the right had allowed the left to draw up the agenda. As a result, according to Sir Keith's analysis, the ideological battle was being lost by default, with disastrous consequences for the moral well-being of the nation. At a time of crisis, it was clearly imperative for the right to go on to the offensive and assume domination of the intellectual battlefield (Joseph, 1976).

Sir Keith was known to be a keen supporter of the education voucher for which the right had been campaigning in earnest since the mid-1970s. Legislation passed in 1980 had enhanced the notion of parental choice by allowing parents to express preferences for particular schools and setting up appeals committees for dissatisfied parents. Shortly after his appointment, Sir Keith used his speech to the 1981 Conservative Party Conference to declare his personal support for the further promotion of 'parent power':

> I personally have been intellectually attracted to the idea of seeing whether eventually, *eventually,* a voucher might be a way of increasing parental choice even further . . . I know that there are very great difficulties in making a voucher deliver – in a way that would commend itself to us – more choice than policies already announced will, in fact, deliver. It is now up to the advocates of such a possibility to study the difficulties – and there are *real* difficulties – and then see whether they can develop proposals which will really cope with them. (Joseph, 1981)

Yet this was to be one occasion when the right did *not* get its way (a point to which we will return in Chapter 5); and at the 1983 Conservative Party Conference, Sir Keith was reluctantly forced to concede that 'the voucher, at least in the foreseeable future, is dead'. Interviewed after leaving office, he was keen to emphasize that all the various schemes devised by his political advisers had to be abandoned for *political* rather than for *financial* reasons:

> I wanted vouchers simply because you transfer in one go from the producers to the consumers . . . But I was a frustrated enthusiast, because I was forced to accept that, largely for political reasons, it wouldn't be practicable . . . Not, as some think, for financial reasons . . . Certainly not . . . Finances didn't enter into it. Finances certainly didn't enter into it. No, it was political. In the sense . . . that you would have to have very controversial legislation, which would probably take two or three years to carry through, with my Party split on the issue and the other Parties all unanimously hostile on the wrong grounds . . . And all the producer forces would be hostile. And then one would have had to decide either to go by way of imposition – from an appointed date, there shall be vouchers everywhere – or one could have gone forward with a pilot scheme. And a pilot scheme would probably have been wrecked by producer hostility and could have produced only a mouse. And I didn't think that I had the moral courage to impose the voucher. Of course, it wouldn't have been like imposing comprehensivisation: it would have been imposing *freedom* – that's the main difference between the two. (Quoted in Chitty, 1997a: 82–3)

With education vouchers off the political agenda, at least 'in the fore-seeable future', Sir Keith Joseph had time to give his personal support to other educational initiatives, notably the drive to make the secondary school curriculum more vocational for students of 'average' and 'below average' ability. In this respect, his thinking was not that far removed from that of ministers, civil servants and political advisers in the final years of the 1974–9 Labour administration. He allowed the Manpower Services Commission (MSC) to wield considerable power and influence during his period as Education Secretary (1981–6), and the MSC's main achievement in the area of curriculum reform was the Technical and Vocational Education Initiative (TVEI). Designed to stimulate work-related education and make the school curriculum more 'relevant' to post-school life, the TVEI was introduced as a series of 14 pilot projects in a number of carefully selected schools in the autumn of 1983. By the time Sir Keith left office, it involved 65,000 students in 600 school and colleges.

The 1988 Education Reform Act

It was left to the less ideologically committed and decidedly more prag-matic Kenneth Baker, who replaced Sir Keith Joseph as Education Secretary in May 1986, to introduce the most radical educational measures of the Thatcher period. In fact, Kenneth Baker inaugurated a period of about ten years when the Conservative Government appeared to be gripped by a frenzied need to legislate on every aspect of educa-tion, with a new and often complex education act arriving on the statute books almost every year. According to Professor Sally Tomlinson, the main aims of all this legislation, beginning with the 1988 Education Act, included:

> Consolidating a market ideology to be achieved by parental choice, estab-lishing central government control over curriculum and assessment, further eroding the powers and responsibilities of local authorities, teachers and their trainers, demanding accountability from individuals and institutions, espe-cially the universities, and encouraging selection under a rhetoric of diver-sity. (Tomlinson, 2001: 43)

As we shall see in Chapter 4, these basic aims have not changed signif-icantly since the arrival of a New Labour government in 1997.

The 1988 Act itself made the decisive break with the principles which had underpinned the education service since the Butler Education Act of 1944. With its 238 clauses and 13 schedules, covering everything from the 'spiritual welfare' of the next generation to the definition of a 'half day', it took up nearly 370 hours of parliamentary time and gave the Secretary of State 451 new powers. It actually covered England and Wales only, although parallel bills with many similarities had also been prepared for Scotland and Northern Ireland. In attempting to redesign the education service from top to bottom, it attracted more bitter and widespread professional opposition than any piece of legislation passed since the introduction of the National Health Service in the second half of the 1940s.

To encapsulate its basic purpose, the 1988 Act sought to erect (or reinforce) a hierarchical system of schooling subject both to market forces and to greater control from the centre. As far as the creation of choice and diversity was concerned, much attention, both in the media and among academics, was focused on the creation of a new tier of schooling comprising City Technology Colleges (CTCs) and grant-maintained or 'opted-out' schools.

Already announced nearly two years before the 1988 Act become law, the new CTCs were designed to be 11–18 schools financed partly by private capital, independent of local authority control and providing a new choice of school in 'deprived' inner-city areas. They were to have their own conditions of service and salary scales for teachers, with overall control vested in governing bodies dominated by representatives from industry. They were encouraged to select 'well-motivated' and hardworking pupils and give them a standard of education supposedly denied to most children from impoverished urban backgrounds. The first CTC, in Kingshurst, Solihull, opened in September 1987, but although the original plan was that 20 such Colleges would be open by 1990, the scheme met with very real difficulties in finding suitable sites and a sufficient number of wealthy backers, and only 15 eventually got off the ground. (It is interesting to note that the idea was to be revived in a modified form by New Labour; and this will be discussed in Chapter 4.)

The grant-maintained schools introduced in the 1988 Act were those schools which chose to opt out of the locally maintained education system and receive their funding direct from central government. The governing body would act as a private trust and control the budget and policy of the school. It is fair to say that considerable controversy and confusion surrounded the precise nature of this new type of school in the weeks leading up to the 1987 General Election. At one pre-election press conference, Mrs Thatcher argued that the heads and governing bodies of those secondary schools that 'opted out' of local authority control should be free to establish their own admissions policies and would not necessarily be prevented from raising extra funds from parents, thereby giving rise to much speculation in the media that the new plans might well include a fee-paying element (reported in *The Guardian*, 23 May 1987). Then Kenneth Baker conceded during a BBC Radio Four *World at One* discussion, broadcast on 10 June 1987, that there would be nothing to stop 'better-off' parents raising additional sums of money for their particular 'opted-out' school so that the headteacher would have the resources to purchase particularly expensive books or items of equipment and perhaps even reward some of the more successful teachers with higher salaries. The anxiety aroused by such comments forced the DES to issue press releases playing down the fee-paying aspect and denying that the chief purpose of encouraging schools to go 'grant-maintained' was to introduce a new form of secondary selection.

In fact, despite all the attention paid to the new tier of schooling, from the point of view of creating a new education system, the most significant provision in the 1988 legislation was probably the introduction of LMS, or Local Management of Schools, involving a new and ingenious scheme for financial delegation whereby local authorities would be required to distribute funds to their primary and secondary schools by means of a weighted, per capita formula. Governing bodies were then to be responsible for controlling the budgets delegated to them. This important development, taken in conjunction with the provision for open enrolment, was viewed by many commentators at the time (see, for example, Maclure, 1988: 42–3; Walford, 1990: 98–100) as a subtle means of adapting the education system in such a way as to make a future transition to education vouchers possible without undue disruption. A school could no longer be 'maintained' as an institution independently of the choices which parents exercised. Under the 1988 scheme for financial delegation, the per capita payments were still to be paid to the school; but the circumstances had been engineered in which it would be a relatively simple matter to give the money directly to the parents instead. This has not quite happened in ways favoured by the right; but it is still true that the 1988 Act can be seen as 'a stage in the process of privatising by stealth' (Walford, 1990: 102).

Among those who played a major role in drawing up the provisions of the 1988 Act, there was considerable resentment at the last minute inclusion of clauses pertaining to the creation of a compulsory national curriculum. This would consist of three core and seven foundation subjects for all pupils aged 5–16 (for further details, see Chapters 6 and 7), to be assessed at the end of four key stages, Key Stage Four ending with the General Certificate of Secondary Education (GCSE) examination which had been introduced as a single system of examining at 16 in 1986. A National Curriculum Council and a School Examinations and Assessment Council would oversee the arrangements, but the Secretary of State was granted considerable power to decide ultimately on actual curriculum content.

As one of Mrs Thatcher's principal education advisers and a leading member of the neo-liberal faction of the New Right, Stuart Sexton has argued that the National Curriculum constituted a quite separate and unnecessary piece of legislation, serving merely to divert attention from the free-market objectives he and others had been working towards:

In my view, the 1988 Education Reform Act was really *two* Acts of Parliament. Now one of those Acts of Parliament I and others had been working on in the latter days of Keith Joseph . . . for the better management and financing of our schools, and there you will find grant-maintained schools and all the rest of it. That was the Bill and the Act we cared about. The second Act of Parliament . . . which got pushed in at the last minute . . . was all to do with central control over the curriculum; and now I claim no credit for that, and neither do the others that were working with me under Keith at that time . . . There was this constant wish on the part of many civil servants at the Department of Education and Science going back years and years, although even they didn't expect the new National Curriculum to be quite so detailed. And the new Secretary of State Kenneth Baker accepted their pressure to have the National Curriculum welded on to the Bill we'd been working on . . . And it was a late introduction . . . and it really went through *in spite of* the politicians, rather than *because of* the politicians . . . And it diverted attention away from the really important parts of the legislation . . . You see the curriculum should be one of the school's selling-points with its own particular consumers . . . Schools should be able to respond to what they perceive the market is looking for . . . The National Curriculum undermines what we were trying to achieve. (Sexton, 1995)

Choice and diversity under John Major

Very little was known about John Major's political and social philosophy when he replaced Margaret Thatcher as Leader of the Conservative Party and Prime Minister in November 1990. Would his arrival in Downing Street usher in a gentler, more compassionate form of Conservatism, involving a return to 'one-nation' values and a renewed concern for social cohesion and social unity? Would the policies pursued by his administration – and particularly those relating to education and health – mark a genuine departure from the radical privatizing agenda of Mrs Thatcher's third term in office? There were a number of leading Conservatives who longed for a period of calm and consolidation; and it has been argued that part of the reason for the Conservatives' (unexpected) success in the 1992 General Election lay in the fact that they were able to convince a sizeable proportion of the British electorate that there had already, in a sense, been a change of government in 1990.

The former Prime Minister herself was in no doubt that John Major would be more or less forced to adhere to her agenda since, as she argued in her famous post-election *Newsweek* article of 27 April 1992, there was simply no such thing as Majorism:

I don't accept the idea that, all of a sudden, John Major is his own man. He has been Prime Minister for just 17 months, and he inherited all those great achievements of the past eleven and a half years which have fundamentally changed Britain, ridding it of the debilitating, negative aspect of Socialism . . . There isn't such a thing as Majorism. There couldn't be at the moment. My colleagues and I turned round the whole philosophy of government. We restored the strength and reputation of Britain. We did it on fundamental principles. They bear *my* name, but they are, in fact, older than I am. Mr Major has accepted these principles, written them into his manifesto, held it up and said: 'It's all me'. What he means is that the things he put in there were *his* choice. But I believe it is *my* legacy he will be forced to take forward. (Thatcher, 1992: 14–15)

It can be argued that Mrs Thatcher had no real need to worry about her successor's respect for her legacy where education policy was concerned. John Major's philosophy was, in fact, an interesting mixture of a concern to promote Thatcherite privatizing measures and a more traditional Conservative belief in the self-evident values of a merito-cratic society. In his ideal world, schools would increasingly compete for pupils by offering various specializations, with parents being encouraged to consult league tables as reliable guides to local authority, school and pupil performance. At the same time, during his administration there would be a continued blurring of the boundaries between the private and state sectors.

One of the key education policies of the 1992–7 Major administration was that of selection by specialization. The need for all Socialists to come to terms with the concept of specialization at the secondary level was, in fact, the theme of an article by the Education Secretary, John Patten, published in the *New Statesman and Society* in July 1992:

Selection is not, and should not be, a great issue for the 1990s as it was in the 1960s. The S-word for all Socialists to come to terms with is, rather, 'special-isation'. The fact is that children excel at different things; it is foolish to ignore it, and some schools may wish specifically to cater for these differ-ences. Specialisation, underpinned by the National Curriculum, will be the answer for *some* – though not *all* – children, driven by aptitude and interest, as much as by ability. (Patten, 1992: 20)

The White Paper, *Choice and Diversity: A New Framework for Schools,* published on 28 July 1992, claimed that since the Conservative victory in 1979, five great themes had characterized educational change in England and Wales: quality, diversity, increasing parental choice, greater autonomy for schools and greater accountability. It vilified the comprehensive system for 'presupposing that children are all basically the same and that all local communities have essentially the same educa-tional needs' (Department for Education, or DfE, 1992: 3). It also asserted that 'the provision of education, and particularly secondary education, should be geared more to local circumstances and individual needs: hence a commitment to diversity in education' (DfE, 1992: 3-4). At the same time, it was at pains to emphasize that *specialization* should never be confused with *selection*:

The fact that a school is strong in a particular field may well increase the demand to attend, but it does not necessarily follow that selective entry criteria have to be imposed by the school. The selection that does take place is parent-driven. The principle of open access remains. As the demand to attend increases, so the school may simply require extra resources to cope with the range of talent available. (DfE, 1992: 10)

The White Paper announced plans to build on the work of the 15 City Technology Colleges by establishing a network of secondary schools with enhanced technology facilities, to be known as 'technology schools', and a network of secondary schools established with business sponsorship, to be known as 'technology colleges'.

One of the key objectives of the 1992 White Paper, and of the 1993 Education Act which translated its proposals into legislation, was to increase the number of grant-maintained schools. The Major Government was very disappointed that there had been no rush, over the preceding four years, to opt for grant-maintained status, especially in Labour-controlled local authorities. By the 1992 election there had been only 428 decisive 'opt-out' ballots in England and Wales and, where these had been carried out, voters in 97 schools had been opposed to opting-out, with only 331 voting in favour. In Scotland, no school had gone grant-maintained. New ways had to be found of rescuing a failing policy. It was therefore decided that institutions seeking to become new 'technology colleges' would do so as 'grant-maintained' schools. At the same time, new grant-maintained schools could be created in response to parental demand and on the basis of local proposals, thereby paving the way for the establishment of state-funded schools aiming to foster, for example, Muslim, Buddhist or evangelical Christian beliefs, or wishing to promote particular educational philosophies.

The policy of providing a greater choice of schools, particularly in the secondary sector, was reiterated in a 1996 White Paper, *Self-Government for Schools,* published by Gillian Shephard who had replaced John Patten as Education Secretary in July 1994. In an early section headed 'Choice, Diversity and Specialisation', it was argued that:

Children have different abilities, aptitudes, interests and needs. These cannot all be fully met by a single type of school, at least at secondary level. The Government wants parents to be able to choose from a range of good schools of different types, matching what they want for their child with what a school offers. This choice should include schools which select by academic ability, so that the most able children have the chance to achieve the best of which they are capable. (DfEE, 1996b: 2)

By the time the Conservatives left office in 1997, there were 164 grammar schools in England and Wales, together with 1,155 opted-out schools accounting for 19.6 per cent of pupils in secondary schools and for 2.8 per cent of primary pupils, 15 City Technology Colleges, 30 Colleges specializing in languages and 151 new Colleges specializing in technology. At the same time, it has to be admitted that many comprehensive schools did not really deserve the appellation, so it was indeed a very divided system that New Labour inherited from 18 years of Conservative rule. Such a system could, of course, have been radically transformed by the new Government; but, as we shall see in the next chapter, New Labour chose instead to continue with Conservative policies, with much talk of choice and diversity, ladders and escalators.

4

Education and New Labour

On 1 May 1997, the Labour Party gained a landslide general election victory which brought to an end 18 years of Conservative rule in Britain. Securing 43 per cent of the national vote, its 419 MPs gave it a House of Commons majority over all other parties of 179. With only 31 per cent of the national vote and just 165 MPs, this was the Conservatives' most dismal general election performance since their defeat at the hands of Sir Henry Campbell-Bannerman's Liberal Party in January 1906. While all commentators agreed that the result was a major and largely unexpected triumph for Tony Blair's New Labour Party, there were conflicting views as to its causes and actual significance. Above all, did it represent a massive endorsement of the policies that New Labour had been promoting since the death of John Smith in May 1994; or was it simply a decisive rejection of the policies and style of the 1992–7 Major administration which had never really recovered from the economic crisis of September 1992? In this chapter, we look *beyond* the excitement engendered by the change of government and ask to what extent New Labour's education agenda marked a real departure from the policies pursued by the Thatcher and Major administrations.

Aspects of continuity

In a short Fabian Society pamphlet with the all-embracing title *Socialism*, published in July 1994 shortly after his election as Labour Party Leader, Tony Blair had set out to argue that the socialism of Marx, of centralized state control of industry and production, was dead. In Blair's view, this outdated form of socialism misunderstood the nature and development of a modern market economy; it failed to recognize that the state and public sector can become a vested interest capable of oppression as much as the vested interests of wealth and capital; and it was based on a false view of class that became too rigid to explain or illuminate the nature of class division today. In its place, Blair proposed a set of values or beliefs – loosely defined as 'ethical socialism' – based around the notion of a strong and active society committed to promoting the needs of the individual and of enlightened self-interest. The basis of this new form of socialism, or, to use Blair's preferred spelling, 'social-ism' – lay in the view that individuals were 'socially interdependent human beings' and that 'the collective power of all should be used for the individual good of each'. Blair claimed that if and when he became Prime Minister, he did not want to run 'a Tory economy with a bit of social compassion'. He was, in fact, confident that 'the public is once again ready to listen to notions associated with the Left – social justice, cohesion, equality of opportunity and community. They do not want to go back; they want to move on' (Blair, 1994: 2, 6).

Yet in the years that followed, Blair was unable or unwilling to resolve the obvious contradictions involved in affirming a commitment to 'social justice' and 'community' while, at the same time, pursuing competitive market policies in education (and, indeed, in other signifi-cant areas of the Welfare State). He came increasingly anxious to change the Labour Party's image and appeal to a wider section of the middle classes by upholding the virtues of choice and competition and playing down the Party's commitment to comprehensive schooling. Ann Taylor was moved from her post as Shadow Education Secretary in 1994 as soon as Blair assumed the leadership of the Party; and some of those who had worked closely with her since the 1992 election argue (see, for example, Tomlinson, 2001: 65) that the problem lay with the 1993 consultative paper *Opening Doors to a Learning Society* (Labour Party, 1993), which the new leader heartily disliked and which can be viewed very much as the last 'Old Labour' document on education, rejecting, as it does, any government approach to educational policy-making which is 'driven by consumerist dogma, by oppressive dictation by the central state, and by a false and inadequate theory of choice' (Labour Party, 1993: 2).

Between 1994 and 1997, Tony Blair and his new Shadow Education Secretary, David Blunkett, worked tirelessly to set the Party's official education policy on what they saw as a less traditional and more 'voter-friendly' course. There was to be a new and remarkably fervent commit-ment to the idea of specialist secondary schools; and ways had to be found of continuing with the Conservatives' specialist and grant-main-tained schools under more acceptable guises. The first 'New Labour' document on education, published in June 1995 with the very meaning-ful title (which would not have seemed out of place heading a

Conservative education White Paper) *Diversity and Excellence: A New Partnership for Schools* (Labour Party, 1995), proposed that in future all existing categories of state school should be replaced by just *three* types of school:

- community schools, based on the existing county schools
- aided schools, based on the existing voluntary aided schools
- foundation schools, offering a new bridge between the powers available to secular and church schools.

Each of these choices would be open to all state schools to opt for; and schools would be offered the chance to ballot their parents about the official designation and future status of their school. It was anticipated that foundation school status would have special attractions for many, if not all, grant-maintained schools, specialist schools and City Technology Colleges. Such schools would be given powers to employ staff in line with current practice in aided schools; and would not necessarily be subject to the same admissions policies as those operating for community schools (Labour Party, 1995: 15–16).

The 1995 document also dealt with the vexed question of what to do with the remaining 164 grammar schools. While it was reiterated that the Labour Party was 'implacably opposed to a return to selection by the eleven-plus examination', it was also made clear that a future Labour government would *not* deal with the grammar schools as an issue of national policy: 'While we have never supported the grammar schools in their exclusion of children by examination, change can come only through local agreement. Such a change in the character of a school could follow only a clear demonstration of support from the parents affected by such a decision' (Labour Party, 1995: 11).

This strange and clumsy formula infuriated many of the left-wing delegates to the October 1995 Labour Party Conference. Accordingly, in his reply to the somewhat acrimonious education debate on 4 October, David Blunkett sought to placate his sceptical audience by saying: 'Read my lips. No selection, either by examination or interview, under a Labour government.' The strategy worked; and a revolt, organized around demands for the remaining grammar schools to be incorporated into the comprehensive system, collapsed – on the clear understanding that *its chief purpose had already been achieved.*

Yet, in the months that followed, it became increasingly clear that 'no selection' actually meant 'no further selection', and that when David Blunkett began using this new phrase in speeches and media interviews, he was not guilty of a simple slip of the tongue: he was, in fact, announcing *a change of official education policy.* As the former Deputy Party Leader, Roy Hattersley, pointed out in one of a number of articles written for *The Guardian* in November 1997 (Hattersley, 1997), the meaning of the two seemingly similar slogans was, in fact, 'diametrically opposed'. The phrase 'no selection' signified an end to the existing 164 grammar schools; 'no *further* selection' was *'a guarantee of their retention'.* In Roy Hattersley's view – and it was one that prompted an agonized riposte from the Shadow Education Secretary – David Blunkett was 'a superb exponent of injured innocence'. He had given a very clear and specific pledge to see him through a very difficult and potentially damaging education debate, knowing full well that Tony Blair would never allow him to honour it. In his own letters to *The Guardian,* and later on the BBC Television *Breakfast with Frost* programme, broadcast on 30 November 1997, Mr Blunkett argued that when he had used the words 'no selection' in 1995, he had actually intended them to mean 'no *further* selection'. There had therefore been *no* change of policy ordered by Tony Blair. It is still interesting to note that when the Deputy Party Leader, John Prescott, spoke in Oxford in 1996, on the twentieth anniversary of James Callaghan's Ruskin College speech, the first draft of his speech repeated Blunkett's original promise. He was forced to remove it from the final text on the orders of the Party Leader (see Hattersley, 1997; MacLeod, 1997).

By the time of the 1997 General Election, it was clear that New Labour was committed to pursuing many of the Conservatives' more divisive education policies, with education being allowed to continue as a market commodity driven by consumer demands, and parental choice of schools being facilitated by greater teacher accountability and the publication of league tables of test and examination performance. Many of those reviewing an edited book published in 1999 with the title *State Schools: New Labour and the Conservative Legacy* (Chitty and Dunford, 1999) noted with approval the cartoon specially drawn for the cover by *Guardian* and *The Times Education Supplement* cartoonist, Martin Rowson, which seemed to neatly summarize the essential message of the book's contributors. A gowned and mortar-boarded head-teacher (unmistakably Margaret Thatcher) is shown handing a prize to a beaming, blazered student (unmistakably Tony Blair). The prize is a neat scroll of Conservative education policies.

It was emphasized even before the election that, in the event of a Labour victory, several key personnel would remain in their posts at the major education quangos: Anthea Millett at the TTA (Teacher Training

Agency), Nicholas Tate at the QCA (Qualifications and Curriculum Authority) and Chris Woodhead, a highly controversial figure commanding very little respect among classroom teachers, at Ofsted (Office for Standards in Education), which had been set up by the 1992 Education (Schools) Act as a new 'independent' body responsible for contracting independent teams to inspect all primary and secondary schools.

During the election campaign itself, Tony Blair repeatedly declared that 'education, education, education' were to be 'the top three priorities' of a Labour government, with a special emphasis on improvements in the primary school; and this was also the message that the Party was anxious to put across in the New Labour election manifesto *Because Britain Deserves Better* (1997).

The five-page Introduction to this important document by Tony Blair himself, with the heading 'Britain will be better with New Labour', argued in the very first paragraph that Britain *could* and *must* be better: with 'better schools, better hospitals, better ways of tackling crime, of building a modern welfare state, of equipping ourselves to be a new world economy'. It went on to make the proud boast that New Labour had been created to meet the challenges of 'a new and rapidly-changing world', of 'a new millennium symbolising a new era opening up for Britain'. The chief purpose of New Labour was to give Britain a new political choice: the choice between 'a failed Conservative government, exhausted and divided in everything other than its desire to cling on to power' and 'a new and revitalised Labour Party' that had been resolute in 'transforming itself into a party of the future'. This new dynamic Party was putting forward a programme for 'a new centre and centre-Left politics'; this was a set of proposals in each area of policy offering a distinctive approach that differed '*both* from the solutions of the Old Left *and* from those of the Conservative Right'. This was precisely why New Labour *was* new. It believed in 'the strength of its values', while at the same time recognizing that 'the policies of 1997 could not be those of 1947 or even of 1967'. Where education was concerned, there was to be a strong emphasis on 'standards', not 'structures', in both the primary and the secondary sectors, accompanied by a rejection both of 'the idea of a return to the eleven-plus examination' and of 'the monolithic comprehensive schools that take no account of children's differing abilities'. The Introduction ended with a promise by the Labour leader – as an essential component of the Party's new 'contract with the people' – that, over the five years of a Labour government, education would be 'the number one priority' and that the Party would 'increase the share of national income spent on education' while decreasing it on 'the bills of economic and social failure' (Labour Party, 1997: 1, 2, 3, 5).

The manifesto highlighted six policies as being indicative of New Labour's clear determination to make education its 'number one priority' (Labour Party, 1997: 7):

* a reduction in class sizes to 30 or under for all 5-, 6- and 7-year-olds
* the provision of nursery places for all 4 year-olds
* an attack on low standards in schools
* access for all to computer technology
* the provision of lifelong learning through the establishment of a new University for Industry
* increased spending on education as a direct consequence of a fall in the cost of unemployment.

The 1997 White Paper

In the first few weeks of the new Blair Government, legislative priority was given to implementing a promise that the Conservatives' Assisted Places Scheme would be abolished and the money thereby released used to fund reduced class sizes for 5–7-year-olds.

Then in July, just 67 days after assuming office, the Department for Education and Employment published an 84-page White Paper, *Excellence in Schools,* setting out the education agenda for the lifetime of the Parliament. Although many commentators were understandably impressed with the speed with which this White Paper was produced, we shall see in the next chapter that many of the policies had already been formulated in the period before the election, notably at a Labour Education Summit held in April, and that many of the key ideas and slogans had already appeared in books authored by Michael Barber and Peter Mandelson.

In a Foreword to the document, the new Secretary of State (see Box 4.1), David Blunkett, emphasized the importance of rejecting all excuses for 'under-performance' in schools:

To overcome economic and social disadvantage and to make equality of opportunity a reality, we must strive to eliminate, and never excuse, under-achievement in the most deprived parts of our country. Educational attainment encourages aspiration and self-belief in the next generation; and it is through family learning, as well as scholarship through formal schooling, that success will come . . . We must overcome the spiral of disadvantage in which alienation from, or failure within, the education system is passed from one generation to the next. (DfEE, 1997: 3)

Box 4.1   Secretaries of State, 1997–2008

David Blunkett   May 1997–June 2001
Estelle Morris   June 2001–October 2002
Charles Clarke   October 2002–December 2004
Ruth Kelly   December 2004–May 2006
Alan Johnson   May 2006–June 2007

In June 2007 the Education Secretary became the Secretary of State for Children, Schools and Families

Ed Balls   June 2007–

The White Paper began by listing the six principles that would be underpinning New Labour's reform agenda in education (DfEE, 1997: 11–12):

* education will be at the heart of government
* policies will be designed to benefit the many, not just the few
* standards will matter more than structures
* intervention will be in inverse proportion to success
* there will be zero tolerance of underperformance
* government will work in partnership with all those committed to raising standards.

It was then confidently predicted that by the year 2002 (DfEE, 1997: 14):

* there will be a greater awareness across society of the importance of education and increased expectations of what can be achieved
* standards of performance will be higher.

The White Paper then went on to outline a wide range of proposals and recommendations affecting the future education of 3–16-year-olds:

1 There would be effective assessment of all children starting primary school from September 1997, with all schools required to carry out 'baseline assessments' from September 1998.
2 There would be challenging national targets for the performance of 11-year-olds in English and maths. By the year 2002, some 80 per cent of 11-year-olds would be reaching the standards expected for

their age in English, and 75 per cent of 11-year-olds would be reaching the standards expected in maths. (The 'standards expected' in this section referred to National Curriculum Level Four in English and maths tests. In 1997, around 63 per cent of children reached this Level in English and 62 per cent reached the Level in maths.)

3 Literacy and numeracy would be a priority for all pupils. Each primary school would be expected to devote a structured hour a day to literacy from September 1998 and introduce a daily numeracy hour in September 1999. The drive to improve children's literacy and numeracy skills would be assisted by rigorous assessment and testing at the ages of 7 and 11.

4 School performance tables would be more useful, showing the rate of progress children had made alongside their *absolute* levels of achievement. Key Stage Two tables would be published locally, but in a format which facilitated national comparisons.

5 Every school would be inspected by Ofsted at least once every six years. Between inspections, the performance of schools would be regularly monitored by local education authorities (LEAs) on the basis of objective performance information. By April 1999, each LEA would be working to an Education Development Plan (EDP) agreed with the DfEE and the schools, showing how standards in all schools were intended to rise.

6 LEAs would be expected to give early warnings to governors of schools 'causing concern' and intervene where necessary. Where schools showed insufficient evidence of recovery, it might be necessary to consider a 'Fresh Start' policy. This 'Fresh Start' could take one of a number of different forms. It might mean closing the school and transferring all the pupils to nearby 'successful' schools. In less extreme cases, it might involve one school taking over the 'underperforming' school to 'set it on a new path'; or closing the school temporarily and then re-opening it either on the same or on a different site, but with a new name and under new management.

7 The DfEE would become more pro-active and outward-looking through the work of the Standards and Effectiveness Unit and of the Standards Task Force (STF). The Standards and Effectiveness Unit, headed by Michael Barber, was intended to underline the promise, reiterated several times in the White Paper, that 'standards' rather than 'structures' were to be a major goal of the Government. The Standards Task Force was intended to promote good practice and guarantee the 'delivery' of literacy and numeracy targets. It had already been established, with the Secretary of State as Chair and

with Chris Woodhead, the Chief Inspector of Schools, and Tim Brighouse, the Director of Education for Birmingham, as the two Vice-Chairs. (This was thought at the time to constitute a somewhat 'explosive' mixture, Tim Brighouse being viewed as a broadly left-wing defender of LEAs, classroom teachers and 'disadvantaged' pupils and Chris Woodhead being seen as a right-wing critic of LEAs, teachers and 'progressive' methods: see, for example, Carvel (1998). In the event, it was not long before Brighouse felt obliged to resign.)

8 At the secondary level, the comprehensive principles would be 'modernized' to ensure that all children, whatever their talents, were able to develop their diverse abilities.

9 Setting of pupils by ability should be 'the norm' in all secondary schools; and, in some cases, it would be worth considering in primary schools.

10 There would be a pilot programme of about 25 Education Action Zones (EAZs) charged with the task of 'motivating young people in tough inner-city areas'. These would be phased in over two to three years and set up in areas with a mixture of underperforming schools and the highest level of disadvantage. They would operate on the basis of an 'action forum' to include parents and representatives from 'the local business and social community', as well as representatives from 'the constituent schools and the LEA'. A typical zone would have two or three secondary schools with supporting primaries and associated Special Educational Needs (SEN) provision.

11 There would be 'an extensive network of specialist secondary schools' developing their own distinctive identity and expertise. These would initially focus on technology, languages, sports or arts, and would be 'a resource for local people and neighbouring schools to draw on'. They would be expected to give priority to those youngsters demonstrating 'the relevant aptitude'.

12 There should be better developed information and communications technology within a clear national strategy.

13 There would be a new grade of 'Advanced Skills Teacher' to reward the best classroom teachers.

14 A General Teaching Council would be set up to represent the views of teachers at a national level.

15 Streamlined procedures should be introduced for tackling the problem of 'incompetent teachers'.

16 There should be 'home-school contracts' to involve parents in expectations about the standard of education on offer.

17 In future, there would be three types of state school: community, aided and foundation. Community schools would be similar to the existing county schools; aided and foundation schools would employ their own staff and own their own premises. These three categories would eventually incorporate *all* LEA and grant-maintained schools.

18 National guidelines on admissions policies would be set by the Secretary of State. Aided and foundation schools would be able to put forward their own policies in the light of these new guidelines.

19 Where grammar schools still existed, their future would be decided by local parents, not by the LEAs.

20 Ways should be found of creating new partnerships between state and independent schools.

As we have already seen, one of the key themes both of the New Labour election manifesto and of the 1997 White Paper was that 'standards' were more important than 'structures'; yet, as I have argued elsewhere (Chitty, 1997b), it is very difficult to know what the term 'structure' means in this context and why it is not inextricably linked to 'standards':

> If the term refers to the structure of the education system *as a whole,* one is tempted to ask what sort of national framework we would now have in Britain if large numbers of parents, teachers, local education authorities and politicians had not cared about 'structures' in the 1950s and 1960s and campaigned for a less divisive system of secondary schooling. If it refers to the 'structure' of individual schools (which in any case cannot be viewed in isolation from the system as a whole), then we are being asked to consider a false dichotomy. Standards and structures are interrelated and can be understood only in relation to each other. A comprehensive school which is, in reality, a secondary modern school in a still selective local system with inadequate resources to perform a wide variety of tasks is less likely to achieve excellent results of the kind measured by Ofsted than will another school in the same area which occupies a safe and privileged position in the local hierarchy of schools. It is one of the major shortcomings of the school improvement/school effectiveness movement that it often treats schools as if they operated in some sort of social and political vacuum. (Chitty, 1997b: 71)

It has to be conceded that the 1997 White Paper enjoyed a relatively warm reception in the press, among teachers' leaders and from parents' organizations. Choosing the headline 'Ambitious plan excites teachers', a report in *The Guardian,* for example, began with the ringing declaration that: 'The Government yesterday won the first round of its battle to raise standards in schools, when the teaching unions and local education authorities rallied to support a white paper promising hugely ambitious improvement targets and draconian penalties for under-performance' (8 July 1997). Doug McAvoy, General Secretary of the National Union of Teachers, hailed the Government's firm commitments on class sizes, equitable funding and fair and open admissions policies. David Hart, General Secretary of the National Association of Headteachers, said that: 'Combined with the clear promise of more resources to come, the White Paper provides support for the profession, alongside the pressure of targets and league tables which is urgently needed' (reported in *The Guardian*, 8 July 1997).

CASE (the Campaign for State Education) said it was 'heart-warming' to be able to endorse many of the proposals contained within the White Paper: the very idea of policies 'being designed to benefit the many, not just the few'; the establishment of a General Teaching Council; value-added assessments of pupil performance; a national strategy for information and communications technology in schools; and more family learning initiatives in the early years and primary sectors. Yet this broad welcome accorded the Government's plans was not without some strong reservations. While calling the White Paper 'a real step forward', a CASE pamphlet also listed some of the key measures the Campaign could *not* support: home-school 'contracts'; specialist secondary schools encouraged to select pupils on 'aptitude': no governmental support for an end to existing grammar schools; more parents on school governing bodies and LEAs without looking at the need to encourage these parents to be more in touch with other classroom parents. The CASE leaflet went on to ask two important questions: 'Where is the evidence that there is value in promoting diversity by allowing schools to develop a particular identity, character, and expertise?' and 'Why do we need three types of state school: community, aided and foundation?' (CASE, 1997: 1).

There was much support from parents' organizations for the new emphasis on literacy and numeracy at the primary level, although this was accompanied by some misgivings that aesthetic and creative aspects of the curriculum would be marginalized (this will be discussed more fully in Chapter 6). The Government showed that it shared none of these reservations when it announced in January 1998 that pupils under the age of 11 would no longer be required to adhere to the detailed national syllabuses in history, geography, design and technology, art, music and physical education.

The first major Education Act of the Blair Government, with legislative proposals based on the reforms outlined in the White Paper, was introduced into Parliament in December 1997 and became law in July 1998. In seven parts, it contained 145 sections and 32 schedules. It is interesting to note, bearing in mind the Government's repeated assertion that standards mattered more than structures, that this Act was, in fact, chiefly concerned with structures, 89 of the 145 sections being devoted to the new categories of maintained schools, their establishment, financing, staffing, admissions and selection arrangements. The comprehensive school as such did not figure in the Act.

Selection and specialization

As we saw at the end of Chapter 3, the new Government inherited 164 grammar schools, 15 City Technology Colleges and 181 specialist schools and colleges. No attempt was to be made to overthrow the Conservative policy of 'selection by specialisation'; and the Government was soon on target to have 500 specialist schools in place by September 2000 and 650 by September 2001. These schools would be encouraged to play to their strengths and recognize children's 'particular aptitudes'. Admissions policies could then include a small degree of selection based on these 'perceived aptitudes'. According to *Excellence in Schools*: 'We will ensure that schools with a specialism will continue to be able to give priority to those children who demonstrate the relevant aptitude, as long as that is not misused to select on the basis of general academic ability' (DfEE, 1997: 71).

Clause 102 of the 1998 School Standards and Framework Act gave legislative backing to this pledge by stating that a maintained secondary school may 'make provision for the selection of pupils for admission to the school by reference to their aptitude for one of more prescribed subjects' where:

- the admission authority for the school are satisfied that the school has a specialism in the subject or subjects in question
- the proportion of selective admissions in any relevant age group does not exceed 10 per cent.

This provision caused considerable disquiet among teachers and educationists even as the 1997 Bill was making its way through Parliament. It was argued by many that the Government's concept of specialist schools would simply create (or exacerbate) an unbalanced academic and social mix in inner-city schools. In a class-divided and highly competitive society, or so the argument went, specialisms could never be equal: they would rapidly become ranked in a hierarchy of status. Moreover, the Government's long-term plans were based on the false assumption that children could actually be tested for *particular talents* rather than for *general ability*. This flew in the face of the vast body of research evidence, a point emphasized by Professor Peter Mortimore, the then Director of the Institute of Education in London, in an article written for *Education Guardian* in March 1998:

> Except in music and perhaps art, it does not seem possible to diagnose specific aptitudes for most school curriculum subjects. Instead, what seems to emerge from such testing is a general ability to learn, which is often, but not always, associated with the various advantages of coming from a middle-class home. How can headteachers know if the 'aptitude' of a ten-year-old in German shows anything more than the parents' ability to pay for language lessons? (Mortimore, 1998)

Concerns about various forms of secondary selection, both 'overt' and 'hidden', had been expressed by many headteachers completing the detailed questionnaires sent out as part of a large-scale survey of comprehensive schooling in Britain carried out in 1994 (see Benn and Chitty, 1996; 1997). At that time, there were already all the selective mechanisms associated with parental choice, open enrolment and admissions to grant-maintained schools, City Technology Colleges and schools with a clear religious bias. Together with John Patten's plan to encourage comprehensive schools to specialize in one or other of a number of specific curriculum areas, all these new initiatives seemed to be designed to create a damaging hierarchy of competing schools. Above all, there was the continued existence of over 160 grammar schools, a situation which New Labour showed no inclination to interfere with.

After nearly three years in government, education ministers finally conceded in 2000 that arguments about grammar-school selection were part of a previous agenda and not worth pursuing. In the report of an interview granted to *The Sunday Telegraph* in March of that year, headlined 'Our war against grammars is over, says Blunkett', the Education Secretary argued that it was time to abandon 'Labour's historic campaign against grammar schools'. Blunkett said that he was determined to 'bury the dated arguments of previous decades' and reverse 'the outright opposition to grammar schools' that had been 'a touchstone of Labour politics for at least 35 years'. He went on:

I'm not interested in hunting the remaining grammar schools . . . I'm desperately trying to avoid the whole debate in education once again, as it was in the 1960s and 1970s, concentrating on the issue of selection, when it *should* be concentrating on the raising of standards . . . Arguments about selection are part of a past agenda. We have set up a system which says 'if you don't like grammar schools, you can get rid of them'; but it isn't really the key issue for the year 2000. The *real* issue is what we are going to do about the whole of secondary education . . . There are only 164 grammar schools – let's get on with the job of giving a decent education to all the kids. (*The Sunday Telegraph*, 12 March 2000)

This revealing interview was timed to appear *two* days after the announcement of the voting figures in the very first ballot on the future of a grammar school held in accordance with the Labour Government's policy of leaving the future of 11-plus selection in the hands of local parents. The long-term future of Ripon Grammar School in north Yorkshire, founded in 1556 and one of the oldest in England, was guaranteed as parents voted by a clear majority of around two to one to reject the proposition that, henceforth, the school be required to admit children 'of all abilities'. On a 75 per cent turnout, 1,493 of the 3,000 parents (who were entitled to vote because their children attended one or other of 14 'feeder' state primary or independent preparatory schools) voted to reject the proposition, with only 748 voting in favour. This majority was so clear-cut that the 'pro-comprehensive' parents immediately abandoned plans to challenge the outcome, but the Ripon Branch of the Campaign for State Education did complain that more than 25 per cent of those parents entitled to vote came from *outside* the area, while a similar proportion educated their primary-age children in the independent sector. It was also pointed out that the secondary modern school in Ripon had recently been 'upgraded' by being awarded 'specialist school' status. All such considerations were, not surprisingly, ignored by the new Education Minister, Estelle Morris, when she issued a statement accepting the result of the Ripon ballot: 'The Government respects the decision of parents to retain the current admission arrangements at Ripon Grammar School . . . At all stages of the debate, the decision has been a matter for the parents, and they have all had the chance to express their views' (reported in *The Daily Telegraph*, 11 March 2000). In the light of this setback in Yorkshire, and of a distinct lack of encouragement from the Government, it seemed highly unlikely that groups of parents in other parts of the country would risk wasting time and money on a similar enterprise.

The 2001 Green Paper

A new front in the transformation of the education system was opened up with the publication, in February 2001, of a DfEE Green Paper: *Schools: Building on Success: Raising Standards, Promoting Diversity, Achieving Results.* As we saw earlier in this chapter, the 1997 White Paper set clear and challenging national targets for the performance of all 11-year-olds in English and maths. The Government was now able to report that as a result of such initiatives as the National Literacy and Numeracy Strategies, more pupils than ever before were leaving primary schools both literate and numerate. Statistics showed that 75 per cent of children achieved Level Four or above in English in 2000 compared to just 57 per cent in 1996, before New Labour came to power. The comparable figure for maths in 2000 was 72 per cent, compared to only 54 per cent in 1996. These figures meant that in English 160,000 more children and in maths 155,000 more children were now meeting the standard expected of them. Moreover, progress in primary school English and maths was fastest in the most disadvantaged areas of the country. The lowest scoring LEA in Key Stage 2 English was now doing better than the national average in 1996 (DfEE, 2001: 13).

Having achieved these considerable improvements at the primary level, the Government's 'mission' (outlined on page 4 of the Green Paper) was to bring about 'a similar transformation in secondary schools'. With this end in view, much of the publicity surrounding the publication of the 93-page document concentrated on the need to 'modernise' the comprehensive school, though it has to be admitted that some of the language used at the official press launch held on 12 February 2001 did much to offend many of Labour's traditional supporters. In particular, many were surprised and shocked by the failure of the Prime Minister to distance himself from the deliberate and insulting claim made by his official spokesperson, Alastair Campbell, that 'the day of the bog-standard comprehensive' was clearly over. Indeed, by arguing himself that the Green Paper was actually ushering in 'a post-comprehensive era', Tony Blair was giving welcome ammunition to all the opponents of comprehensive schooling, provoking stark headlines in the right-wing press such as 'Death of the Comprehensive' in *The Daily Mail* (13 February 2001) and 'Comprehensives have failed, says Blair' in *The Daily Telegraph* (13 February 2001). From now on, according to the Prime Minister, everyone should take note that 'promoting diversity' was indeed synonymous with 'raising standards' and 'achieving results'.

The authors of the 2001 Green Paper were anxious to stress that the drive to improve standards in primary schools would continue unabated under a second Blair administration. By the year 2004, around 85 per cent of all 11-year-olds would be expected to achieve the standard set for their age (Level Four or above) in English and in mathematics; and 35 per cent would be reaching Level Five in each subject. Many primary-school teachers expressed concern at what was perceived to be the Government's 'inflexibility'; but the new Education Secretary, Estelle Morris, was to reiterate the Government's tough targets for Key Stage Two in a letter sent to MPs in March 2002 (reported in *The Times Educational Supplement,* 8 March 2002).

That being said, and despite the continued emphasis on literacy and numeracy at the primary level, the chief focus of the Green Paper was on 'transforming secondary education' (the title of its Chapter 4). In this respect, we can discern a number of major themes and policy alignments running through the document, notably:

- a rejection of the principles underpinning the era of the 'one size fits all comprehensive'
- a concern to see the promotion of diversity among secondary schools and the extension of 'autonomy' for 'successful' schools
- a desire for private and voluntary sector sponsors to play a greater role in the provision of secondary schooling.

As a prime means of promoting 'diversity', the Government intended to accelerate the Specialist Schools Project so that there would be around 1,000 specialist secondary schools in operation by September 2003 and 1,500 by September 2006. In addition to an increase in the number of such schools, there would also be a broadening of the range of specialisms available. To add to the existing specialisms of technology, modern languages, sports and the arts, schools would now be able to opt for one of three new specialist areas: engineering, science, and business and enterprise. Business and enterprise schools would be expected to develop strong curriculum-business links and also to develop teaching strengths in business studies, financial literacy and enterprise-related vocational programmes.

As an extension of the Specialist Schools Programme, the Government intended to introduce in due course a new category of Advanced Specialist School which would be open to 'high-performing' schools after operating for five years as 'specialist schools'. They would be expected to 'volunteer' to take on a number of innovative ideas from a 'menu' drawn up centrally by the new DfES. In return, they would receive an additional capital investment to strengthen their role as 'centres of excellence'. An important aspect of their work might well be initial teacher training, with many of these institutions playing a leading role as Training Schools.

Then, as yet another element in this bewildering array of new creations, there were the new Beacon Schools, intended to develop and spread 'good practice' among neighbouring establishments. David Blunkett had announced in March 1999 that there were to be around 1,000 Beacon Schools in operation by September 2002. It was now intended that there would be 1,000 of these Schools in existence by September 2001, a year ahead of schedule.

The Green Paper was also anxious to see an increase in the number and variety of schools within the state system sponsored by the Church of England and other major faith groups. Some 560 secondary schools were already provided by the Church of England or the Catholic Church; and the Government wished to see more Muslim, Sikh and Greek Orthodox Schools brought inside the state system and funded on the same basis as existing 'aided' schools.

In addition to more 'faith-based' schools, which acted as their own 'admissions authority', the Government was also anxious to promote an increase in the number of schools that owed their existence to private sponsorship. The City Academy Programme, launched in March 2000 and clearly modelled on the Conservatives' City Technology Colleges project, enabled sponsors from the private and voluntary sectors to establish new schools whose basic running costs would then be met fully by the state.

At the same time, the Government intended to develop a new model which would enable an external private or voluntary sector sponsor to take over responsibility for a 'weak' or 'failing' school with a fixed-term contract of, say, 5–7 years and renewal subject to performance. This would be based on the situation at King's Manor School in Guildford where '3Es', a charitable offshoot of the City Technology College at Kingshurst in Solihull, had been given responsibility for setting up a new school in February 1999.

Other policies for tackling 'under-performance' and 'failure', such as the 'Excellence in Cities' Programme launched in March 1999, were also given prominence in the Green Paper, though comparatively little space was accorded to the Education Action Zones Initiative which had formed an important part of the *Excellence in Schools* White Paper back in July 1997. Reports in the national press that the EAZ experiment was to be dropped brought furious denials from a number of the leading zone directors; but in November 2001 the Schools Minister, Stephen Timms, told a conference of zone directors that none of the contracts for the existing 73 zones would be renewed when they expired at the end of their 5-year period, and that the more successful initiatives would simply be subsumed within the 'Excellence in Cities' Programme (reported in *The Times Educational Supplement,* 16 November 2001).

There would be exacting new targets for secondary schools operating 'in challenging circumstances'. By 2003, all such schools should have at least 15 per cent of their students gaining five or more A* to C grade GCSEs; by 2004, at least 20 per cent; and by 2006, at least 25 per cent. (2001 Green Paper)

As far as the internal organization of secondary schools was concerned, the Government wanted to see more setting within subjects, including 'express sets' for 11–14 year-olds to enable the 'most able' in each year group to advance *beyond* the level set for their age and, where possible, take Key Stage Three Tests early. At Key Stage Four, students could still take a number of GCSEs but, increasingly, they would be able to mix 'academic' and 'vocational' GCSEs with work-based qualifications.

The 2001 White Paper and the 2002 Education Act

Many of the themes and specific policy proposals outlined in the February 2001 Green Paper were reiterated and expanded upon later in the year, first in a new White Paper *Schools Achieving Success,* published on 5 September, and then in a new Education Bill, published on the 23 November. This Bill, in turn, served as the basis for the 2002 Education Act which received Royal Assent on 24 July 2002.

Readers of the White Paper were left in no doubt that the idea of extending choice and diversity at the secondary level would be pursued with a single-minded determination. Indeed, the word 'diversity' appeared *seven* times in the space of a short three-page introduction. In the words of the DfES: 'devolution and diversity' were 'the essential hallmarks of the White Paper'; 'ours is a vision of a school system which values opportunity for all and embraces diversity and autonomy as the means to achieve it'; 'we need to move away from the outdated argument about diversity versus uniformity'; and so on in a similar vein (DfES, 2001: 1, 2, 3).

New targets were set for the implementation of key elements of the

Government's second-term programme. There would be at least 1,000 specialist schools in operation by September 2003 and at least 1,500 by the year 2005, this latter date being a year earlier than at first envisaged. In addition to the new specialisms on offer in engineering, science and business and enterprise, there would be a fourth: mathematics and computing. The number of Beacon Schools in existence in September 2001 – roughly 1,000 – already included 250 secondary schools; and the number of these secondary Beacons would be expanded to at least 400 by the year 2005.

The document reiterated the need for challenging new 'floor targets' for student performance, the term used to describe *minimum* performance levels to be achieved by all secondary schools, irrespective of the nature of their catchment areas. By 2004, all schools should have at least 20 per cent of their students achieving five or more A* to C grade GCSEs; and by 2006, at least 25 per cent. (2001 White Paper)

Considerable controversy was to surround one of the key proposals in the White Paper and the 2001 Education Bill: the promotion of 'faith-based' schools as a way of creating 'a truly diverse secondary system' (see Gillard, 2002). An amendment to the Bill, tabled by the former Health Secretary, Frank Dobson, and the Liberal Democrat education spokesperson, Phil Willis, required all new Church schools to reserve at least one-quarter of their places for children of other faiths or of none, but it was to be heavily defeated in the House of Commons on 6 February 2002 by 405 votes to 87; this was a government majority of 318, with the Conservative Opposition voting with the Government. It is clear that the promotion of diversity poses a number of awkward questions as to precisely *which* groups should be allowed to sponsor and have a say in the running of state schools; this will be discussed more fully in Chapter 5.

The 2002 Education Act covered a vast range of issues and performed a useful function in tidying up some of the problematic areas surrounding the legislative proposals in the 1998 School Standards and Framework Act. Two main issues highlighted in the new legislation concerned school organization and changes to the curriculum. The Act stated that where a new secondary school was required, the relevant local authority would be obliged to advertise, so that any interested party could put forward proposals for a new school. Any legitimate promoter, including a community or faith group, an LEA, or another public, private or voluntary body, could publish proposals. All such proposals would then be judged on the basis of their educational merits, the 'value for money' factor and the outcome of consultation. At the same time, the

Act created a legislative distinction between Key Stages One to Three on the one hand, and Key Stage Four on the other, thereby making it possible to make major changes to the Key Stage Four curriculum in the future and further disband the framework created in 1988 (this will be discussed in Chapter 7).

Difficulties facing the Education Secretary

It was early in the summer of 2002 that the Education Secretary, Estelle Morris, began to attract adverse publicity for her handling of a number of difficult problems and situations, some of which were of her own making. In particular, she was finding it very difficult to resolve the problems of diversity versus uniformity in matters relating to the organization of secondary schools and to the implementation of the secondary-school curriculum.

Prior to delivering an important speech to the Social Market Foundation at the end of June, the Education Secretary wrote an article for *The Observer* in which she unwittingly exposed one of the fundamental contradictions in the Government's position. She argued that in the pursuit of 'opportunity for all' comprehensive schools had concentrated on their essential 'sameness' and failed to offer children an education 'tailored to individual needs'. She went on:

Comprehensive schools don't cherish their differences. Equality of opportunity will never be achieved by giving all children the same education. It *is* achieved by tailoring education to the needs of the individual. The old tripartite system could never have done that. Comprehensive schools could, but so far haven't. In the fight for equal opportunity, we may have emphasised the *equality* too much and the *opportunity* too little. This is characterised in our attitude to excellence. Too often, it is confused with elitism and with failing to understand that recognising and celebrating those who achieve does not hold back others . . . So . . . we must keep the entitlement curriculum that comprehensive education offers all children. But we have to encourage every single one of our secondary schools to develop their own sense of mission and play to their strengths. That is why we will invest in specialist schools and training schools, beacon schools and city academies, each school choosing its own special identity within the comprehensive family. We have to get away from the perception that 'one size fits all schools' and the concept of 'ready-to-wear, off-the-shelf comprehensives'. (Morris, 2002b)

What is not explained here is how the expansion of the specialist schools programme and the steady abandonment of the National Curriculum at

Key Stage Four are compatible with the continued promotion of an 'entitlement' curriculum.

In the speech itself, delivered on 24 June, the Education Secretary claimed that the comprehensive system had failed in its mission to 'raise standards for all' and promised to end the era of the 'one-size-fits-all' comprehensive by introducing greater diversity into the system through new specialist schools and city academies. Yet although this was an important message, the focus of most newspaper headlines the following day was an ill-judged aside, which was not scripted, which echoed the 2001 'bog-standard comprehensive' jibe by the Prime Minister's powerful Communications Chief, Alastair Campbell. Ms Morris said: 'I know that all secondary schools are not identical. As a former teacher, I go into some schools and think: "I would like to work here"; but there are some I simply wouldn't touch with a bargepole.' Not surprisingly, this remark provoked anger and dismay from the majority of the teacher unions. In the words of Doug McAvoy, leader of the National Union of Teachers:

> This is an outrageous statement which ill becomes the Secretary of State for Education and Skills. Our teachers devote their energies to doing the utmost for their pupils. There will be many wondering whether they are teaching in a school the Education Secretary wouldn't 'touch with a bargepole'. Her statement will leave many of them asking the obvious question: 'if she would not teach here, why should we?' . . . Her statement is totally demoralising and ignores the efforts made by our teachers, many of whom work in extremely difficult circumstances. (Quoted in *The Times*, 25 June 2002)

The following month, Chancellor Gordon Brown announced a record increase in government spending for the Department for Education as part of the Comprehensive Spending Review. An extra £14.7 billion for education meant an annual increase in spending of 6 per cent until 2006. Yet in a statement to the House of Commons by the Education Secretary on 16 July 2002, it was made clear that this extra investment would be tied to an acceptance by the teacher unions of the need for a restructured teaching profession, including an enhanced role for teaching assistants, and for a 'post-comprehensive' structure of schools at the secondary level. 'We need to make a decisive break with those parts of the existing comprehensive system that still hold us back', Ms Morris told MPs. 'This substantial extra investment must also be matched by a firm commitment from our national partners to a restructured teaching profession and a reformed school workforce – more flexible, more diverse, more focused on raising standards' (reported in *The Guardian*,

17 July 2002). In the event, only the National Union of Teachers (NUT) refused to reach an agreement with the Government on a new role for teaching assistants, one of the factors which was to cause Ms Morris's successor, Charles Clarke, to refuse to attend the NUT's annual Easter Conference in April 2003.

It was also in the summer of 2002 that Estelle Morris was suddenly faced with a crisis over the marking and grading of A Level scripts. Figures released on 15 August showed that the pass rate had risen from 89.8 to 94.3 per cent (the biggest ever yearly rise), with the proportion of A grades increasing from 18.6 to 20.7 per cent. This caused Ruth Lea, Head of the Policy Unit at the Institute of Directors, to label A Level as 'the exam you almost cannot fail'. But then a front-page story in *The Observer* on 1 September sparked off a major controversy by alleging that a large number of sixth-formers had had their papers deliberately 'marked down' so that the exam boards would not face the criticism that the exam had become 'too easy'.

Of the three boards involved in the marking of A Level scripts – the Oxford and Cambridge and RSA Board (OCR), the Assessment and Qualifications Alliance (AQA) and Edexcel – media attention focused largely on the OCR Board where, or so it was alleged, there had been widespread marking down of students' coursework grades. Amidst all the accusations and counter-accusations, it soon became clear that the introduction of the new AS Levels in 2000 was an important factor to be taken into consideration. For the first time, A Levels were now fully 'modular', taken by many students in six units of study. The first three constituted the AS or Advanced Subsidiary level, taken in the first year of the Sixth Form; three units taken in the second year then marked the completion of the A2 or Advanced Terminal Level. The introduction of the AS Level exam had given many sixth-formers the opportunity to drop their weakest subjects at the end of their first year of study, thereby ensuring that final results would be artificially high. This seemed to have taken the exam boards – and particularly the OCR Board – by surprise.

Under pressure from union leaders and headteachers – and, in particular, the headteachers of a number of Britain's leading independent schools – Estelle Morris ordered three separate inquiries to ascertain whether or not the OCR Board had indeed deliberately reduced grades for some A Level coursework to bring down the overall pass marks and had done so having been subjected to what was perceived as pressure, both subtle and overt, from either the QCA or the Government. The first inquiry, carried out by Ken Boston, the QCA's new Chief Executive, found no evidence to substantiate these allegations and instead blamed teachers for failing to fully understand 'the demands that were now required for the coursework element in the new A2'.

During the month of September, the debate over alleged 'malpractice' became increasingly bitter and acrimonious, and one of the 'casualties' of the crisis was Sir William Stubbs, Chairperson of the QCA, who was forced to resign on 27 September for his part in the creation of what the Education Secretary described as a 'breakdown of trust' between the QCA and the three exam boards. Sir William, however, blamed the Education Secretary for her handling of the whole affair and for trying to influence the outcome of the further inquiries carried out by Mike Tomlinson, the former Chief Inspector of Schools.

The Tomlinson investigation in fact decided that the new A and AS Levels were 'an accident waiting to happen' because they were so flawed and had been imposed on schools and colleges without adequate preparation. Accepting that there had been some interference in the grading of coursework, the first Tomlinson Report argued that thousands of sixth-form students should have their A Level modules re-assessed. In the event, fewer than 2,000 students were given higher grades, and only 165 sixth-formers were eligible to switch from their second to their first choice of university.

One *positive* outcome of the A Level fiasco was the re-emergence of the debate about the nature of post-16 qualifications. Ideas were put forward for the introduction of a 'British Baccalaureate', involving the study of a broader range of subjects; and, in an interview with *The Sunday Times* (22 September 2002), Professor David Hargreaves, a senior government adviser on school examinations, argued that the A Level would indeed be replaced by a British or English version of the International Baccalaureate 'within ten years'. Serious consideration of the proposal was to be given further support in a 14–19 discussion document published in January 2003 (this is discussed further in Chapter 8).

Alleged interference with the grading of A Level scripts was not the only problem that the Education Secretary faced in the summer and early autumn of 2002. Figures released on 26 September showed that the Government had failed to meet its literacy and numeracy targets for 11-year-olds (discussed in Chapter 7). Discussion of this in the media was overshadowed by a controversy over whether or not Ms Morris had promised to resign in the event of such a clear failure. Then there was the failure of the Criminal Records Bureau to complete background checks on all new teachers by the start of the Autumn Term in the wake of a number of serious crimes involving children, and particularly the murder of two little girls from Soham in Cambridgeshire. Finally, the

Education Secretary was heavily criticized for what was seen as an inept intervention in the affair of the two students at Glyn Technology School in Epsom, Surrey, who had been expelled after plaguing a male teacher with death threats and then allowed back into school after consideration of the case by an appeals panel set up by the governing body.

It is fair to say that despite the publicity given to her difficulties, everybody was taken by surprise when Estelle Morris suddenly resigned on 23 October, arguing by way of explanation that she was incapable of providing the right strategic management needed to run a big government department. In her resignation letter to the Prime Minister she said:

> In many ways I feel I achieved more in my first job as a minister than in the second. I've learned what I'm good at, and also what I am less good at. I'm good at dealing with the major issues and in communicating to the teaching profession. I am less good at strategic management of a huge department, and I am not good at dealing with the modern media. All this has meant that with some of the recent situations I have been involved in, I have not felt I have been as effective as I should have been, or as effective as you need me to be.
> (Reported in *The Guardian,* 23 October 2002)

Her successor, Charles Clarke, was generally regarded as being a much tougher and more combative personality. He certainly set himself a punishing work schedule in his early months in office. Two important documents were published in January 2003, one a consultative document on the 14–19 curriculum (DfES, 2003a) and the other a White Paper on the future of higher education (DfES, 2003b), and these will be discussed in Chapters 7 and 8 respectively.

A renewed commitment to choice and diversity

During Charles Clarke's period as Education Secretary (October 2002–December 2004), it was becoming increasingly clear that, as far as both main political parties were concerned, the twin formulations of choice and diversity, particularly when applied to secondary provision, were *the* key concepts capable of securing wide popular appeal. And two documents appeared in the Summer of 2004 which reflected this prioritization of choice and diversity as the guiding principles for future education policy: *Right to Choose*, published by the Conservative Party on the 29 June (Conservative Party, 2004) and *A Five Year Strategy for Children and Learners*, published by the Department for Education and Skills on 8 July (DfES, 2004a).

The first section of *Right to Choose*, headed 'The Case for Change', contained a decidedly gloomy analysis of the existing educational scene, arguing that after seven years of a Labour government, and despite a 40 per cent increase in public spending, standards in education remained 'unacceptably low'. The authors highlighted the fact, revealed in a MORI survey for the General Teaching Council published in January 2003, that a third of teachers believed they would no longer be teaching in five years' time. According to the survey, there were two principal reasons why teachers were anxious to leave the profession after such a relatively short period of time. The first was the workload resulting from 'unnecessary bureaucracy'. Every year, schools received more than 2,000 pages of instructions, regulations and circulars from Whitehall – twelve pages for every working day. And the second reason given by teachers was 'worsening pupil behaviour'. Around two-thirds of teachers apparently believed that standards of discipline, particularly in secondary schools, were falling.

The Conservative publication went on to claim that parents were responding to declining school standards, exacerbated by high staff turnover, by adopting one or other of a number of viable strategies. Some were able to move house into the catchment area of 'a good school'. Others found they were lucky in 'the lottery of the admissions appeal system'. Some went so far as to leave the state system entirely. And this left millions of pupils 'trapped in under-performing schools' – left behind while their more fortunate peers got the start in life that 'should be the right of all British children' (Conservative Party, 2004: 5).

Bearing all these issues in mind, the Conservative Party's education policy was now said to have three main elements: the Right to Choose, Freedom for Professionals and the Right to Supply.

Taking each of these elements in turn, the first of them meant that under a Conservative government, the parents of all school-age children – at primary, secondary and sixth-form levels – would have the right to choose 'the best school for their child'. In effect, parents would be able to spend a notional sum of around £5,500 a year as they saw fit. This could go towards the fees at a private school or be used at an existing or newly-established state school of their choice. Those schools which persistently failed their pupils would be taken over by new management – or lose their right to taxpayer funding (Conservative Party, 2004: 18).

The section on 'Freedom for Professionals' contained a number of specific policy proposals. Schools would receive a 'per pupil tariff', including a capital maintenance element and an adjustment 'to take account of specific local and pupil circumstances'. Headteachers would know their budgets at the start of the school year and would be able to set their budget priorities 'based on the needs of their schools and not on the preferences of ministers'. A Conservative government would scrap targets on schools imposed from Whitehall. It would also end the Surplus Places Rule whereby popular schools were forbidden to expand while there were empty places at other local schools. Appeals Panels would be abolished, thereby 're-establishing the authority of heads and governors to deal with disruptive pupils'. Heads and governors would be able to vary the pay and conditions of staff and, above all, would have total freedom to determine their own admissions policies (Conservative Party, 2004: 38–9).

Under the section on 'The Right to Supply', any school, charitable or commercial, that could show itself capable of providing a good education for the same cost as that incurred by a state school would be entitled to receive taxpayer funding. This meant a Conservative government would finally break the link between state funding and state provision, allowing the creation of new schools run by a variety of providers, including faith groups, parents and private companies (Conservative Party, 2004: 40).

Turning now to the New Labour *Strategy* Document, we learn from the Foreword by the Secretary of State that the 'central characteristic' of the new education system which the Government was planning would be 'personalization' – 'so that the system fits to the individual, rather than the individual having to fit to the system'. In order to ensure that there really would be 'different and personalized opportunities available for all', the system had to be 'both freer and more diverse', with 'more choices between types of provider'. The twin goals of the education service had to be more choice for parents and pupils; a greater variety of schools (DfES, 2004a: 4).

The 110-page *Strategy* argued that five key principles of reform would underpin the drive for a step change in children's services, education and training:

- greater personalization and choice, with the wishes and needs of children's services, parents and learners centre-stage.
- the opening up of services to new and different providers and ways of delivering services.
- freedom and independence for frontline headteachers, governors and managers, with clear simple accountabilities and more secure streamlined funding arrangements.

- a major commitment to staff development, with high quality support and training to improve assessment, care and teaching.
- partnerships with parents, employers, volunteers and voluntary organizations to maximize the life chances of children, young people and adults. (DfES, 2004a: 7)

The most contentious proposal in the *Strategy* was to create 'independent specialist schools in place of the traditional comprehensive' (DfES, 2004a: 8). The Document actually highlighted an increase in the numbers of two types of school, specialist schools and City Academies, as the chief means of enhancing choice and diversity in the secondary sector. The number of specialist schools had already increased from 196 when Labour came to power in 1997 to 1,955 as the projected figure for September 2004 (see Box 4.2); and it was envisaged that there would be a further massive expansion over the next four years. The number of City Academies – 17 in September 2004 – would have increased to around 200 by the year 2010. And it was hoped that 95 per cent of state secondaries would be either independent specialist schools or City Academies by the year 2008 (DfES, 2004a: 56).

What is striking about the Conservative and New Labour policy documents is that the language used was more or less interchangeable, with the two political parties sharing the same ideals and aspirations. Both documents talked about the need for greater personalization, choice and flexibility, particularly in the secondary sector. Both documents talked about the need to abandon the idea of a uniform system of comprehensive secondary schools, the Conservative manifesto arguing that it was time to see an end to 'large, one-size-fits-all, state institutions' (Conservative Party, 2004: 5) and the New Labour *Strategy* claiming that we had to move away from the 1960s model for secondary schools which was 'a monolithic one', with the focus on 'a basic and standard product for all' (DfES: 2004a: 3). For both documents, the way forward involved the creation of new types of schools run by a variety of sponsors, including philanthropic individuals, educational trusts, faith groups, parents and private companies. Writing in *Education Guardian* in January 2005, and reflecting on the Government's most recent plans for the education system, Tim Collins, the Shadow Secretary of State for Education, argued that the policies were 'the latest instances of New Labour mouthing Tory slogans', although not actually offering schools the full independence a Conservative government would offer' (Collins, 2005).

After Tony Blair's third successive General Election victory in May

Box 4.2   Number of Specialist Schools by specialism, from September 2004

Technology (maths, science and design technology)   545*
Arts   305*
Sports   283*
Science   224
Languages   203*
Maths and computing   153
Business and enterprise   146
Combined specialisms   38
Engineering   35
Humanities   18
Music   5*

Total   1,955

Notes:
Asterisk indicates that a school offering this specialism is allowed to select up to 10 per cent of its pupils on the basis of their aptitude for the subject. Some specialisms have been introduced more recently than others, which explains the smaller numbers for (for example) humanities and music.

Source: DfES, 2004a: 47.

2005, albeit with a reduced Commons majority of just 67, the New Labour modernizing agenda in matters relating to education continued to dominate the policy-making process – and with new strategies for creating even greater diversity within the system. The 2005 Labour Party Election Manifesto, with the title *Britain Forward Not Back* had reiterated that Labour wanted all secondary schools to become 'independent specialist schools with a strong ethos, high-quality leadership, good discipline (including school uniforms), setting by ability and high-quality facilities as the norm' (Labour Party, 2005: 35). But Labour Party supporters were *not* prepared for the radical nature of the rhetoric employed in the October 2005 White Paper *Higher Standards, Better Schools for All: More Choice for Parents and Pupils* (DfES, 2005b).

In his Foreword to the White Paper – a 116-page document which heralded the fortieth Education Act since 1980 – Prime Minister Tony Blair argued that we were at an historic turning point: we now had an education system that had 'overcome many of the chronic inherited problems of the past' and, after eight years of investment and reform, it was poised to become 'world class' – if we only had 'the courage and vision to reform and invest further and put the parent and the pupil at the centre of the system'. Further reform must build on the freedoms that schools had already received and extend them radically; and, to under-pin this change, 'the local authority must move from being a provider of education to being its local commissioner and the champion of parent choice'. According to the Prime Minister, comprehensive schools had been introduced to deal with the weaknesses of the post-war divided secondary system, but their introduction had been too often accompa-nied by all-ability classes, which had meant that 'setting by subject abil-ity was rare' and 'overall standards were far too low'. The Government was now determined to 're-energize comprehensive education' which meant that all secondary schools had to have 'challenging targets for improvement' and develop 'a clear mission'. This also meant creating a greater diversity of secondary schools; and the aim now was to set up a system of 'independent non-fee paying state schools', with all secondary schools deciding whether they wished to acquire a Trust – similar to those that supported the new Academies – or become a self-governing foundation school (DfES, 2005b: 1–4).

The White Paper went on to make a number of far-reaching propos-als building on the Prime Minister's vision, though it was not always clear how the new 'freedoms' being offered to schools could work out in practice. It would now be open to any existing secondary school – and this would apply to primary schools as well – to create its own Trust or link the school with an existing Trust. These new Trusts could be formed by businesses, charities, faith groups, universities or parent and commu-nity organizations. They would have many of the same freedoms as those currently enjoyed by Academies and be able to appoint the govern-ing body, control their own assets, employ their own staff and set their own admissions criteria while having regard to the Admissions Code of Practice (DfES, 2005b: 25).

All new schools would be self-governing foundation schools, Trust Schools, voluntary- aided schools or – where appropriate – Academies. Those schools deemed to be 'failing' would be given twelve months in which to improve, and if such improvement proved unrealizable, a 'competition for new providers' would have to be held and the school would be reopened as an Academy or as a new Trust School backed by a private charity or business group (DfES, 2005b: 10, 36).

The White Paper came in for a remarkable amount of detailed criti-cism – from a significant section of the Labour Party both inside and outside Parliament, from the National Union of Teachers and from a large number of prominent educationists and comprehensive school campaigners.

The promotion of Academies – to reach 200 in number by the end of the decade – was seen by many as a deliberate means of *privatizing* the education service (to be discussed more fully in Chapter 5). It was feared that giving schools greater control over their admissions criteria could easily result in an admissions 'free-for-all', with enormous implications for the selection of pupils and the segregation of schools. And there was tremendous anxiety about the loss of local accountability involved in encouraging private sponsors and faith groups to set up their own educational 'brands', grouping schools together in ill-defined Trusts. For the National Union of Teachers, the White Paper was 'extraordinarily wrong-headed'; and the Union wanted each local authority to be able to establish the admissions policy for *all* the schools in the maintained sector in its area, including all foundation schools, voluntary-aided schools and existing Academies (White and Taylor, 2005). The Editor of the educational journal *Forum* was concerned that there was no talk in the White Paper about human educability, one of the underpinning principles of the comprehensive reform, with Chapter 1 including the highly questionable assertion that pupils could be divided into three main categories: 'the gifted and talented, the struggling and the just average' (Chitty, 2006: 5; DfES, 2005b: 20). And Professor Sally Tomlinson of Oxford University pointed out that the White Paper was full of 'repetitions and stunning contradictions', with, for example, paragraph 9.3 asserting that 'we will support local authorities in playing a new commissioning role in relation to the creation of a new system of schools at the heart of their local communities'; and then, on the next page, paragraph 9.7 telling local authorities that they had 'a duty to promote choice and diversity in the delivery of school places', where necessary to get children out of their local community (Tomlinson, 2006: 52; DfES, 2005b: 104-5).

Education Secretary Ruth Kelly, who had taken over the post from Charles Clarke in December 2004, found it very difficult to defend the Government's new proposals. In the view of John Dunford, General Secretary of the Association of School and College Leaders (Dunford, 2006: 34), she was so taken aback by the strength of the opposition to the idea of greater independence for schools that she was often forced to undermine the Prime Minister's radical vision by emphasizing the *similarities* between the new Trust Schools and existing foundation schools. Even so, she received a very hostile reception from local government officials and councillors when she tried to defend the Government's plans at the North of England Education Conference in Newcastle on 6 January 2006 (reported in *The Guardian*, 7 January 2006).

When the Education and Inspections Bill was published on 28 February 2006, it was clear that the basic architecture of the original White Paper's intention remained in place; but there were, in fact, three key respects where the drafters of the legislation *had* taken account of criticisms of the White Paper. There was now to be an agreement to require schools to 'act in accordance with the Admissions Code', rather than just 'have regard to it'; and there was a proposed ban on interviewing for selection (other than for boarding places). At the same time, the local authorities could propose new *community* schools if new schools were needed or a 'failing' school had to be replaced, but only following the approval of the Secretary of State.

That being said, the Bill still contained a number of worrying features as far as supporters of a genuine comprehensive system were concerned. Secondary schools in England would still become more fragmented, with local authorities unable to ensure fairness and justice at a local level. Informal selection could still be practised and would undoubtedly continue because of the intense competition between schools for the most 'motivated' pupils, the weak and vulnerable inevitably suffering in the process. The Secretary of State retained a veto over the creation of traditional community schools; and the future clearly lay with the spread of 'independent state schools', even if they were to be known by the existing name of 'foundation schools', instead of as Trust Schools, a term which had attracted deep hostility. Above all, there was still the fear that foundation school governing bodies and school assets could fall under the control of unsuitable external interests such as entrepreneurs with a specific capitalist agenda or faith groups with a fundamentalist message.

Amidst all the fuss over admissions and foundation school privileges, an important section of the new Bill actually received very little media attention, even though it could have a damaging effect on traditional comprehensive schools. The little-noticed clauses in Part 5 dealing with the provision of the new specialized vocational diplomas (to be discussed more fully in Chapter 9) probably meant that many comprehensive schools would find it very difficult to offer the full range of curriculum entitlement at the post-14 stage. There were, in fact, many who believed that the Prime Minister's long-term aim was to move vocational education for 14–19 year olds into further education where it could be provided more cheaply. The post-war bipartite system of grammar schools and secondary moderns could then be transformed into secondary schools for those on the 'academic' path; while further education colleges took the place of secondary modern schools for those labelled as 'non-academic'.

Despite all the opposition within the Labour Party, the Education and Inspections Bill passed its Second Reading in the House of Commons on 15 March 2006 – but only with the support of the Conservative Opposition. A total of 52 Labour MPs joined the Liberal Democrats in voting against the Bill, and 23 Labour MPs abstained. It had been thought at the beginning of March that the rebellion would be even larger; but a number of White Paper critics, including the leading comprehensive school campaigner David Chaytor, decided to support the Government in the hope that the Bill could be improved at the committee stage – a sanguine expectation that proved to be naïvely optimistic. On 23 May 2006, 69 Labour MPs voted for a rebel amendment to the Bill requiring schools to hold a ballot of parents before acquiring independent trust status. And then on 24 May, 46 Labour MPs voted against the third reading of the Bill, creating the largest rebellion ever suffered by a Labour government at third reading.

The new Brown administration

Tony Blair had indicated before the 2005 General Election that he would not be leading New Labour into a fourth general election contest. And Gordon Brown finally took over as unopposed Labour Leader and Prime Minister on 27 June 2007. Ed Balls replaced Alan Johnson as Schools Secretary in the revamped Department of Children, Schools and Families, and he must have been aware that there were a number of important issues concerning school admissions and local accountability that were still unresolved.

As I write, it is obviously far too early to provide a detailed assessment of the new Brown administration's attitude towards education and social policy; but it is possible to comment on certain emerging trends.

Gordon Brown had, in fact, already given a clear indication of his broad educational philosophy in his final Mansion House Speech as Chancellor of the Exchequer delivered on 20 June 2007. And any hopes on the Left of the Labour Party that he would seek to reverse some of the more controversial school reforms of the Blair era had been squashed by his promise that he would pursue the Blair agenda with renewed vigour. In particular, it was stressed that one of the clear priorities of the new administration would be the expansion of the Academies Programme, with universities and colleges being encouraged to play 'a fuller part in the sponsorship of the new schools' (quoted in *The Guardian*, 21 June 2007). In fact, where Academies were concerned, the Government's message was not always as clear-cut and consistent as proponents would have wished (to be discussed more fully in Chapter 5). On 2 October 2007, Schools Minister Lord Adonis made an enthusiastic speech in which he emphasized that universities and private schools that wished to sponsor Academies would no longer have to contribute £2m towards the starting costs (reported in *The Guardian*, 2 October 2007). And on 19 November 2007, he welcomed the Conservative plan to extend the Academies Programme so that eventually most schools would be released from the control of local authorities (reported in *The Guardian*, 19 November 2007). Yet in the same month, an urgent review of Academies was ordered by Ed Balls amid growing concern at the heart of government that this was one of the education policies that could be said to be failing to target 'the most disadvantaged pupils' (reported in *The Guardian*, 13 November 2007).

After ten years of costly education initiatives, it was apparent to ministers that too many, largely working-class, youngsters were still leaving school with few or no qualifications. The new Brown Government was certainly determined to encourage all young people to stay on at school or join training programmes beyond the age of 16 and to offer so-called NEETs (those not in education, employment or training) a way back into work or education. Indeed, there would be legislation to effect this change over a period of eight years. One of the proposed new laws in the education section of the Queen's Speech delivered on 6 November 2007 would require all young people to stay in education or training until 17 by 2013 and until 18 by 2015. Parents would have a new legal duty to help make sure their children stayed on in education until they were 18; and employers would be required to let young people attend training for at least one day a week. Teenagers who refused to comply would face spot fines of £50 and possible court fines of £200. There would also be a legal duty on schools and colleges to inform truancy officers and career guidance workers if a student dropped out. In a speech delivered to the Fabian Society the day before the Queen's Speech, Ed Balls said: 'we need a new culture throughout schools which makes sure that the 10-year-olds of today understand fully the risks and consequences for them of *not* being in education or training' (reported in *The Guardian*, 6 November 2007.

Another set of problems for Ed Balls to deal with centred on the complex issue of school admissions. A new School Admissions Code had come into force on 28 February 2007 and was intended to apply to all maintained schools for admissions in 2008. In theory, it also applied to Academies and was seen by some as an attempt to bring Academies into line with maintained schools, although it was not clear how the Code could be enforced in existing Academies since these schools were governed by their own special Funding Agreements which were, in effect, private legal agreements between the Secretary of State and the Sponsor and could not be altered by either party unilaterally. That being said, the new Code did contain proposals designed to ensure that 'admissions authorities – whether local authorities or schools – operate in a fair way that promotes social equity and community cohesion'. It extended the role, membership and powers of Admissions Forums, it stipulated that catchment areas must be fairly drawn, and it put a stop to various 'unacceptable over-subscription criteria', such as the consideration of parental background and income.

On 11 March 2008, the Department of Children, Schools and Families announced that 81.6 per cent of families in England had received an offer of their first preference school on the 'national offer day' (3 March). At the same time, more than 25,000 of the 560,000 pupils applying in 2008 had been placed in a secondary school to which they did not apply. However press coverage on 12 March mostly concentrated on an accompanying announcement which revealed that, having examined the admissions criteria for 570 primary and secondary schools in three local authorities – Northamptonshire, Manchester and the London Borough of Barnet – the Department had found that a 'significant minority' of schools appeared not to be complying with the new School Admissions Code, of which a 'disproportionate number' were faith or foundation schools. The illegal practices identified included: interviewing pupils, failing to give priority to children in care, demanding information about parents' professions and incomes, and asking for financial contributions.

An editorial in *The Guardian* on 3 April 2008, with the title 'Beyond Blair', argued that education ministers in the Brown Government appeared to be 'shuffling away from' the educational policies of Tony Blair. Gone was the former Prime Minister's insistence that vocational and academic qualifications must remain separate. Gone was the idea that schools must always act as though they were in cut-throat competition with one another. Above all, gone was the idea that it was perfectly acceptable for certain schools to employ all manner of questionable strategies in order to select 'a disproportionate number' of pupils from 'desirable and well-heeled families'. Only the threat of a parliamentary mutiny had persuaded a reluctant Tony Blair to accept a strengthened legal code for school admissions. Now the Schools Secretary seemed determined to ensure that the Code was strictly enforced, with the Schools Adjudicator, who had previously reviewed decisions only when asked to do so by disappointed parents, now being transformed into 'a proactive policeman'.

Yet, if some ministers were aware of the need for change, the Prime Minister himself seemed to be firmly of the opinion that the Blairite legacy – and particularly where it applied to education and health – must be preserved and built upon. Writing in *The Financial Times* in March 2008, Gordon Brown argued that it was now time to implement 'the third act in public sector reform'. According to his analysis of the situation, the first act – indeed the Government's first task in 1997 – had demanded 'a programme of investment and repair designed to remedy decades of neglect and to establish a basic level of standards below which no school or hospital would fall'. This had inevitably meant using national targets, league tables and tough inspection regimes to monitor progress. To ensure that the Government obtained maximum value from each pound spent and that struggling services were turned round, the second stage of the reform programme had focused on 'tackling under-performance and on reducing variations in standards'. It was now time to go further and move to the third stage of reform where, in the case of education, choice and diversity were enhanced and new providers were brought in to create the dynamism for transforming under-performing schools. In the near future, the Government would announce new plans that would 'empower and enable more of our best headteachers to help turn around low-performing schools, that would create new trusts and federations around successful schools, and, in areas of greatest need, drive forward an even faster expansion of the Government's Academies Programme' (Brown, 2008). This was Gordon Brown's vision for undermining monopoly provision in a revitalized education service.

5

The Privatization of Education

The idea of privatizing significant parts of the education service did not occupy a major role in the educational and political discourse of the 1960s and 1970s when many of the post-war certainties were subject to reappraisal, although, as we saw in Chapters 2 and 3, there was a spirited campaign on the Far Right of the Conservative Party to promote the cause of the education voucher as a means of enhancing parental choice and undermining the powers of the local education authorities.

Privatization in the 1980s

In the 1980s, and with the idea of experimenting with the voucher failing to gain the support of Education Secretary Keith Joseph, what could be described as privatization assumed at least two major forms: the purchasing at *private* expense of educational services which ought to be free within the *public* system; and the purchasing at *public* expense of educational services in *private* institutions (see Pring, 1983; 1986; 1987; Chitty, 1989a: 178–89; 1997c). There was possibly even a third category, which was privatization in the sense of impoverishing the maintained sector to such an extent that anxious parents with adequate means felt more or less obliged to select some form of private education for their children. In all its many forms, the privatization of education could be usefully defined as the systematic erosion, and possibly even abandonment, of the commitment to a common educational service based on pupil needs, rather than upon private means, and accessible to all young people on the basis of equal opportunity. And all this was taking place in the 1980s against a background of sustained criticism of the achievements of the state system and as part of the process of subjecting the education service to the same kind of harsh market pressures as those to which any commercial enterprise would be subjected. State schools were desperately trying to earn the respect of parents at a time when the

Government of Margaret Thatcher was providing strong ideological and financial support for private education and encouraging 'exit' from state institutions.

The first category included the various ways in which parents and private firms were being asked to pay for both essential and non-essential services within the public sector: special lessons or additions to the curriculum, resources and books, repairs and maintenance, basic facilities and buildings, even teaching posts (see Pring, 1987: 292). It could be argued that there were a number of extra-curricular activities – for example, visits to the theatre or school trips abroad – for which parents could not reasonably object to being asked to make a contribution. Yet in many cases, parents were being expected not simply to enrich the curriculum for a few but actually to help ensure basic curriculum provision for all. The National Confederation of Parent Teacher Associations (NCPTA) estimated that, by the middle of the 1980s, £40m a year was being required of parents for what were regarded as essentials: books and equipment and lessons (Mountfield, 1991: 45). And successive HMI reports in the 1980s also pointed to the need for parents to contribute large sums of money in order to compensate for a desperate shortage of books and other essential items. The Report of the 1985 Survey, for example, published at a time when Keith Joseph was being much criticized for his refusal to demand more money for education from the Treasury, showed that the gap between rich and poor schools was widening because of differing parental contributions. Schools in affluent middle-class areas were clearly in a better position to compensate for LEA economies:

> Contributions overall ranged from £50 to £15,000 per year, the latter sum being on top of a capitation allowance of £38,000. In one exceptional case, one secondary school received £45,000, which was 25 per cent more than its capitation, and a considerable proportion of this sum came from covenants made by parents . . . Schools in the shire counties received proportionately the greatest level of contribution: over one-third of the schools visited received contributions in excess of £6 per pupil, while this was so in only one-fifth of the schools in the metropolitan districts and London authorities. Compared with in previous years, schools in all three types of authority were receiving more contributions from parents than ever before. (DES, 1986: 46)

It seems clear that these contributions were being used to provide or enhance a wide variety of teaching resources and activities:

> Most commonly, the money was being used to help towards the cost of educational visits, and this was followed by the purchase of computers,

audio-visual equipment, library and reference books, PE and games equipment, school mini-buses, musical instruments, textbooks and reprographic equipment. The most notable change since 1984 was the increased number of references to parental contributions being used to improve school premises. For example: in one school, the whole of the first floor was rewired using the funds provided by the parents, while in many others, parental contributions were used to provide the materials needed to redecorate parts of the school. (DES, 1986: 47)

The most obvious example of the second category was, of course, the Assisted Places Scheme, the most radical and controversial of the measures introduced by Margaret Thatcher's first Education Secretary Mark Carlisle (1979–81) (already discussed in Chapter 3). Being a major feature of the 1980 Education Act and launched in 1981, the Scheme was, as we have seen, all about providing central government money to enable a select group of 'financially eligible' and 'academically able' students to benefit from a private education. It was, in fact, a considerable administrative achievement that in September 1981 4,185 of the 5,417 places available in 223 English independent schools were actually taken up by the parents who had applied to take advantage of the Scheme. By the end of the 1980s, when the Scheme was almost fully in operation, 26,899 young people were holding assisted places at a cost to the Government in 1987–88 of just under £50 million (Edwards, Fitz and Whitty, 1989: 2).

In a paper published in 1990, Caroline Benn reviewed the various ways in which both central government and local authorities were engaged in promoting the *private* at the expense of the *public* sector and estimated the cost to the taxpayer of providing separate and supposedly superior educational opportunities for a small minority of young people. For this purpose, she took into account not just the Assisted Places Scheme of recent origin, but also a number of long-established practices such as the purchase by the state of places at private day or boarding schools for the children of high-ranking civil servants and military personnel often serving overseas. A 1983 paper by Richard Pring came up with a minimum yearly subsidy bill of around £200m (Pring, 1983: 15). An earlier article by Rick Rogers in *New Statesman*, taking into account both *direct* and *indirect* subsidies, including tax losses from the independent schools' entitlement to 'charity status', had arrived at a national yearly bill of £654m (Rogers, 1980). For Caroline Benn, both these figures were conservative estimates, and she provided detailed statistical evidence for setting the 1990 figure as high as £1.3bn (Benn, 1990: 68).

Private Finance Initiative

In the course of the 1990s, private capital recognized that, as many markets for traditional consumer goods were reaching saturation point, the expanding markets of the future would be in services such as education and health. It had looked to the Conservative Party to introduce tax rebates for parents who opted for the private sector or to issue vouchers that could be used as payments for the whole or part of the cost of a child's education in independent schools. But New Labour under Tony Blair promised a better solution. Instead of competing for custom in the uncertain conditions of the private market, firms would get the chance to run public services in return for a more or less guaranteed stream of income from the state.

The most obvious example of how private capital could make such a low-risk investment was the Private Finance Initiative, in many ways the most radical and far-reaching of the privatization schemes of the last 20 years, involving the use of private sector funding and ownership to provide new buildings and facilitate major refurbishments right across the public sector. Put simply, PFI involved the injection of private capital into a wide range of essential public services, notably education, health and transport, in return for, among other things, lucrative long-term service contracts and the welcome prospect for the private company or group of private companies concerned of a considerable period of financial stability and steady growth. PFI contracts, involving buildings and facilities management, were normally designed to last for between 25 and 35 years, during which time the private sector company or companies would be handsomely reimbursed by the relevant public agency (invariably an LEA or health trust). In the case of schools, the company or consortium responsible for the construction of the new building would normally take over the maintenance and management of the premises, and this would involve responsibility for many important aspects of facilities management, such as: repairs, grounds maintenance, catering, cleaning, utilities, furniture and IT equipment.

The UK Private Finance Initiative had actually been launched by the Conservative Government of John Major in late 1992. It was expanded by New Labour after Tony Blair came to power in 1997, although the PFI policy was never discussed openly during the 1997 general election campaign. After 1997, PFI schemes were grouped together under the umbrella title Public Private Partnership (PPP), although it should be noted that PPPs have come to embrace a much wider range of possible contractual and collaborative relationships between public authorities and private sector companies. The first two schools to be financed by PFI contracts were opened in 1999; and the new government building programme (Building Schools for the Future) was expected to make use of PFI funding.

One of the principal advantages of PPP as far as governments were concerned was that it reduced capital spending – or, rather, postponed it to future years. PPP projects also had the distinct advantage of not counting as capital spending under the Maastricht criteria for public sector borrowing. At the same time, they were also very attractive to local authorities in so far as they provided much-needed funding for capital building, which might well not otherwise be forthcoming. The initial claim for PFI or PPP schemes was that they both provided 'value for money' and delivered more efficient services. At a conference in 2000, the Finance Directors of Birmingham and Glasgow Local Authorities, both major users of PFI, cast doubts on the 'value-for-money' claims being made for the schemes, while also conceding that there really was no alternative source of income. George Black, the Finance Director for Glasgow, said: 'I'm not sure it is value for money. But it's the only game in town. It's the way you get money back into your services' (quoted in Ball, 2007: 47).

There have, of course, been a number of drawbacks to this new way of securing private finance for infrastructure projects. PFI and PPP schemes have often been more expensive than have publicly-funded projects of a similar nature. It has cost local authorities more to borrow from the private sector than from the Government, and, on top of that, there have often been the fees for consultants and the profit taken by the private companies themselves. It was estimated in 2001 that PFI projects cost at least 10 per cent more than schemes financed in more traditional ways (see Hatcher, 2001: 67). It is important to realize that PFI or PPP projects have received government approval only by demonstrating 'value for money', so many have been forced to reduce costs by operating schools more 'efficiently' on facilities management contracts which have employed fewer staff, more staff on flexible contracts and which have included the right to increase income generation through heavy charges for private and community use of school premises.

By late 2004, there were 86 PFI schools projects in England worth £2.4 billion involving over 500 schools, 15 in Scotland worth £553 million and two in Wales. The overall value of PFI deals in 2004 was estimated by the Treasury to be £7.7 billion, including £900 million for educational and skills projects (see Ball, 2007: 46). So far, Academies have opted to stay clear of PFI preferring to keep total control over the building and management of their schools.

What, then, is the overall significance of the PFI phenomenon? In the words of Professor Stephen Ball: 'the multi-faceted nature of PFIs has re-worked the landscape of public sector provision and has become part of the re-positioning of local government as service commissioners' (Ball, 2007: 47–8). And the Government has been quite frank in acknowledging that PFI or PPP has entailed a radical redefinition of provision in the public service, with local authorities forced to accept a massive reduction in their service provision role:

> PPP is one of the Government's main instruments for delivering higher quality and more cost-effective public services, with the public sector as an *enabler* and, where appropriate, guardian of the interests of the users and customers of public services. It is not simply about the financing of capital investment in services, but about exploiting the full range of private sector management, commercial and creative skills. (Press Release, Lord Chancellor's Department, 8 February 1998)

And there has also been a global dimension to private capital's colonization of the public sector, with England being far from alone in envisaging a changed and diminished role for the state. As the World Bank has said: 'although the state still has a central role in ensuring the provision of basic services – education, health, infrastructure – it is not obvious that the state must be the *only* provider, or indeed a provider at all' (quoted in Hatcher, 2001: 63).

Other privatizing initiatives in the 1990s

Following on from the NCPTA and HMI evidence of the 1980s, a large-scale survey of comprehensive schools and colleges carried out in the academic year 1993–4 and already referred to in Chapter 4 (see Benn and Chitty, 1996; 1997) found evidence of a dearth of resources and of a mounting dependency on donations from wealthy parents and from local and national businesses. In their replies to the 1993 questionnaire, hundreds of schools admitted that they depended upon money raised by parents for a wide range of curricular and extra-curricular activities. In explaining what parental funding was used to provide, headteachers revealed that top of the list was provision and/or maintenance of the school minibus; followed by purchase of PE and sports equipment; contributions towards the cost of school trips in both this country and abroad; support for the Library Fund, along with provision of essential school textbooks; purchase of computer software; contributions towards the costs of building and maintenance and repairs; and, lastly, purchase of AVA (audiovisual aids) equipment (Benn and Chitty, 1996; 1997: 317).

The companies that donated large sums of money to schools invariably received good publicity in return and sometimes a chance, indirectly, to promote the future of private industry, or just their own particular niche. All their generosity was accepted as essentially non-political. Yet the message left behind was not always strictly neutral. For example: several schools participating in the 1993–4 survey mentioned one supermarket giant's donated study-pack 'Siting a Supermarket'. It clearly embodied a political argument, and yet very few schools decided that it needed a counterbalancing study-pack (or lesson) putting the case that could be made *against* green-field developments for supermarkets. Support from outside donors could never be truly 'value-free'; and critics of private donations pointed out that problems could arise in a number of cases: for example, where schools or colleges might wish to question offers from firms in the forefront of world controversy (with weapons connections, image problems relating to working practices, or with connections to the meat or animal trade), but would feel unable to do so because of financial need (Benn and Chitty, 1996; 1997: 320; Mountfield, 1991: 48).

A report from the National Consumer Council published in May 1996 and reported on at length in *The Independent* (24 May 1996) warned teachers about 'a rising tide of US-style commercialism in British classrooms', as businesses took advantage of 'a squeeze on school funding' to target vulnerable pupils with educational resource packs which were either 'biased' or 'plastered with company logos'. According to the Council, there had been an explosion of commercially-sponsored resources for schools since 1990 – around 5,000 items for technology alone – with industry spending about £300m a year on sponsorship aimed at primary and secondary schools. The Report emphasized the need for new guidelines for teachers, governors and parents to help them recognize 'high-quality sponsored material' and reject the literature which might encourage unhealthy habits, play on children's fears or cause parents to be 'pestered to buy the sponsor's products'. It was clear that some firms were using sponsored material to persuade pupils to eat unhealthy food; while others were simply failing to mention 'basic arguments against their activities'. Cadbury's *World of Chocolate* resource pack for 11- to 12-year-olds said: 'Chocolate is fun to eat at any time of the day and gives you the energy and important nutrients that your body needs to work properly'. *Energy and the Environment* from British

Nuclear Fuels Ltd failed to mention the one key drawback of nuclear waste: that it takes up to hundreds of thousands of years or more to decay and become safe. Voucher schemes for computers and schoolbags run by Tesco's and Sainsbury's respectively rewarded 'those schools where parents could be pestered to shop at particular supermarkets. At the same time, they disadvantaged pupils who did not live near those supermarkets'. In launching the NCC Report, the Council's chairperson, David Hatch, admitted that commercially-sponsored teaching packs could be invaluable at a time when school funds were scarce, but argued for a debate on 'the creeping tide of commercialism in our classrooms' to ensure that commercial sponsorship did not take the place of state funding for core education activities. He pointed out that in parts of America, pupils were bombarded with advertisements throughout the day, sometimes on compulsory schools television programmes which included advertising. 'We want to protect British classrooms from these excesses. The classroom should be a place of learning, not a free-for-all for business interests' (Judd, 1996; Chitty, 1997: 57–8).

Much attention was focused in the media on the news that the tobacco giant BAT Industries had agreed to provide £100,000 sponsorship for one of the new Technology Specialist Schools announced in May 1996 by Conservative Education Secretary Gillian Shephard (BAT having already donated more than £2 million to the Macmillan City Technology College in Middlesbrough) (reported in, for example, *The Times*, 21 May 1996). The decision to welcome BAT Industries as a sponsor was described in an editorial in *The Times Educational Supplement* (24 May 1996) as 'a gift for the political satirists', at a time when the Government was spending millions of pounds discouraging teenagers from smoking. And this raises the whole question of the problems associated with the private sponsorship of schools, which will be covered in the next section.

It was also in the 1990s that the Conservative Government of John Major effectively 'privatized' the inspection process for schools. As we saw in Chapter 4, the Education (Schools) Act of 1992 established Ofsted (Office for Standards in Education) as a new 'independent' body responsible for contracting independent teams to inspect all primary and secondary schools. The number of HMIs was to be greatly reduced, from nearly 500 to 175; and the relationship between the schools and the Inspectorate was to be radically transformed, with many headteachers feeling that the new body showed little real awareness of the challenges they faced.

In 1998, Surrey County Council invited companies to bid for the contract to run a 'failing' comprehensive school, King's Manor in Guildford (already referred to in Chapter 4). And in February 1999, it was announced that the contract had been won by 3Es Enterprises Ltd, a private company set up as the commercial arm of Kingshurst City Technology College which had opened in the West Midlands Borough of Solihull in the Autumn of 1988. The Managing Director of 3Es was, in fact, the husband of the Principal of the Kingshurst CTC. And, once again, this brings us on to the debate as to whether private companies should be able to run state schools, which has become the most controversial aspect of private sector involvement in education and will form the subject of the next section.

Finally, as part of this brief survey of the privatizing agenda of the 1990s, it is worth noting that it was announced in November 1999 that Cambridge Education Associates – a consultancy that was also the largest contractor for school inspections – was the preferred bidder to take over all (or nearly all) the functions of Islington Local Education Authority in north London, arguably the first major privatization of an LEA. Hackney Local Education Authority was already in the process of having *some* of its services privatized, but Islington was the first to have its day-to-day running taken over by a private contractor. Announcing the decision to the media, the then Schools Minister Estelle Morris said that the DfEE and Islington were determined that this would mark 'a new beginning'. She went on to tell reporters that she hoped services would be privatized 'in up to 15 more local education authorities'. Privatization was the obvious solution to the long-standing problems which many local education authorities faced (reported in *The Independent*, 27 November 1999).

The Academies Programme

The statutory basis for the Labour Government's Academies Programme launched in March 2000, and referred to briefly in Chapter 4, was the collection of legislative powers taken from the 1988 Education Reform Act and originally intended to facilitate the establishment of a nationwide network of City Technology Colleges. And this is a point of some significance because the Academies initiative was in many of its essentials a New Labour version of the Conservatives' CTC Project.

It was at the 1986 Conservative Party Conference that the then Education Secretary Kenneth Baker unveiled his plans for a pioneering network of City Technology Colleges, to be situated largely in deprived inner-city areas. As we saw in Chapter 3, the CTCs were designed to be new schools for 11–18-year-olds, financed to a large extent by private capital and independent of local authority control. The response from private firms was expected to be very positive; and it was confidently predicted that 20 such Colleges would be up and running by the beginning of the 1990s.

In the event, this confidence turned out to be completely misplaced and, as a number of commentators argued at the time (see, for example, Chitty, 1989b), the original CTC concept was doomed to failure largely because it would be impossible to find the required number of suitable sites and a sufficient number of wealthy sponsors.

Where funding was concerned, most major firms simply boycotted the CTC scheme anxious, in many cases, not to harm their good relations with schools under local authority control; and so widespread was the feeling of reservation and doubt that, of 1,800 firms initially approached, only 17 responded positively. Even where money *was* forthcoming, it was never in the quantities Kenneth Baker hoped for. The original idea was that wealthy backers would put up between £8 and £10 million towards capital costs; but it rapidly became clear that the Government would have to be satisfied with £2 million or less. For example: in the case of the Djanogly CTC in Nottingham, which opened in September 1989, the Government was forced to donate £9.05 million from the Treasury to augment the £1.4 million which was subscribed by private companies.

On the issue of sites, it proved quite impossible to find suitable and inexpensive locations in the sort of areas envisaged in the original plans; and as matters deteriorated, the Government was forced to set up CTCs wherever circumstances permitted. According to Cyril Taylor, who had become special CTC adviser to Kenneth Baker in February 1987, the original plans were simply 'incapable of realization'. He was quoted in *The Times Educational Supplement* on 17 June 1988 as saying that 'costs of refurbishing and equipping redundant schools and green-field sites were woefully underestimated by the Department of Education and Science'. The aim now was to 'buy up schools still in use and "phase in" the CTCs over a period of up to six years' (Nash, 1988).

In fact, the CTC at Kingswood in Bristol, which opened in September 1993, was the last CTC to be authorized, bringing the total to 15. And it seemed at that time that the idea of private firms sponsoring individual schools or colleges was no longer a viable proposition.

Then, in March 2000, the then Education Secretary David Blunkett launched the City Academies Programme. The Project was conceived as 'a radical approach' to breaking 'the cycle of underperformance and low expectations' in inner-city schools. In a speech delivered to the Social Market Foundation on 15 March 2000, the Secretary of State outlined his vision for the new schools:

> These Academies, to replace seriously failing schools, will be built and managed by partnerships involving the Government, voluntary, church and business sponsors. They will offer a real challenge and improvements in pupil performance, for example through innovative approaches to management, governance, teaching and the curriculum, including a specialist focus in at least one curriculum area . . . The aim will be to raise standards by breaking the cycle of underperformance and low expectations. To be eligible for government support, the Academies will need to meet clear criteria. They will take over or replace schools which are either in special measures or clearly underachieving. (http:/www.dfes.gov.uk/speeches; see also Rogers and Migniulo, 2007: 7)

The first of three Academies opened in September 2002. Nine followed a year later, and five more opened in September 2004, making a total of 17 during Tony Blair's second term in office. As we have already seen in Chapter 4, the *Five Year Strategy for Children and Learners*, published in July 2004, indicated that the Government intended to have 200 Academies 'open or in the pipeline' by the year 2010, despite the fact that no evaluation had been made of their cost-effectiveness. Some would replace 'under-performing schools'; others would be entirely new, particularly in London where there was a demand for new school places and where it was expected that there would be 60 new Academies by 2010 (DfES, 2004a: 9, 51).

Writing in *The Guardian* on 9 July 2004, Francis Beckett pointed out (Beckett, 2004) that, while it might seem curious that New Labour ministers would seek to resurrect the Conservatives' CTC Project, they were at least determined not to repeat some of the Conservatives' more obvious mistakes. Where funding was concerned, for example, we have already noted that Kenneth Baker was being unduly optimistic if he genuinely believed that his private sponsors would be prepared to pay 'all or most' of the estimated £10 million cost involved in setting up a CTC in the late 1980s. The Conservatives quickly found that business did not relish paying up anything like as much and were forced to drastically revise their expectations downwards. As we have seen, they finally settled on the more modest sum of £2 million, which, coincidentally, was the figure New Labour decided on for City Academies in 2000, though £2 million was obviously worth far less by then and was a far smaller proportion of the total cost.

Many of the new Academies (the word 'city' soon being dropped to allow for the creation of new schools in rural areas) were very popular with parents and massively oversubscribed; but they also aroused genuine concern in certain quarters, and where there was disquiet, it tended to focus on issues of sponsorship and accountability. A front-page story entitled 'Should these people be running state schools?', which appeared in *The Independent* on 8 July 2004 and which was written by the newspaper's Education Editor Richard Garner, argued that by the end of this decade, the secondary education landscape in England would have been transformed, with 'a whole swathe of state-maintained schools handed over to private sponsors to run'. The people and institutions in charge of our schools would be 'the bankers, the churches, the millionaire philanthropists and the leaders of the country's private schools'. The 'people' referred to in the title of the piece were: Graham Able, the Headteacher of Dulwich College in south London, who was anxious to justify his School's charitable status by setting up a new Academy in east London; Sir Frank Lowe, the founder of an advertising agency who had given £2 million to Capital City Academy in Brent, north London, opened in September 2003; Peter Sutherland, the Head of the global investment bank Goldman Sachs, who had Downing Street support for ploughing £2 million into running a sixth-form college in Tower Hamlets, east London; and Sir Peter Vardy, the millionaire car dealer who had just acquired control of King's Academy in Middlesbrough, opened in September 2003, and whose first school, Emmanuel City Technology College in Gateshead, had been accused on a number of occasions of allowing, and indeed encouraging, the teaching of 'creationism' in science (Garner, 2004).

Of these individuals singled out by Richard Garner, it is undoubtedly Sir Peter Vardy who has attracted the most sustained criticism in the years since the Academies Programme was first launched in 2000. Sir Peter was, in fact, the first person to come forward and offer to sponsor one or more City Academies after David Blunkett made his initial announcement; and he rapidly earned the respect and admiration of Tony Blair. His car dealer firm, Reg Vardy plc, financed the setting up of the Emmanuel Schools Foundation, which took its name from the first school for which Sir Peter acted as sponsor. The main reason for so much of the controversy surrounding Sir Peter is that he is an outspoken creationist. He sincerely believes that the Bible is telling the literal truth when it says that the universe was created by God in six days; and he believes that this event occurred in 4004 BC (see Beckett, 2007, p. 72). It follows that this is the theory (truth) that the Emmanuel Foundation expects children to be taught in its colleges. Nigel McQuoid, who became Head of King's Academy in 2003, said that 'schools should teach the creation story as literally depicted in Genesis' (reported in *The Guardian*, 15 January 2005). Liberal Democrats, senior church figures and a group of prominent scientists demanded a government inquiry when it was reported in *The Guardian* in March 2002 that Emmanuel City Technology College had hosted a 'creationist conference' and that Sir Peter had said at this event that all his teachers were expected to promote 'biblical fundamentalism' (*The Guardian*, 9 March 2002). Questioned in the House of Commons about the use of taxpayers' money to fund the teaching of 'creationism' at Emmanuel College, the Prime Minister neatly sidestepped the question and said:

> I think it would be very unfortunate if concerns over that were seen to remove the very, very strong incentive to make sure we get as diverse a school system as we possibly can . . . In the end, it is a more diverse school system that will deliver better results for our children, and if you look at the actual results of the College, I think you will find they are very good. (Reported in *The Guardian*, 14 March 2002)

Then a further storm was provoked by a report in *The Times* in July 2004 that Sir Peter had arranged for a document entitled *Christianity and Curriculum* to be available on the website of Emmanuel College which suggested, along other things, that Britain was probably saved from an invasion by Adolf Hitler in the Second World War by 'an act of God'. The document emphasized the importance of using 'a frame of reference in which God is sovereign' when teaching history, going on to say that: 'in this context, it becomes important to consider why Hitler paused at the English Channel in 1940 before embarking on an invasion of Britain. Could it not be that God was calling a halt to this march of evil?' (reported in *The Times*, 24 July 2004). It is interesting to note, as a sort of coda to this discussion, that a third school which Sir Peter acquired, Trinity Academy in Thorne and Moorends, Doncaster, which opened in September 2005, soon ran into difficulties with many people in the catchment area. In May 2006, more than 200 parents attended a meeting to complain that the Academy was 'excluding large numbers of pupils' and 'pushing an aggressive religious agenda'. If they didn't share the Academy's beliefs, where else were their children to go? (see Beckett, 2007: 79–81).

Tony Blair told delegates at Labour's 2005 Party Conference that the new Academies were helping children in the country's most deprived communities. 'The beneficiaries are not fat cats,' he said. 'They are, in fact, some of the poorest families in the poorest parts of Britain' (reported in *The Guardian*, 28 September 2005). Yet it was later revealed that the percentage of pupils from less affluent families had actually dropped, in some cases dramatically, at almost two thirds of the Academies, when compared with the so-called failing schools they replaced (*The Guardian*, 31 October 2005).

As we saw earlier, there were already 17 Academies in existence by the beginning of 2005. A further 10 opened in September 2005 and 19 in September 2006, bringing the total to 46. In a Speech to the Specialist Schools and Academies Trust Conference in November 2006, Tony Blair announced a doubling of the target figure to 400 – but with no specific reference to the timescale. Interestingly, it was envisaged that some of these Academies would be aimed at catering for pupils aged from three to 19.

In his final Mansion House Speech as Chancellor of the Exchequer, delivered on 20 June 2007 and already discussed in Chapter 4, Gordon Brown said that one of the 'clear priorities' of his new administration would be the expansion of the Academies Programme, with higher education being encouraged to play 'a fuller part in the sponsorship of the new schools (reported in *The Guardian*, 21 June 2007). The new Prime Minister was to be mindful of the need to legitimize the Academies Project in the face of those who argued that it had so far been dominated by sponsors from business who knew little or nothing about education; and, for this reason, it had been decided to allow universities to sponsor Academies at a discount rate.

Then in a speech to the Headmasters' and Headmistresses' Conference (HMC) delivered on 2 October 2007, the then Schools Minister Lord Adonis (in many ways the chief architect of the Academies Project) said that any independent school that came forward to run an Academy would not be required to contribute £2 million towards the starting costs. In an interview with *The Guardian* ahead of the Speech, Lord Adonis said:

> Successful independent schools will be exempt from the £2 million sponsorship requirement when they set up or support an Academy. It is their educational DNA we are seeking, not their fee income or their existing charitable endowments. (*The Guardian*, 2 October 2007)

Coming so soon after the announcement of a similar concession to universities, this was seen by many as part of a concerted attempt to move away from the original and somewhat discredited profile of Academy sponsors who, as we have seen, were largely entrepreneurs with little experience of running schools.

The Academies Project seems to be assured of government support, whatever the outcome of the next General Election, in that it has the support of the Conservative Opposition. One of David Cameron's most controversial moves as Conservative Party Leader has been to make it clear that Academies are the schools of the future, while, at the same time, abandoning the Party's long-standing commitment to establish new grammar schools throughout the country. Addressing a conference of the CBI (Confederation of British Industry) in May 2007, the then Shadow Education Secretary David Willetts said that the Conservatives would be happy to 'adopt Tony Blair's Academies' and would 'run them better than would be the case under Gordon Brown' (reported in *The Guardian*, 17 May 2007).

Moreover, a recent government statement about 'failing' secondary schools has been seen as signifying a real boost to the Academies programme. A front-page story in *The Observer* on 8 June 2008, headed 'Schools get ultimatum: improve or face closure', predicted that 'hundreds of the worst-performing schools in England – those where fewer than three out of ten pupils gained at least five A* to C GCSE grades, including English and maths – would soon be told that they faced closure within the next three years if they failed to improve. When it came, two days later, on 10 June, the announcement by Ed Balls, Secretary of State for Children, Schools and Families, identified 638 out of 3,100 secondary schools in England as 'seriously underperforming', and offered the local authorities concerned the option either to provide intensive support to these schools or to replace them with Academies or Trust Schools. In the words of the Secretary of State:

> If local authorities do not take radical action, then in the end, we will have the powers ourselves to intervene . . . We don't want to see excuses about poor performance; what we do want to see are clear plans to raise standards in every school with a clear expectation that, if by 2011, there are still schools stuck below 30 per cent . . . and there's not been a radical transformation at that point, our expectation will be that the school closes and then reopens as a National Challenge Trust School or as an Academy. (Reported in *The Guardian*, 10 June 2008)

Mr Balls predicted that about 200 of the 638 failing schools would not, in fact, improve fast enough and would have to be replaced by Academies; while there was funding to allow 70 schools to close and be reconstituted using the new trust school model. This move clearly represented a further quickening of the pace of the Academies Programme since, with 83 Academies already open, the Government was now on target to have around 300 up and running by September 2010. It was also now clear that Ed Balls and Gordon Brown wanted to be seen as furthering Tony Blair's reform agenda, with plans that were true to the spirit of the 2005 White Paper and the 2006 Education Act.

Capita and ETS

The Government has not always been lucky with the private firms it has chosen to carry out its work. It came in for much criticism at the beginning of 2004 when it was confirmed that Britain's biggest outsourcing company, Capita, had been awarded a £177m contract, the largest in education to date, to manage the Government's twin strategies for improving standards of reading and writing and numeracy in the country's primary and secondary schools. In assuming complete responsibility for the national primary and Key Stage Three strategies from April 2005, Capita Strategic Education Services would be expected to help ministers hit their targets for literacy and numeracy. The new contract would involve hiring thousands of reading and maths consultants to 'advise' schools and local education authorities on how to deal with 'under-achieving pupils' and how to raise the test scores at the ages of 11 and 14. Capita has always had a reputation for being New Labour's 'favourite' public sector contractor; and it is estimated that it has made at least £3 billion from all manner of lucrative government contracts secured since 1997 (see Beckett, 2007: 43; Ball, 2007: 71). Yet it has been widely criticized for its performance on several of these contracts and opposition politicians have questioned its competence on a number of occasions. It was held responsible for the botched introduction of the Criminal Records Bureau – which caused the system for checking the background of new teachers and other staff working with children to break down in the Autumn of 2002 – and for the problematic administration of London's congestion charge in its early days. Liberal Democrat education spokesperson, Phil Willis, pointed out that the award of the 2004 contract also posed issues about conflicts of interest, since Capita was understood to be in the frame as a potential sponsor of a new Academy. It later transpired that Capita's founder and executive chairperson, Rod Aldridge, had pledged £2 million to an Academy in Blackburn, choosing to do so through his personal charitable trust. Aldridge was awarded an OBE in 1994; but he was forced to resign as chairperson of Capita in 2006 after a secret £1 million loan to the Labour Party was made public and became the subject of a police investigation (see Smithers, 2004; Ball, 2007: 71–2, 152–4; Beckett, 2007: 42–3).

Then came the ETS fiasco in the Summer of 2008. It was revealed in the middle of July 2008 that the Government had been forced to delay the publication of the year's SATs results for 11- and 14-year-olds, after Educational Testing Services (ETS), the American firm which had been awarded a five-year £165m contract to mark the tests, had failed to meet the 7 July deadline for all test results to be back with the schools. Details of the 'crisis' caused by ETS incompetence were revealed by Ken Boston, Head of the Qualifications and Curriculum Authority (QCA), at an emergency meeting of the House of Commons Children, Schools and Families Select Committee held on 14 July 2008. Among the 'enormous number of problems' identified by the QCA had been problems with marker recruitment and retention; large numbers of markers being given the wrong information about the location and time of training; a delay in getting papers to markers; unmarked scripts being returned to schools; and inadequate call centre capacity. At one point, the National Assessment Agency (NAA), the division of the QCA responsible for overseeing the tests, had found that ETS was sitting on over 10,000 unopened emails from schools and markers complaining of problems with the administration of the marking. But Ken Boston went further than simply blaming the American firm for its lack of administrative competence and embarrassed ministers by suggesting that ETS's failure was partly a 'symptom' of the inordinate stress caused by the Government's determination to test 9.5 million pupils a year as the basis for the compilation of the all-important league tables. Asked if the test system was now broken, Mr Boston replied: 'the test system is certainly under very great stress, and what has happened this year is a symptom of that' (reported in *The Guardian*, 15 July 2008).

In the ensuing days, there were many stories in the media highlighting examples of the bizarre assessment of pupils' work. It was even claimed by Barry Sheerman, Chairperson of the Children, Schools and Families Select Committee, that 'students who had only recently passed their A Level exams' had been recruited to mark the tests for 14-year-olds (*The Guardian*, 17 July 2008). Then a front-page story which appeared in *The Daily Telegraph* on 17 July 2008 included extracts from essays by two 11-year-old pupils at Moss Side Primary School in Chorley in Lancashire where, it was said, 'the marking served to illustrate the marking crisis facing SATs' (see Box 5.1). *The Telegraph* pointed out that the essay from Child A, which was 'littered with spelling mistakes, poor punctuation and shoddy grammar', was awarded a higher mark than that given to 'the literate, imaginative piece of writing' from Child B.

Box 5.1   When marking invalidates the test

Child A wrote an essay that included: "If he wasent doing enthing els hed help his uncel Herry at the FunFair during the day. And then hed stoody at nigh.'

Child B wrote an essay that included: 'Quickly, it became apparent that Pip was a fastastic rider: a complete natural. But it was his love of horses that led to a tragic accident. An accident that would change his life forever.'

Child A received a higher mark than the one awarded to Child B.

When he appeared in the House of Commons on 22 July 2008 to answer questions about the SATs crisis, Ed Balls pointed out that the QCA had been responsible for awarding the marking contract to ETS and that he was not in a position to say if the contract would now be terminated. Then a week later, on 29 July, it was revealed that ETS had been relieved of the task of re-marking tens of thousands of the test papers – an onerous responsibility which had been handed over to the National Assessment Agency. The SATs results for 11-year-olds were finally published on 5 August 2008 which was hardly a satisfactory end to the story, since few headteachers had any faith in their accuracy and they were still not available for more than 7,000 children. It was announced on 16 August 2008 that the Government had terminated its contract with ETS. And it was partly as a result of the marking fiasco that Ed Balls announced in the House of Commons on 14 October 2008 that the Government had decided to abolish SATs examinations for 14-year-olds, thereby effectively overturning two decades of education policy.

6

The Changing Worlds of Education Policy

This chapter has *two* chief purposes: to examine how educational policy has been made since the end of the Second World War, and to broaden the discussion of educational policy-making and implementation to embrace the situation in Scotland in addition to that in England and Wales. Many studies of education and the social order since the passing of the 1944 Education Act have tended to concentrate on policies affecting England and Wales, even if the word 'Britain' sometimes appears in the title; and there has been relatively little published work which systematically studies the education system in Britain as a whole. As David Raffe has argued (Raffe, 2000: 10), this is actually an opportune moment to examine the major similarities and differences among the major British systems, since even the concept of a more or less single integrated system operating in England and Wales is now ripe for re-appraisal. Recent developments promoting the extension of devolved power in the UK, with the establishment in 1999 of a Scottish Parliament along with Assemblies in Wales and Northern Ireland, all with responsibility for education and training (though without *legislative* powers in the case of Wales) could well have the logical consequence of a marked reduction in the power wielded by the Department for Education and Skills in London.

Patterns of decision-making in the 1940s

Returning briefly to the situation in Britain in the early 1940s, we need to emphasize that the Second World War created the necessary conditions for the enthusiastic reception of social reform. Apart from any other considerations, the War showed up the defects of existing social services, while at the same time increasing the sense of social solidarity and a climate of common endeavour. At the risk of oversimplifying the situation, it seems fair to say that wartime politicians and their civil servants could be divided into two main groups: those working closely with the Prime Minister, Winston Churchill, and concerned primarily with the active prosecution of the War; and those, mainly on the left, who were delighted that the Labour leader, Clement Attlee, occupied a prominent position in Churchill's War Cabinet throughout the War, first as Lord Privy Seal and then after February 1942 as Deputy Prime Minister, and were chiefly occupied with the domestic scene and with plans for social reconstruction.

Churchill certainly showed little interest in the minutiae of domestic policy, and he had neither the temperament nor the sense of obligation to assume in areas of social and education policy the sort of role which he had defined for himself in strategic and diplomatic affairs. In the words of a telling comment on his priorities by left-wing Labour politician Aneurin Bevan when writing in the weekly journal *Tribune* (4 October 1940): 'His ear is so sensitively attuned to the bugle note of history that he is deaf to the raucous clamour of contemporary life.' It was left to others, and mainly the Labour members of the Cabinet's hard-working Reconstruction Committee, to concern themselves with the crucial issues which were to become central features of the post-war Welfare State: social security for all, a National Health Service, full adult employment and improved educational opportunities (see Simon, 1991: 71).

The one leading Conservative politician who *was* concerned to play a part in the creation of a new social order was R.A. (Rab) Butler who was moved from his post as Under-Secretary at the Foreign Office to become President of the Board of Education in the summer of 1941. As we saw in Chapter 2, Butler later wrote of his excitement at being given the opportunity to 'harness to the educational system the wartime urge for social reform and greater equality' (Butler, 1971: 86). The account he gave in his 1971 book of memoirs, *The Art of the Possible,* of his visit to Downing Street in July 1941 to be given his new portfolio also clearly indicates that the Prime Minister attached little real importance to the post and that his chief focus was on the contribution the Board of Education might make to the war effort:

> The Prime Minister saw me after his afternoon nap, and was audibly purring like a great tiger. He began, 'You have been in the House for fifteen years and it is time you were promoted.' I objected gently that I had, in fact, been there for only twelve years, but he waved this aside. He said, 'You have been in the Government for the best part of that time, and I now want you to go to the

Board of Education. I think that you can leave your mark there. It is true that this will be *outside* the mainstream of the War, but you will at least be independent. Besides,' he continued, with rising fervour, 'you *will* still be in the War. You will move poor children from here to there' – and he lifted up imaginary poor children and evacuated them from one side of his blotting pad to the other – 'and this will be very difficult'. He went on: 'I am too old now to think that education can improve people's natures. I think everyone has to learn to defend himself. I should not however object if you could introduce a note of patriotism into the schools . . . Tell the children that Wolfe won Quebec.' . . . I said that I would like to influence what was taught in the schools, but that this was always frowned upon. Here he looked very earnest and commented: 'Of course – but *not* by instruction or order, but always by *suggestion.*' . . . I then said that I had always looked forward to going to the Board of Education if I were to be given the chance. He appeared ever so slightly surprised at this statement, showing that he felt that in wartime a central job, such as the one I was leaving at the Foreign Office, was the most important. But he looked genuinely pleased that I had shown so much satisfaction, and seemed to think the new appointment entirely suitable. He concluded the interview by saying: 'Come and see me to discuss things – not details, of course, but the broad lines.' (Butler, 1971: 86; see also Howard 1987: 109–10)

There is continuing controversy as to whether or not the 1944 Education Act actually deserves to be labelled 'the Butler Act'; and much of this centres on the role of civil servants in the formulation of national education policy (a recurring theme of this chapter).

The main offices of the Board of Education were evacuated to Bournemouth for the duration of the War; and there is no doubt that ideas for future legislation were discussed at great length by a group of powerful civil servants meeting at the Branksome Dene Hotel in late 1940 and early 1941. Butler's authorship of the 1944 Act was first challenged by historian Peter Gosden in his 1976 study of education in the Second World War, where he argued persuasively that Butler's main role after 1941 was to protect and implement *existing* departmental policies (Gosden, 1976). Then in 1981, R.G. Wallace elaborated on this thesis in an important *History of Education* article by asserting that: 'Butler exerted little influence on the education aspects of the 1944 Act. It is not *his* Act in the sense that it embodies his policies or was designed by him . . . He was rather the protector of other men's plans' (Wallace, 1981: 283).

In support of this argument, it is worth noting that as early as June 1941, *before* Butler had any chance to influence policy-making at the Board, a lengthy, detailed document known as the Green Book and entitled *Education after the War*, was being circulated 'confidentially' among those working in Bournemouth on plans for a new Bill. The Green Book actually contained many of the proposals which were first presented to Parliament in December 1943 and eventually became the 1944 Act.

Foremost among the critics of the Wallace standpoint is Kevin Jefferys who has argued that important decisions about the scope and content of educational reform were still to be taken *after* July 1941. According to Jefferys: 'The working out of the proposals for reform after July 1941 indicates that the principal authors of the 1944 Act were *not* the civil servants who had met in Bournemouth, but the ministers and officials who jointly arrived at the main decisions during 1942 and 1943' (Jefferys, 1984: 423).

It is, of course, possible to argue that the later work of Kevin Jefferys does not *totally* undermine the thesis that much of the broad agenda enacted in 1944 – the need for 'secondary education for all', the need to plan for the raising of the school-leaving age to 15, and so on – had indeed been set out in the so-called Green Book while Butler was still working at the Foreign Office. As Michael Barber has pointed out in his own study of the origins of the 1944 Education Act (Barber, 1994: 36), the wartime Board of Education had a strong reputation among contemporary politicians for being in the control of its permanent staff; and a new President such as Butler would not have found it easy or expedient to challenge that control. At the same time, Butler *did* have an important role to play in securing widespread support for the Board's main proposals. He was particularly skilful in promoting the reforms in a way which left most of the interested parties believing that they had indeed received a considerable proportion of what they had asked for. The relatively calm passage of the Bill through Parliament was due in large measure to his careful preliminary work and to his patience and resourcefulness during long and often tedious House of Commons debates. Much of his time was spent in negotiating a diplomatic solution to the thorny problem of the relationship between state and Church schools; but he was careful to avoid opening up such controversial issues as the future of 'public' and multilateral schools. Once the Act had received Royal Assent in August 1944, Butler was gratified and somewhat taken aback to receive a telegram which read: 'Pray accept my congratulations. You have added a notable Act to the Statute Book and won a lasting place in the history of British Education. Winston S. Churchill' (quoted in Butler, 1971: 122).

The post-war tripartite partnership

For nearly half a century, the provisions of the 1944 Education Act dominated the education system of England and Wales (and the same was true of the 1945 and 1946 Education Acts where Scotland was concerned). Yet it would be wrong to give the impression that the day-to-day implementation of this legislation was purely a 'top-down' affair, with all or most important policy decisions taken by politicians and civil servants working at the centre. As we touched upon briefly in Chapter 2, administratively the legislation of the 1940s set up what is usually described as 'a national system, locally administered'. Until the late 1970s, the role of local education authorities did indeed seem unassailable (see Chitty, 2002b), and the structure of educational decision-making that developed in the post-war period involved a tripartite 'partnership' – sometimes referred to as 'a triangle of tension' (see, for example, Briault, 1976) – between central government, local government and individual schools and colleges (with this *third* element in the 'partnership' sometimes replaced in academic studies by the organized teaching profession). This same model of partnership, implying a genuine dispersion of power and responsibility, also existed in Scotland; although it is often claimed (see, for example, McPherson and Raab, 1988: 29) that the Scottish system has traditionally been more centralized than the English.

According to the constitutional expert, Vernon Bogdanor, writing in the *Oxford Review of Education* in 1979, the 'efficient secret' of the British system, and the main reason why 'tension' surfaced only periodically, was that no one individual participant could enjoy a monopoly of power in the decision-making process, so that:

> Power over the distribution of resources, over the organisation and over the content of education was to be diffused amongst the different elements and no one of them was to be given a controlling voice . . . Such a structure . . . offered clear and obvious advantages, not only for the administrator concerned primarily with the efficient working of the system, but also for the liberal, anxious to avoid the concentration of power in a few hands, and the pluralist, insistent that different interests should be properly represented. For parallel to the formal relationships between central and local government, embodied in statute and convention, there grew up a network of professional communities whose role it was to soften the political antagonisms which might otherwise render the system unworkable . . . The diffused structure of decision-making led, it could be argued, to better decisions because it ensured a wide basis of agreement before any changes were made.
> (Bogdanor, 1979: 157–8)

It is true that a number of special factors contributed to the prevailing mood of co-operation and consensus. The relative absence of damaging political conflict in the 1950s and early 1960s was greatly helped not only by the general climate of expansion, but also by the availability of sufficient financial resources to ensure the successful implementation of expansionist policies. At the same time, the post-war period was one when the number of powerful interest groups was fairly small, and it was comparatively easy to secure consensus among a cosily restricted network. As Vernon Bogdanor goes on to observe:

> The system of consultation worked best when only a small number of interests were involved whose rank and file were content to defer to elites, and could, therefore, always be relied upon to act 'sensibly'. This process of elite accommodation reached its apogee during the post-war period, when, or so it was believed, many important policy decisions in education were taken over lunch at the National Liberal Club by a troika consisting of Sir William Alexander, Secretary of the Association of Education Committees, Sir Ronald Gould, the General Secretary of the National Union of Teachers, and the Permanent Secretary at the Department (or Ministry) of Education. If these three agreed on some item of educational policy, it would, more often than not, be implemented. Such at least was the general belief; and even if it was a caricature, it is at least significant that it was widely held. (Bogdanor, 1979: 161)

Policy-making at the centre

It seems clear that by the time 13 years of Conservative rule came to an end in 1964, educational policy-making was largely in the hands of government ministers, top civil servants, local education authorities and a select group of union leaders. Educational issues had attracted widespread debate in the final years of the Conservative Government; and there was certainly more importance attached to the education portfolio than was the case in the 1940s. In April 1964, the Department of Education and Science was created as a single department, responsible for education, science and the universities when the old Ministry of Education and the Office of the Minister for Science were amalgamated and took in various responsibilities from other departments. Quintin Hogg (formerly Viscount Hailsham) became the first Secretary of State for Education and Science and held the post until the Conservative Government of Sir Alec Douglas-Home was defeated in the October 1964 General Election.

In the autumn and early winter of 1970, Maurice Kogan, Professor of

Government and Social Administration at Brunel University, undertook a series of lengthy conversations with first Anthony Crosland and then Edward Boyle which were subsequently reported in *The Politics of Education,* published in 1971 (Kogan, 1971). Kogan's declared purpose was to explore with 'two of the ablest politicians to emerge since the 1939–45 War', who had between them shouldered responsibility for education for almost *all* of the five-year period between July 1962 and August 1967, what they saw as the main aspects of their role as Ministers and/or Secretaries of State for Education. These conversations, along with Kogan's illuminating introduction, have done much to shape our understanding of the role of the central authority in policy-making and in the day-to-day management of education. Both Boyle and Crosland were talking about a period which many have come to view as a high point of the consensus on education and its management which developed in the wake of the 1944 Education Act and which was reflected in the assumptions and tactics of these two talented politicians. It is, of course, debatable whether or not that cross-party 'consensus' still existed at the time when Kogan's Penguin Education Special was published.

In his own interview with Professor Kogan, Edward Boyle was genuinely enthusiastic and grateful about the *positive* contribution that local government had made to educational decision-making. He argued that 'quite a lot of important ideas in education have come *up* from the local authorities and haven't all come *down* from the Ministry' (Kogan, 1971: 125); and he spoke, in particular, about the pioneering work on a variety of educational issues of such authorities as Bristol, Hertfordshire, Leicestershire, Oxfordshire, Southampton, the West Riding and the Isle of Wight. According to Boyle, 'one of the strengths of the movement behind secondary reorganisation was that the initiatives were coming from the local authorities themselves'. A really good example of 'a successful local initiative' was the Leicestershire Scheme launched in 1957 which 'did not involve all-through comprehensives but successfully did away with the eleven-plus' (Kogan, 1971: 125–6). Pressed further by Professor Kogan on this issue of the desirability of local autonomy, Boyle admitted that there had to be *some* sense of direction from central government, but he held firm to his basic thesis, one that was to find little favour with his more doctrinaire successors as Conservative education ministers:

> I agree there is and has to be some central framework . . . But I would always hope that governments for the most part can play along with what local

authorities genuinely want to do, rather than to have to impose too many things on them that they don't want to do. (Kogan, 1971: 127–8)

It was left to the Labour Education Secretary Anthony Crosland to issue Circular 10/65 in July 1965 which went too far for Boyle's liking, even though it only *requested* local authorities to prepare plans for comprehensive reorganization in their areas (see Chitty, 1998). Crosland's own conversation with Kogan does, in fact, provide us with a fascinating insight into the lively debate that went on *within* the DES in the first half of 1965 as to whether the Circular should *require* or *request* local authorities to produce their reorganization plans. We know that Crosland finally sided with those officials opting for 'request', and he told Kogan that, in coming to this decision, he had been strongly influenced *both* by his meetings with the Association of Education Committees *and* by his judgement of 'the general mood of the local authority world' (Kogan, 1971: 189). While those working at the DES were still divided on the issue, he stated in the House of Commons in a debate held at the end of March: 'I am perfectly confident that local authorities will respond voluntarily and co-operatively to our request to submit reorganisation plans' (reported in *The Times Educational Supplement*, 26 March 1965). Asked by Kogan later if he regretted *not* taking statutory powers in 1965, Crosland was most emphatic:

> No. You must remember that at that time, most local authorities were Labour-controlled and sympathetic to what we were doing – as indeed were some Tory authorities. So the plans were coming in at least as fast as we could cope with them. For the whole time I was at the DES (Curzon Street), the thing was going as fast as it could possibly go. The limitation was one of human and physical resources, and not one of statutory powers. But, of course, the situation changed later when the disastrous local election results of 1968 and 1969 put the Tories into power almost everywhere. (Kogan, 1971: 191)

Looking back on *his* time at the DES, Edward Boyle told Kogan that there were essentially *two* traditions in the Department: 'the 'social justice' tradition, wanting to widen opportunity, giving young people the greater opportunity to acquire intelligence; and the 'technical college' tradition – education for investment, education for efficiency' (Kogan, 1971: 123).

In Boyle's view, economic prosperity and demographic factors made it possible, and indeed *desirable,* to satisfy both of these traditions in the 1960s. Pressure of numbers made it essential to reorganize secondary schooling and expand rapidly both further education and higher education. What Boyle could not know in 1971 was that neither of the two traditions was to survive the economic traumas of the 1970s in its original form, and that, by the end of the decade, there was to be profound disenchantment with both the comprehensive reform and the perceived 'failure' of educational expansion to solve the country's economic problems.

The central authority as a 'tension system'

Up to now, we have tended to concentrate on the relationship between Education Secretaries (or Ministers) and their civil servants, and between the central authority and local government; but this is not really an entirely adequate or satisfactory way of understanding the 'education sub-government' of the 1960s and 1970s. In particular, we need to subdivide the central authority of that period into at least three separate power groups at the national level: the politicians and their political advisers; the bureaucrats (DES officials); and the professional Inspectors of Her Majesty's Inspectorate (HMI). This was the model put forward by Professor Denis Lawton in the William Walker Lecture which he delivered to the British Educational Management and Administration Society in 1983, and which was subsequently published in a revised and updated version in 1984 (Lawton, 1984).

Each of the three groups postulated in the Lawton model had its distinct ideology, largely determined by its primary role in the governing structure and by the values which it sought to defend and promote. It was, of course, accepted that the reality might not be as neat and precise as the model implied: some DES officials might at times behave like HMI professionals, and some members of HMI might have views close to those of DES civil servants or even of governing politicians. Nevertheless it was (and is) Professor Lawton's argument that there would still be sufficient and discernible differences between the three factions to make sensible generalizations about them as distinct groups. From the three ideologies could then be derived different views on particular issues or policies. On curriculum policy, for example, one might well find evidence of the politicians' addiction to standards and accountability, the DES concern for specified objectives, contrasted with HMI support for a 'common-culture' curriculum of high quality. Instead of being seen as a monolithic body, the DES would emerge as a site of competing interests. In other words, it would be revealed as a 'tension system', *not* as a 'consensus'.

It is Professor Lawton's concept of a 'tension system' at the centre which will serve as a useful theoretical model for the discussion which follows and to which we will return later in the chapter. It is, in fact, the aim of this section to examine the role and philosophy of each of the three main groups which constituted the central authority from the 1970s onwards: the DES bureaucracy; Her Majesty's Inspectorate; and the group of young but influential advisers to the Prime Minister brought together within the Downing Street Policy Unit established in 1974.

The DES bureaucracy

In 1974, a small team of investigators from the OECD (Organisation for Economic Co-operation and Development) was appointed by the DES to review educational planning in England and Wales and concluded in their Final Report that 'although the powers of government with regard to educational planning are formally limited . . . the central Department of Education and Science is undoubtedly the most important single force in determining the direction and tempo of educational development' (OECD, 1975: 28).

The OECD Report paid particular attention to the role played by the Civil Service in determining that 'direction and tempo':

> The permanent officials of the DES, in the great tradition of British Civil Servants, are 'non-political' in their function. In no other country, it is safe to say, does the Civil Service govern itself more closely by a code of loyalty to whatever government is in power. The protections in the British System against the Civil Service's being captured by a political party go very far . . . Yet it is also true that a permanent officialdom possessing external protections and internal disciplines becomes a power *in its own right.* A British department composed of professional civil servants who have watched the ministers come and go is an entity that only an extremely foolish or powerful politician would persistently challenge or ignore . . . The prestige, acquaintanceships and natural authority of leading civil servants give them a standing in the civil forum that is often *superior* to that of their *de jure* political superiors. They are, in the continental phrase, *notables,* whose opinions must be given special weight, whether or not votes in the next election will be affected . . . There has also to be taken into account the momentum of thought and action within a department composed largely of 'career officials' who have long known one another, who have the same training and prospects, and who work within a common tradition and point of view. (OECD, 1975)

The OECD investigators went on to observe that policy-making in the Department was often both shrouded in secrecy and carried out by officials unable or unwilling to question basic assumptions and attitudes:

The United Kingdom offers an example of educational planning in which the structures for ensuring public participation are strictly limited. This has at least *two* consequences. One is that in certain cases, policy is less likely to be understood and therefore less likely to be wholeheartedly accepted when the processes which lead up to its formulation are guarded as arcane secrets. The second is that goals and priorities, once established, may go on being taken for granted and hence escape the regular scrutiny which may be necessary for an appropriate realignment of policy. (OECD, 1975)

In the same year that the findings of the OECD investigation team were made public in *The Times Higher Education Supplement* (1976), another report critical of the running of the DES was published, this time the work of the Parliamentary Expenditure Committee, sometimes referred to as the Fookes Committee (House of Commons, 1976). The main complaints in the so-called Fookes Report echoed the findings of the OECD team in arguing that the DES was excessively secretive, that it chose to involve only a limited number of people in the planning process and that it was ill-equipped to meet the demands of change (see report in *The Times Higher Education Supplement,* 9 May 1976; and also Raggatt and Evans, 1977: 149–69, 170–91).

Her Majesty's Inspectorate

It is sometimes suggested that the criticisms levelled at the DES in the mid-1970s caused the bureaucrats to start making better use of HMI in the planning process; and this has led some commentators to view the Inspectors as little more than 'data collection agents of the DES'. In a book published in 1981, Brian Salter and Ted Tapper described the Inspectors as 'the organic intellectuals of the DES'. It was difficult, they argued, to avoid the impression that after 1976 (the year of the Ruskin College speech and the beginning of the Great Debate), the Inspectorate became 'much more directly responsive to the Department's policy-making needs and much more alive to providing the right information at the right time' (Salter and Tapper, 1981: 213). Although the Inspectorate was wary of becoming too obviously a slave to DES needs, its traditional and much vaunted independence from the Department was, in fact, being steadily eroded. As 'the organic intellectuals of the Department', the Inspectors had the responsibility for ensuring that DES policies were legitimized in advance by the presentation of the appropriate evidence and arguments. In short, it could be argued that HMI was becoming an integral part of the growing system of central control of education. In the words of Salter and Tapper:

We would argue that HMI's position in the educational system as authoritative supplier of information both to the LEAs and schools on the one hand, and to the DES on the other, is undoubtedly critical. At the local level, HMIs have the functions of inspectors of schools and colleges, interpreters of Department policy to the LEAs, and they are also members of numerous committees such as examination boards and regional advisory councils for further education . . . At the central level, they act as professional advisers to the DES, drawing on their network of local contacts, contribute to Department publications and staff Department courses for teachers. Any move by the DES to systematise further the process of policy construction is therefore dependent upon HMI to acquire and to disseminate the right information at the right time. This would imply that from the Department's point of view, the closer the ties between itself and HMI the better . . . In fact, as the DES moves further in the direction of determining policy at the centre, so it must rely more on its internal means of information collecting, rather than on information supplied by external groups. In this respect, the role of HMIs as the 'field representatives' and 'data collection agents' of the DES is bound to be crucial in its efforts to sustain this move . . . It seems likely . . . that whatever independence the Inspectorate still retains will be further eroded in response to the requirements of the new style of policy-making; though the myth of autonomy may well be retained a long as possible, since it enhances the supposed objectivity of the information on which the Department rests its policy proposals. (Salter and Tapper, 1981: 109–11)

The 1981 Salter and Tapper thesis came in for strong criticism from Denis Lawton and Peter Gordon in their 1987 study of HMI on the grounds that, after the Great Debate of 1976–7, HMI independence was in fact steadily *increasing* rather than *diminishing* (Lawton and Gordon, 1987: 113). As we shall see in Chapter 7, evidence of this growing independence could be found principally in the increasing confidence with which the Inspectorate published its views on the school curriculum, even though these were clearly at variance with the more traditional curriculum model favoured by the DES bureaucracy. According to Lawton and Gordon, this was not 'a chance difference of opinion', but 'a fundamental question of *educational* as opposed to *bureaucratic* values' (1987).

The Downing Street Policy Unit

The third element in the central 'tension system' based on Professor Lawton's useful model consists for our purposes of the Downing Street Policy Unit. It will be shown here that educational reform of a radical nature has always been one of this body's chief concerns and that it has never been frightened to challenge DES and HMI orthodoxy.

The comparatively recent creation, in March 1974, of a new Policy Unit, separate from the Central Policy Review Staff (CPRS) created by Edward Heath in 1970, has been described by Professor Peter Hennessy as 'Harold Wilson's most important and, to date, durable innovation' (Hennessy, 1986: 82). Under the strong leadership, from 1974 to 1979, of Dr Bernard (now Lord) Donoughue, a political scientist from the London School of Economics, it soon became, in Hennessy's words, 'a prime-ministerial cabinet in all but name' (1986).

According to a press release issued from Downing Street in 1974, it was intended that the new Unit would 'assist in the development of the whole range of policies contained in the Government's programme, especially those arising in the short and medium term'. This was a clear attempt to distinguish it from the Central Policy Review Staff based in the Cabinet Office, which was more, although not exclusively, orientated to *longer-term* policy horizons. Bernard Donoughue himself was well aware of the potential role of the Unit as 'the eyes and ears' of the Prime Minister (which was Harold Wilson's own concept), and he made clear his view of the Unit's distinguishing features in his own book of memoirs published in 1987:

> The Policy Unit was obviously the newest part of the Downing Street machine. Previous Prime Ministers had employed individual advisers. However, until Harold Wilson created the Policy Unit in March 1974, there was no systematic policy analysis separate from the regular civil service machine and working solely for the Prime Minister. These are the three characteristics which clearly distinguished the new Policy Unit from what had existed before: it was systematic; it was separate from the Whitehall machine; and it was solely working for the Prime Minister. (Donoughue, 1987: 20)

Donoughue worked frantically during the spring and early summer of 1974 interviewing and recruiting members for the new Unit, the original target being to have six to eight policy specialists, together with a couple of research assistants. As things turned out, education policy – and, in particular, the generation of new ideas – was to be very much under the control of Donoughue himself, working closely with Elizabeth Arnott, recruited from Transport House's social policy research staff. An internal memorandum to Unit members, drafted by Donoughue and cleared by Harold Wilson, described the Unit's chief functions in some detail:

> The Unit must ensure that the Prime Minister is aware of what is coming up from the departments to Cabinet. It must scrutinise papers, contact departments, know the background to policy decisions, disputes and compromises,

and act as a general 'early warning system'. The Unit may feed into the system ideas on policy which are not currently covered, or are inadequately covered . . . The Unit should feed in 'minority reforms' which departments may overlook, or which fall between departmental boundaries, or which are the subject of worthy but unsuccessful Private Members Bills. This is especially the case with issues which concern ordinary people (and of which Whitehall may be unaware). Donoghue, 1987: 21–2)

The political dimension of the Unit's work in the second half of the 1970s was underlined:

> The Prime Minister has assumed responsibility as custodian of the Labour Manifesto. The Unit must assist in that role, always making sure that the Manifesto is not contravened, nor retreated from, without proper discussion and advance warning . . . Throughout its policy work, the Unit will clearly be aware of the political dimension in Government. It must maintain good relations with the party organisation. The individual ministries must not be allowed to become isolated from the Government as a whole and lapse into traditional departmental views. (Donoghue, 1987: 22)

By 1976, the Policy Unit felt strong enough to challenge the orthodox thinking of a number of government departments; and nowhere was this more true than in the case of education. As we saw in Chapter 3, shortly after taking over from Harold Wilson as Prime Minister, James Callaghan received a lengthy memorandum from Bernard Donoughue suggesting (among other things) that it might well be appropriate, given the widespread anxiety being expressed, for the new occupant of Number Ten Downing Street to make the raising of educational standards in state schools an important feature of his public pronouncements. In Donoughue's opinion, this was an important area of hotly contested views where the new Prime Minister would be in a strong position to convey his personal commitment and concern.

With this initiative, the Policy Unit was, in effect, seeking to enlist the support of James Callaghan in the cause of forcing the DES to adopt a more positive and interventionist role in educational policy-making. Donoughue made no attempt to hide his contempt for the cosily restricted network of powerful interest groups which had been such a marked feature of the post-war partnership years. It was his view that much of the blame for the apparent malaise in the education system lay with the malign influence of the teachers' unions in general and of the National Union of Teachers in particular:

> Education policy was conducted by the local authorities and the teachers' unions with the Department of Education . . . being little more than a post-

box between the two. A further problem was that each Minister was burdened with party policy commitments which were based on the assumption that all education problems could be solved by simply throwing money at them, or, to be more precise, giving the cash to the teachers' unions. But in fact the latter, and especially the National Union of Teachers, had become a major part of the problem. In all my many dealings with the NUT . . . I never once heard mention of education or children. The Union's prime objective appeared to be to secure ever decreasing responsibilities and hours of work for its members; and it seemed to me that the ideal NUT world would be one where teachers and children never entered a school at all – and the executive of the NUT would be in a permanent conference session at a comfortable seaside hotel. (Donoughue, 1987: 109–10)

It was clearly Donoughue's view that the National Union of Teachers had allowed itself to be taken over by a powerful group of cynical 'militants' and 'progressives' with little real concern for developing pupils' abilities. Interviewed in January 1986, he argued that:

many of the militants and dogmatists around in the 1970s were really discrediting comprehensive education . . . The doctrine of permissiveness was meaning that people were simply not working hard enough in the education system. In other words, liberalism was becoming a fig-leaf for idleness. It made it so easy for teachers to do very little on the basis that it was unfair to make the pupils do very much. (Donoughue, 1986)

All this meant that too many young people were not being trained in the skills necessary to find useful employment in industry and commerce. The solution was for Callaghan's Government to take the lead in forcing teachers, particularly in urban areas, to be more accountable to politicians, employers and parents, and this might well involve a degree of central involvement in sensitive matters relating to the secondary-school curriculum.

The Prime Minister seems to have accepted the major features of the rather bleak Donoughue analysis of the problems facing state education; and, as we have already seen, he welcomed the novel idea of delivering an important speech on the state of the service at the earliest opportunity. With few new ideas emanating from the DES under Fred Mulley, he was clearly prepared to make effective use of the think-tank inherited from his predecessor. In the words of his 1987 autobiography: 'its thinking was unorthodox and refreshing, and it had considerable influence when I launched the so-called Great Debate on education' (Callaghan, 1987: 405).

The Policy Unit was certainly very active in the period from 1976 to 1979. It was the Policy Unit which, according to Donoughue (1987:

110), secured the appointment of James Hamilton (at that time working in the Cabinet Office) as Permanent Secretary at the DES in June 1976, a move of enormous significance since Hamilton was eager to support Donoughue in the campaign to force the Department to adopt a more interventionist role in education. It was the Policy Unit which, as we saw in Chapter 3, drafted the questions asked of Education Secretary Fred Mulley by the Prime Minister at the important interview which took place in Downing Street on 21 May 1976 (Callaghan, 1987: 409). It was at this interview that Mulley first learned, somewhat to his surprise, that the Policy Unit was drafting a major speech on educational standards for the Prime Minister to deliver later in the year. It was Bernard Donoughue and Elizabeth Arnott who then spent much of the summer of 1976 working on both the education section of the speech which Callaghan delivered to the Labour Party Conference at the end of September and the various drafts of the speech which he gave at a foundation stone-laying ceremony at Ruskin College, Oxford in the middle of October. As indicated in the Callaghan recollection quoted at the end of the previous paragraph, it was the Policy Unit which was influential in promoting the idea of staging a Great Debate on Education, even though the resulting 1977 Green Paper, *Education in Schools: A Consultative Document* (DES, 1977a), was not to be as challenging and assertive in its final form as the Policy Unit would have wished (Donoughue, 1987: 112–13). In the meantime, Shirley Williams had replaced Fred Mulley as Education Secretary and, according to Donoughue (1987: 112), was 'shocked and unhappy' that the Prime Minister and his political advisers had 'trespassed into her ministerial territory, opened a can of worms, and then left her to deal with the consequences'. Sheila Browne, Senior Chief Inspector of Schools from 1974 to 1983, was also concerned about the emergence of a new power-base and asked to see Donoughue to gain some idea of the Policy Unit's true motives and objectives (Browne, 1986).

In all of this frenetic activity in the second half of the 1970s, Donoughue certainly had a strong ally in James Hamilton. The new Permanent Secretary of the DES from June 1976 shared the Policy Unit's concern for a stronger and more aggressive governmental voice in educational matters in general and in curriculum matters in particular. While still working in the Cabinet Office, Hamilton had joined forces with Donoughue in suggesting to the Prime Minister that Fred Mulley should be required in his May 1976 interview to prepare a lengthy DES memorandum on matters causing public concern about state education. Hamilton then arrived at the DES to find his new colleagues among the civil servants engaged in the feverish activity which produced the 63-page confidential document to be known as the Yellow Book (DES, 1976). In the words of a later valedictory article by editor Stuart Maclure, published in *The Times Educational Supplement* on 29 April 1983, 'having helped to set the examination paper, Hamilton then moved to the DES to answer it, or at any rate to take final responsibility for the Department's response'. Shortly after moving to the DES, Hamilton delivered an important speech at the Annual Conference of the Association of Education Committees meeting in Scarborough in which he warned that, in future, his Department would be taking 'a much closer interest' in what was being taught in the nation's schools. According to Hamilton, teachers had traditionally reserved the right to decide what should be taught in the classroom; but now 'the key to "the secret garden of the curriculum" had to be found and turned' (reported in *The Times Educational Supplement,* 2 July 1976). Seven years later, this 'unrepentant centralist' (to use Maclure's telling description) looked back over his eventful period at the DES and at a conference organized by the Association for Science Education in June 1983 regretted that both Labour and Conservative governments had generally shown too much 'delicacy' about making their presence felt in the classroom. It was now to be hoped that the proposal for a new common system of examining at 16-plus would be seized upon as an important centralizing initiative:

> I believe we always erred on the side of safety. I believe that we could, with benefit, have produced a more pungent, a more purposive analysis . . . There is a strong argument for the DES acting more directly in certain limited areas of the curriculum. Otherwise, other agencies will move in to fill the gaps they perceive, possibly to deleterious effect . . . The present exercise of reforming examinations at sixteen-plus should be seen primarily as part of this process of establishing greater central control. (Reported in *The Times Educational Supplement,* 1 July 1983)

As I have argued elsewhere (Chitty, 1989; 1994), for much of the time that Hamilton was Permanent Secretary at the DES, the *political* viewpoint and the *bureaucratic* viewpoint coincided. During the three-year period of the Callaghan administration, there was a clear attempt to create a new educational consensus built around more central control of the curriculum, greater teacher accountability and the more direct subordination of secondary schooling to the perceived needs of industry. With the deepening economic crisis associated with balance-of-payments difficulties and mounting domestic inflation, the DES was prompted to re-examine the bases of centre–local relationships in order to clarify and redefine points of control. It was under James Hamilton that DES civil servants developed a new concern for efficiency, detailed policy-making and the need to make maximum and effective use of limited resources. Despite the strong reservations of Shirley Williams and Sheila Browne, the DES bureaucracy was also prepared to help the Policy Unit in its concerted efforts to undermine the autonomy of schools and local education authorities. It was after 1976 that *accountability* definitely replaced *partnership* as *the* dominant metaphor in discussions about the distribution of power in the education system.

The period from 1976 to 1979 was clearly one of considerable significance in the evolution of the Downing Street Policy Unit as a form of 'prime-ministerial cabinet', yet its power and influence appeared to be threatened by the change of occupant of Number Ten Downing Street in May 1979. Somewhat paradoxically in the light of later developments, when Margaret Thatcher replaced James Callaghan as Prime Minister, her initial inclination was to rely for political advice on her newly-appointed ministers and, by implication, for policy advice on their departments. She accordingly reduced the number and seniority of her political aides at Number Ten and also cut down the size of her Policy Unit. For the next three years (1979–82), while it was headed by Sir John Hoskyns, the Unit appeared to have a much reduced role in policy formulation. Significantly, it had no remit to discuss or formulate education policy (see Chitty, 1989: 12; Knight, 1990: 141, 148). This did *not*, however, mean that the first Thatcher administration lacked advice from those operating *outside* the traditional policy-making networks. It was in the period 1979–81 that Stuart Sexton, Special Adviser to the Education Secretary, Mark Carlisle, was able to establish himself as an *éminence grise* of Conservative education policy. It is, in fact, Sexton who is usually credited with drafting the 'Parents' Charter' that went into the 1979 Conservative Election Manifesto and with the formulation of the Assisted Places Scheme (see Chapter 3; and Knight, 1990: 140).

It was the debilitating experience of working with a predominantly cautious set of ministers (see King, 1985: 101–7) that caused Mrs Thatcher to revise her earlier judgement where the Policy Unit was concerned. By the time of the June 1983 General Election – an election fought in the aftermath of Britain's victory in the Falklands War – she had clearly decided to rely for advice, encouragement and a steady supply of radical new ideas on a growing number of young, committed right-wing analysts who would henceforth occupy all the key positions in the Policy Unit. Significantly Oliver Letwin (who is now one of

David Cameron's ministers in the Conservative Shadow Cabinet and has a reputation for liberal opinions) was transferred from the Conservative Research Department to take up the education portfolio in the Policy Unit, which he retained until January 1986. An outspoken advocate of education vouchers, he was to publish a polemical text in 1988 with the provocative title *Privatising the World*. It was the growth of such new assistance at Number Ten that counterbalanced the Prime Minister's abolition of the CPRS. The demise of Edward Heath's 1970 creation came immediately after the 1983 election, and could be said to be one element in a significant and ongoing shift towards a *presidential* style of government. For it has been pointed out (Jones, 1985: 93) that the CPRS had provided policy advice for the Cabinet as a whole and had served a useful function in a system of *collective* government. While Mrs Thatcher was now *strengthening* her own personal staff resources, she was *weakening* those at the disposal of her ministerial colleagues for the performance of their collective deliberations. With the elimination of the CPRS, allied to a systematic downgrading of the Cabinet's policy-making responsibilities, the stage was now set for a new and important phase in the Policy Unit's history, and one that was to survive the change of government in 1997.

We have a very useful model devised by Denis Lawton (see Table 6.1) to show how each of the three groups at the centre – the 'politicos' (ministers and their political advisers), the bureaucrats (DES civil servants and officials) and the professionals (members of HMI) – had its own distinct ideology, particularly with regard to curriculum issues. This was intended to apply to the early 1980s, just as James Hamilton was coming to the end of his period as Permanent Secretary at the DES and the role of the Policy Unit, under first Ferdinand Mount (1982–3) and then John Redwood (1983–5), was beginning to widen considerably as part of what many now see as a calculated move away from *collective* to *presidential* government. It omits all reference to the Manpower Services Commission, which wielded considerable power between 1982 and 1984, and Lawton could not have predicted the swift demise of 'professional' influence after the 1987 General Election; but it does show which particular issues were 'conflict-generating' in the early 1980s, even if Lawton had no way of knowing in 1983 how they would be resolved within the 'tension-system'.

We also have a very revealing account of how the Policy Unit oper-ated in the mid-1980s which has been provided by David Willetts, now a prominent Conservative MP (Willetts, 1987). Willetts worked in Mrs Thatcher's Policy Unit from April 1984 to December 1986, specializing

Table 6.1   Three ideologies in the education system

	Beliefs	*Values*	*Tastes*
1 Politicos (ministers and political advisers)	market	freedom of choice	independent schools fees
2 Bureaucrats (DES officials and civil servants)	good administration	efficiency	central control examinations standard tests
3 Professionals (HMI)	professionalism	quality education	impressionistic evaluation of schools

Source: Lawton (1984), p. 17.

in Department of Health and Social Security and Treasury issues. At the time of writing his 1987 paper for the journal *Public Administration,* adapted from his prize-winning entry to the 1986 Haldane Essay Competition, he was Director of Studies at the right-wing Centre for Policy Studies.

In his paper, Willetts emphasized that, unlike the by-now defunct CPRS, the Policy Unit did not undertake large-scale, long-term studies. One of its chief functions was to offer policy advice on matters of current concern, working to a timetable 'determined by that night's box, the weekend box, or a meeting planned several days in advance' (1987: 443). It was always very much a part of the Prime Minister's own machine in Downing Street: the advice it proffered did *not* go to Cabinet where it could be rebutted by hostile or unsympathetic departmental ministers. It was considered normal practice that it would receive copies of all papers sent to the Prime Minister concerning domestic policy: according to Willetts, 'members of the Unit must be prepared to stay late and to brief at short notice, so that departments don't believe they can escape Policy Unit scrutiny simply by sending in a paper after 6 p.m., with a reply needed the following morning' (1987: 448). Not that the work of the Unit was determined simply, or indeed largely, by the actions of government departments. Members of the Unit were 'always on the lookout for new policy ideas, the fresh angle, the new policy proposal worth putting before the Prime Minister' (1987: 450). The Unit saw one of its main tasks as being to help the Prime Minister roll back 'the frontiers of the politically impossible'. According to Willetts 'the Policy Unit, because it is directly subordinate to the most senior and astute politician of the lot, is not afraid of putting forward what might initially appear to be politically far-fetched' (1987: 452).

The Department of Education and Science strikes back

Although the future clearly lay with the young idealists of the Policy Unit, it is important to note that there were two occasions in the 1980s – at a time, in fact, when Mrs Thatcher's own position seemed impregnable – when the DES bureaucracy secured a notable 'victory' over the Government's political advisers.

As we saw in Chapter 3, Sir Keith Joseph proved unable to proceed with a viable scheme for introducing the education voucher on a nationwide basis, and one of the reasons for this 'failure' was the determined opposition of the DES civil servants. When asked by the Secretary of State to prepare a detailed paper outlining the problems that would need to be overcome before an education voucher scheme could be introduced, they produced a blocking memorandum that was totally negative and hostile (see Chitty, 1989: 183–6). The abandonment of the voucher in 1983 was viewed by many at the time as a 'victory' for the conservative forces at the heart of the political and bureaucratic establishment. In the eyes of the Far Right, Sir Keith lacked the strength and the energy to take on his own civil servants. According to Marjorie Seldon, Chairperson of FEVER, when speaking on the BBC 2 television programme *Decision-making in Britain*, first shown in March 1983: 'the bureaucrats, if *ordered* to do so, could produce a perfectly workable scheme. There is no difficulty that cannot be overcome with ingenuity' (quoted in Seldon, 1986: 97). And an editorial in *The Daily Telegraph* at the beginning of 1986 argued that:

> Measures dear to the Prime Minister which fell by the wayside between 1983 and 1986 include: education vouchers, student loans, repeal of rent control . . . Though her aspirations reflect *popular* feeling, they run counter to those of the political and bureaucratic classes – the establishment in this country that is now accustomed to rule, whomever *demos* elects. (*The Daily Telegraph*, 13 January 1986)

The other major area of policy where the DES Civil Service got its way (this time in alliance with the Education Secretary, Kenneth Baker) was over the last-minute inclusion in the 1987 Education Reform Bill of the clauses creating a national curriculum. Of the various right-wing pressure groups operating at the time, only the newly-created Hillgate Group viewed this as a 'desirable' reform; for the others, it appeared to undermine the choice and diversity that were meant to be the distinguishing features of the new legislation. Interviewed on a BBC *Panorama* programme, 'A Class Revolution', broadcast on 2 November 1987, Stuart Sexton, by this time Director of the Education Unit of the IEA, made it clear that he and most of his right-wing colleagues remained deeply unhappy about the very idea of a government-imposed compulsory curriculum, and particularly one with as many as *ten* separate subjects. In the course of the lively discussions which had taken place in Downing Street over the previous 18 months, there had apparently been general support for the Hillgate Group's special emphasis on morality and social order; but it was felt that a return to traditional values could be achieved quite easily by encouraging all schools to concentrate on certain key disciplines. On one famous occasion, according to Sexton, Mrs Thatcher had emphasized that her chief concern was the effective teaching of what she labelled 'the 6 Rs': reading, writing, arithmetic, religious education, and right and wrong. This was what she had always meant by the 'core curriculum' for schools; and she was appalled by the much broader version favoured by the DES bureaucracy.

The origins of the 1988 Education Act

As we saw in Chapter 3, the educational policies carried out by Kenneth Baker and his ministerial team after 1986 were greatly influenced by the writings and speeches of that group of economists, philosophers and educationists often referred to collectively as the New Right. This body of thinkers, dispersed among a host of influential pressure groups, had a history going back to the 1950s, but it pursued its objectives with exceptional vigour after the 1979 General Election, aided by its easy access to the Downing Street Policy Unit and Prime Minister Margaret Thatcher and a friendly relationship with important sections of the media. As Professor Andrew Gamble has argued (1988), the New Right claimed to have a coherent strategy for the economic and moral regeneration of Britain, in which education clearly had an important role to play, but it was not without its internal contradictions. It was, in fact, a broad coalition of neo-liberals, interested chiefly in arguing the case for 'a freer, more open and more competitive economy', and neo-conservatives, interested primarily in 'restoring social and political authority throughout society' (1988: 29). So great was its influence in the late 1980s that many believed, if somewhat reluctantly, that any defence of the post-war orthodoxies would henceforth be a damage limitation exercise fought on the New Right's terms.

As far as education was concerned, there were three groups which exerted a powerful influence on the formulation of policy: the IEA, which established its own Education Unit under Stuart Sexton in 1986; the CPS, founded by Sir Keith Joseph, Margaret Thatcher and Alfred Sherman in 1974; and the Hillgate Group, which began to publish manifestos and pamphlets at the end of 1986.

It is difficult to be precise about *which* of these pressure groups was responsible for particular elements of the Government's new education programme; but variations of the new ideas which eventually found their way into the 1987 Education Bill can be discovered in, for example: *The Riddle of the Voucher,* published by the Institute of Economic Affairs in February 1986 (Seldon, 1986); *Our Schools – A Radical Policy,* written by Stuart Sexton and published by the IEA's new Education Unit in March 1987 (Sexton, 1987); and *Whose Schools? A Radical Manifesto,* issued by the Hillgate Group in December 1986 (Hillgate Group, 1986). Kenneth Baker has acknowledged that when he was offered the education portfolio in May 1986, he knew that the IEA, the CPS and the Hillgate Group were the *real* policy-makers as far as the Prime Minister was concerned (Baker, 1993: 163). After one particular meeting with the Centre for Policy Studies Education Study Group, held in the House of Lords in the spring of 1987, he turned to his chief political adviser and said: 'those are the people who are really setting the educational agenda now' (quoted in Wilby and Midgley, 1987: 11). Mrs Thatcher herself told journalists that CPS pamphlets on education – and particularly Sheila Lawlor's attack on the complexity of the National Curriculum (Lawlor, 1988) – were 'compulsory bedtime reading' for her in the spring of 1988 (quoted in Gow, 1988).

The right was extremely fortunate in that after Professor Brian Griffiths became Head of the Downing Street Policy Unit in October 1985, that body was happy and willing to act as a 'conduit' between the various education think-tanks and the Prime Minister herself. Described by Marcel Berlins in an article published in *The Illustrated London News* in June 1988 as 'one of the twenty-five people who really matter in Britain' (Berlins, 1988), Professor Griffiths occupied a small second-floor office above the door to Number Ten and enjoyed daily access to the Prime Minister. An evangelical Christian anxious to promote a moral and theological justification for Thatcherism, he was a former Dean of the City University Business School, a Director of the Bank of England and Chairperson of Christian Responsibility in Public. He had specific responsibility for education within the Unit, and was credited by Mrs Thatcher in her 1993 book of memoirs with devising 'the final extremely successful model of the grant-maintained . . . schools' (Thatcher, 1993: 592). There seems good reason to accept Stuart Maclure's analysis of the vital role of the Policy Unit in the final process of translating New Right ideology into practical policies:

> What eventually emerged in the 1987 Election Manifesto – and therefore ultimately in the 1988 Education Act – was assembled *in secret* in the nine months before the 1987 General Election. There was a determined effort *not* to consult either the DES or the civil servants or chief education officers or local politicians. Under the discreet eye of Professor Brian Griffiths, Head of the Prime Minister's Policy Unit, the outline of a radical reform was set down in bold lines from which there was to be no going back. (Maclure, 1988: 166)

The role of advisers under New Labour

By the time of the 2005 General Election, Tony Blair's Labour Government had 81 special advisers who cost the taxpayer just over £4.4 million a year in salaries. Although this number appeared to be, and indeed was, very large (Iain Duncan Smith said a Conservative administration would reduce it to 60), it did, of course, include a wide variety of categories, with only 11 working in the much-derided communications field as so-called 'spin-doctors' and only a small group of policy specialists housed in the Downing Street Policy Unit.

This new reliance on a rapidly growing number of special advisers has obviously had a marked effect on the role and status of the British Civil Service, which has been under threat since the late 1970s. We know from Mrs Thatcher's own account of her years in Downing Street that she often raged against a service reluctant to join her in dismantling the despised edifice of the post-war 'welfare consensus' (Thatcher, 1993). Her impatience with officials who did not share her own activist zeal helped to destroy the careers of many whose promotion was denied at her personal whim. Yet, as the late *Guardian* columnist, Hugo Young, argued:

> in retrospect, the Thatcher period looks like a model of decorum. There were limits to the disrespect she was prepared to show the bureaucratic system.

> The Foreign Office may have been 'beyond redemption' in her eyes; but other departments in Whitehall continued to operate by well-understood rules about who was 'political' and who was not. (Young, 2002)

Mrs Thatcher came to rely more and more for advice on the type of right-wing political idealist who could be described as 'one of us'; but she understood the right of the civil servant to exercise *impartial* judgement. Despite occasional problematic episodes such as the Spycatcher Affair, the independence of the Cabinet Secretary was respected; and he remained the acknowledged expert on the essential distinction between the role of *partisan* policy advisers and that of *impartial* civil servants. As the final definer of 'propriety', he never had his writ challenged.

All this changed when New Labour came to power in 1997. Although the collective record of Tony Blair's front-bench team did not include a single hour of management or delivery at 'the coalface of national government', and only a handful of ministers could boast of their time in city or local government, the newcomers were convinced that their own theoretical preparations for government were vastly superior to anything the Civil Service could offer. At the same time, they clearly did not understand the overriding need to protect the Civil Service from the threat of 'politicization'. To quote Hugo Young again:

> To make good the Civil Service's supposed defects, New Labour enhanced the cadre of so-called special, or political, advisers. Their number more than doubled – from 35 to 81 since the time of John Major. Some of them matched the practice of decades by bringing genuine expertise in particular policy issues, though few had any more experience than their ministers of delivering anything. In Number Ten itself, the advisers prodigiously multiplied to form, in effect, a para-government, second-guessing departmental civil servants at every turn . . . Most worryingly of all, Blairism has stealthily begun the process whereby the Civil Service, in the power positions at the top, should no longer be impartial, but should become instead an arm of the Party. (Young, 2002)

Others have also been concerned about the threat of 'politicization'. In a speech to the Centre for Management and Policy Studies in London, delivered at the end of March 2002, Sir Richard Wilson, the outgoing Cabinet Secretary, used his authority to call for a Civil Service Act to protect the political neutrality of Whitehall officials, and to restrict both the number and role of ministerial special advisers and the size and influence of the Downing Street Policy Unit. Sir Richard repeatedly stressed the neutrality of the Civil Service, and defined the mandarin class as 'the shock absorber at the heart of the state'. It was the job of the Civil Service to ensure smooth government: 'the Civil Service has to paddle furiously under the surface to make things work, whilst presenting to the world a calm picture of business as usual' (Wintour, 2002). If it was indeed necessary to employ special advisers and 'experts' it should be accepted that their role was 'explicitly party political' and that they should seek actively to protect the Civil Service from 'politicization'. In the words of Sir Richard:

> Special advisers should never behave illegally or improperly . . . Special advisers should not ask civil servants to do anything improper or illegal . . . They should not do anything to undermine the political impartiality of civil servants or the duty of all civil servants to give their own best advice to ministers. (Wintour, 2002)

Where education is concerned, there is considerable evidence of the role of so-called experts in the formulation of policy, but little or no indication that this has compromised the 'neutrality' of the Department's bureaucracy. As we saw in Chapter 4, many commentators were impressed with the speed with which the July 1997 White Paper was produced; but it was also noted that many of the new policies had already been worked out in the months leading up to the May Election, notably at a Labour Education Summit held in April, and that many of the key ideas and slogans had already appeared in books authored by such influential advisers as Peter Mandelson and Michael Barber.

The somewhat ambiguous catchphrase *'standards not structures'* that was an important theme of the White Paper had earlier featured prominently in the first edition of *The Blair Revolution: Can New Labour Deliver?*, co-authored by Peter Mandelson and Roger Liddle and published in May 1996. It was in this provocative book that Mandelson and Liddle set much of the tone of New Labour's educational agenda, arguing that a preoccupation with 'structure' in education had absorbed a great deal of energy to little effect and that the first priority of a Blair administration must be to raise general educational standards:

> New Labour now believes that, throughout schooling, standards are more important than structures. Each school should be made clearly responsible for its own performance and be subject to a mixture of external pressure and support in order to raise it. Performance must be regularly assessed in objective terms that parents can understand and compare with elsewhere . . . New Labour must now spell out with greater clarity what its new educational policies will mean in practice and how its new emphasis on *standards, not structures,* can, in time, transform state education. (Mandelson and Liddle, 1996: 92–3)

Where Michael Barber is concerned, the important text is *The Learning Game: Arguments for an Education Revolution,* also first published in 1996 and described by Tony Blair on the back cover as 'provocative and timely, illuminating and optimistic'. From this book, we get the White Paper idea that *'intervention in schools should be in inverse proportion to success'.* According to Professor Barber:

> The general assumption behind this principle is that most schools have within them the capacity to improve themselves steadily, as long as national government provides a sensible policy and funding framework. The precise nature of intervention in a school which is not succeeding should depend on the extent and character of its failure. (Barber, 1996: 149)

In seeking to understand the provenance of New Labour's education programme, we need to appreciate that there are *three* individuals who stand out as having exerted a powerful influence on the formulation of policy: Michael Barber, David Miliband and Andrew Adonis.

A former Professor of Education at the Institute of Education in London, Michael Barber was appointed by David Blunkett to chair Labour's own Literacy Task Force set up in May 1996. After the 1997 General Election, he became Head of the new 275-strong Standards and Effectiveness Unit within the then Department for Education and Employment, a post he held for four years until 2001, when he became Head of the Prime Minister's Delivery Unit at Number Ten charged with delivering major improvements in *four* key areas: education, crime reduction, health, and transport. Interviewed at the Institute of Education in April 2002 in front of an audience composed largely of his former colleagues, he was asked about the call he made in his book *The Learning Game* for all classroom teachers to sign up to 'the crusade of raising standards in schools'. He answered:

> I think that when I wrote that book in 1996, I thought it would be easier to sign up the teaching profession. I did not understand sufficiently how difficult it is to get change on that scale, that fast. I think the early phase of New Labour from 1997 involved some very tough messages. (quoted in Mansell, 2002)

David Miliband, a former researcher at the IPPR (Institute for Public Policy Research) with a keen interest in issues of education and training for older students, was appointed as a policy adviser to Tony Blair in 1994 and became Head of the Downing Street Policy Unit in 1997. He has been widely credited with drafting the 1997 and 2001 New Labour election manifestos and with putting together the 1997 White Paper,

Excellence in Schools (see, for example, Passmore, 2001; Tomlinson, 2001; Ahmed, 2002). He became the MP for South Shields in 2001 and then, at the early age of 36, a minister of state in the DfES in the May 2002 re-shuffle occasioned by the resignation of Stephen Byers.

His successor as Head of the Downing Street Policy Unit following the 2001 General Election was Andrew Adonis, who had been appointed to advise the Policy Unit on education policy in 1998 and was largely responsible for putting together the 2001 White Paper, *Schools Achieving Success*. His original 1988 appointment caused some disquiet in Labour Party circles because he was known to be an opponent of the traditional comprehensive school. Writing in *The Independent* on 23 November 1998, the former Labour deputy leader Roy Hattersley commented: 'When a new Number Ten political adviser is an established opponent of "official" government policy, the fact is worth mentioning'. Formerly a Fellow of Nuffield College, Oxford and a political columnist on *The Observer*, Andrew Adonis co-authored with Stephen Pollard a book called *A Class Act*, published in 1997, which argued that: 'the comprehensive revolution, tragically, destroyed many of the excellent schools without improving the rest. Comprehensive schools have largely replaced selection by ability with selection by class and house price' (Adonis and Pollard, 1997: 55). There is no doubt that Andrew Adonis wielded enormous power and influence in the formulation of New Labour education policy. It was the contention of a well-researched Channel Four television programme, *Tony: President or King?*, shown on 4 May 2002 and presented by *Observer* columnist Nick Cohen, that education policy was determined by Tony Blair and Andrew Adonis. This view was upheld by all those interviewed for the programme, including Roy Hattersley and David Hart, General Secretary of the National Association of Headteachers (see Chitty, 2002c).

Policy-making in Scotland

It is often argued that Scotland's education system has always been based on 'a widespread respect for learning' and 'an egalitarian social outlook'. While all such generalizations tend to contain elements of 'myth', it is certainly true that post-war Scotland embraced educational reform with an enthusiasm lacking in England and that in such areas as entrance to higher education, Scotland has shown a concern for the rights of 'economically deprived social classes' not evident in other parts of the UK (see Benn and Chitty, 1996: 4; Matheson, 2000: 81).

The Education (Scotland) Acts of 1945 and 1946 applied the principles of the 1944 Education Act for England and Wales to Scottish circumstances, though it is rather misleading to say this, since two of the major innovations – the provision of secondary education for all and the raising of the school-leaving age to 15 – had already been enacted in Scotland in 1939 and then suspended owing to the outbreak of the Second World War (McPherson and Raab, 1988: 73).

As we saw in Chapter 2, it was in the mid-1960s that a *national* political initiative was taken by the central Labour administration to 'go comprehensive'. This took the form of Circular 10/65 (DES, 1965), a call by the DES in London for local education authorities in England and Wales to submit plans for the establishment of comprehensive schools. Although the Education Secretary, Anthony Crosland, had a clear preference for the 'all-through', 11–18 model of reorganization, the Circular itself endorsed five other ways in which secondary schooling might be organized on a non-selective basis. By way of contrast, the implementation of comprehensive education in Scotland was remarkably uniform (see Kerckhoff *et al.,* 1996: 6). Circular 600, issued in the same year by the Scottish Education Department (SED), prescribed only *one* final form of comprehensive organization, which was the six-year, 'all-through', fixed-catchment, comprehensive school for 12–18 year-olds. That said, the Circular did concede that some variant of a two-tier system might be 'an unavoidable interim arrangement', especially in outlying rural areas (SED, 1965: paras 10 and 11).

Interviewed at the end of the 1980s about the effectiveness of Circular 600, former Scottish minister Bruce Millan argued that although the Circular marked the *official* start of reorganization, the door in Scotland was already 'half-open':

> I think there was a more *genuine* disposition in Scotland towards changing over to the comprehensive system than there was in England. The arguments about selection, in other words, I think had been largely won in Scotland by the time we sent out our Circular . Of course, there were a number of schools in the Highlands, and elsewhere, where there was already something very much more approaching what one would call a comprehensive school; and it was perhaps for that reason that we had less hostility towards the idea in Scotland than they had in certain areas of England – and, indeed, far from hostility, a general acceptance of the idea. (Quoted in McPherson and Raab, 1988: 374)

The situation in Scotland today differs from that in other parts of the UK in a number of significant ways. For one thing, very few Scottish children attend private schools, and there is a high degree of confidence in the state sector (see Scott, 2001). Unlike England, Scotland has no plans to increase the number of specialist secondary schools or to use private money to run schools. There is no national curriculum in Scotland, the curriculum from 5 to 14 being based on five broad curriculum areas, and from 14 to 16 on eight 'modes' of study. The Scottish Executive has also signalled a move away from compulsory national testing by giving primary schools the opportunity to set their own academic targets, and the main agenda for the academic year 2001–2 was to focus on increasing the powers of headteachers and also on introducing a national standardized report to help parents understand their children's progress. Where post-16 courses and qualifications are concerned, there is a principal difference between Scotland, where the curriculum comprises shorter academic courses (Highers) and vocational modules; and the rest of the UK where it comprises longer academic courses (A2 and AS Levels) and vocational programmes leading to group awards.

So even before the Scottish National Party's recent electoral success and the formation of an SNP administration, it has been obvious that the education policy in Scotland will always be very different from that south of the border. The 32 all-purpose local authorities set up in 1996 enjoy greater autonomy than do their counterparts in England; and this autonomy extends to the headteachers of schools who are widely admired for their professionalism (see Paterson, 2002: 37). With the exception of the Private Finance Initiative, there is far less emphasis on the role of the private sector in educational reform; there is very little support for the view that greater differentiation among secondary schools is a pathway to higher academic success; and there is much greater respect within governing circles for the capabilities of classroom teachers. There is no enthusiasm for the creation of Academies or Trust Schools; there has been strong opposition to the idea of 'top-up' fees for new university undergraduates; and the testing programme in schools has had a very different underlying philosophy, with league tables being scrapped in 2003.

There seems, in fact, to be a real sense of confidence and pride among Scottish ministers, with *no* attempt to play down the differences between Scotland and England. For example: it was proudly announced in June 2007 that class sizes in the first three years of Scottish primary schools could soon be cut to a record low of just 18. Fiona Hyslop, the Scottish Education Secretary, said £25m would be spent recruiting more teachers to give young children 'the time and attention to flourish'. And this announcement was reported in *The Daily Telegraph* (21 June 2007) at the same time as it emerged that in England, 23,250 pupils aged five to seven were still being taught in classes which exceeded the legal limit of 30. On 5 August 2008, nearly 160,000 Scottish students received results in their standard and higher grades showing a rise in the pass rate for highers – the equivalent of A Levels in England – from 71.7 per cent in 2007 to 73.4 per cent in 2008. Fiona Hyslop was quick to point out that the Scottish Government was very pleased with the results and did not wish to get dragged into a row about exam standards in England:

> A Level grade inflation is an issue of concern to the English examination system. But we have a strong system which is improving steadily. We do not wish to get dragged into a debate about grade inflation in England. (Reported in *The Guardian*, 6 August 2008)

There has even been a BBC Radio Four programme, broadcast on 16 August 2008, devoted to the theme of the 'superiority' of the Scottish system of schooling. Much of the content of the programme was, of course, anecdotal and highly subjective, but it is interesting to note that among those interviewed who had taught in both England and Scotland, it was generally agreed that life in Scottish schools was far less stressful, with teachers freed from the pressures of SATs and league tables.

The New Labour education project in England is based on two fundamental assumptions: that the comprehensive reform has failed, and that teachers are largely to blame for poor pupil performance in many schools. Neither of these perceptions exists in Scotland. Public support for a common system of secondary schools is still strong; and there has also been strong public support for a recent agreement on teachers' pay and conditions offering higher pay and more teacher autonomy in return for a willingness by teachers to work more flexibly. There has been little sympathy in Scotland for those policy developments under both Conservative and New Labour administrations tending to privatization, competition and individualism which are seen as 'undesirable and against the spirit of Scottish civil society' (Ozga, 1999: 48). It is Professor Lindsay Paterson's view that 'the normal pattern of schooling in Scotland will remain the non-selective, neighbourhood-based primary and secondary schools', though with 'some erosion of the neighbourhood principle through parental choice of school' (Paterson, 2002: 36). He goes on to argue that 'the whole system will continue to be seen as a distinctive part of Scottish civic identity, the responsibility for which rests firmly in the Scottish Parliament and not even partly at Westminster or in Whitehall' (ibid.).

Recent developments in Wales

Since devolution in 1999, the Welsh and English systems have been steadily diverging and Jane Davidson, the Minister for Education and Lifelong Learning in the Welsh Assembly, has sought to take Welsh education in its own, distinctive direction. Taking on her key role in October 2000, Ms Davidson soon abolished the publication of school league tables for secondary schools (Wales has never had them for primary schools); and made it clear that she rejected the English plan to encourage the establishment of specialist and faith-based schools.

In September 2001, on the same day that Estelle Morris launched the White Paper *Schools Achieving Success* (discussed in Chapter 4), Jane Davidson delivered *The Learning Country,* in effect Wales's own White Paper, a 72-page document outlining ambitious plans for Wales's 2,000 schools, 27 colleges and 13 higher education institutions (National Assembly for Wales, 2001). These were among the main proposals:

- a new 'foundation stage' for children aged 3–7 would focus on 'learning through play'
- there would be no more tests for 7-year-olds, with pupil progress to be measured instead by teacher assessments
- class sizes in junior schools would be reduced to 30 or fewer by the autumn of 2003
- no primary class would contain more than 25 pupils by the autumn of 2007
- there would be improved transition arrangements between primary and secondary schools
- there would be no literacy or numeracy strategy for 11–14-year-olds
- there would be a strong commitment to comprehensive secondary schools
- the private sector would not be permitted to set up new schools
- there would be no specialist schools or city academies in Wales
- ACCAC, the Welsh Curriculum Authority, would be asked to press ahead with plans to develop a Welsh 'Baccalaureate', to include not only General National Vocational Qualifications (GNVQs), AS and A2 Levels, but also education in Welsh identity and culture, community work, key skills and modern languages.

Responding to the document, Gethin Lewis, Secretary of the National Union of Teachers Cymru, said: 'We are overjoyed at the news that tests for seven-year-olds will be scrapped. We also welcome the fact that the Government in Wales is finally listening to teachers and praising the role they play in society' (quoted in Slater, 2001: 14). Councillor Jeff Jones, Wales's Local Government Association's Education Spokesperson, commented: 'I am pleased that the Minister has made clear her strong commitment to the existing system of comprehensive education . . . We don't have "bog-standard" schools in Wales . . . Specialist schools and privatisation are not required here' (Slater, 2001).

Interviewed for an article in *Education Guardian,* published at the beginning of October 2002, Jane Davidson emphasized her determination to eschew English solutions:

> There would be real risks in a shift to extensive and untested measures delivered solely through the private or other sectors . . . We have a comprehensive system that we are fully proud of, and which has served Wales very well . . . I don't believe that the private sector has a role in the delivery of education in Wales. (Quoted in Woodward, 2001: 2)

In a lecture to celebrate the life and work of Brian Simon, delivered at the Institute of Education in London on 7 February 2004, Jane Davidson went further in outlining her vision for the future of education and training in Wales. She pointed out that the strategy laid out in *The Learning Country* was for a programme of reform over at least a decade since change in education took a long time to achieve and a long-term approach was necessary. She emphasized that the new administration remained committed to 'a dynamic, all-ability comprehensive system, with an emphasis on the school being firmly embedded in its local community'. A number of the pledges contained in *The Learning Country* were in the process of being honoured. The percentage of junior pupils in classes of over 30 had fallen from 29 per cent in September 2000 to 13 per cent in September 2003. Key Stage One tests had been undertaken for the last time in the Summer of 2002 – and this was, in fact, three years ahead of a similar development in England. It was also envisaged that there would soon be major changes to the nature and purpose of the Key Stage Two tests and that there would be 'a move away from' the traditional national tests at Key Stage Three. The administration was convinced that 16 was an 'inappropriate' break point in education and that 14 to 19 should be seen as *one* phase, with the development of academic and vocational courses with 'parity of esteem' between them and a programme of 18 pilot projects to test the feasibility of a Welsh Baccalaureate. Jane Davidson ended her Lecture by claiming that *The Learning Country* was 'a hugely challenging education agenda', because it meant 'doing things differently in Wales' – 'building on our success, but prepared to tackle failure'. She was indeed proud of the country's 'distinctive approach':

> I want to see our vision of Wales as a learning country realised – where learners come first, where the experience of learning is broadening and enriched, where standards are high, teachers are equipped to work effectively and headteachers are able to drive forward improvement . . . We also have to ensure that our policies are evidence-based, that they secure social inclusion and that they drive forward equality of opportunity and the provision of new access routes to learning for all. . . . I also hope that in the future, some other countries' educational developments will be informed by Wales. (Davidson, 2004: 51)

Shortly after the delivery of this Lecture, in July 2004, the Welsh Assembly took the decision to end all national testing *before* the GCSE years. In a report to the Assembly, ACCAC (the Qualifications, Curriculum and Assessment Authority for Wales) had talked about the negative impact on the curriculum of too many teachers simply 'teaching to the test'. It said that there was strong evidence that many primary schools were concentrating on the core subjects (English, Welsh, maths and science) at the expense of other areas of the curriculum (ACCAC, 2004). Defending the administration's proposal to replace the end-of-primary and Key Stage Three tests with teacher assessment, Jane Davidson told the Assembly that 'the testing regime put teachers under pressure to teach to the test, narrowed the curriculum and had a negative effect on learning' (quoted in Mansell, 2007: 242).

7

The Evolving Curriculum from 5 to 14

It is both extraordinary and, in a sense, a major source of shame and embarrassment that the National Curriculum for England and Wales, details of which constituted such an important part of the 1988 Education Reform Act, has found itself subjected by successive governments, both Conservative and New Labour, to so many radical and destabilizing changes in the course of its short history of just 15 years. Most of these far-reaching changes have affected Key Stage Four (concerning the schooling of students aged 14–16) which has never actually been implemented *in its original form*; and these changes will be discussed in Chapter 8. But there have also been very significant developments affecting the 5–14 curriculum, and it is these changes which will form a major part of this chapter following a fairly brief account of the curious background to the initiatives of the late 1980s.

Teacher 'control' of the curriculum

As we saw in Chapter 2, the 1944 Butler Act provided no guidance as to the actual *content* of either primary or secondary education. The word 'curriculum' does appear in the Act (on page 20), but only in passing and at the end of a section (Section 23) depriving the central authority of direct responsibility for what was taught in schools. The Elementary Regulations had been abolished in 1926 and the Secondary Regulations were simply allowed to lapse in 1944, so primary and secondary teachers were able to enjoy a considerable degree of autonomy in curriculum matters in the post-war period, even if (or so it can be argued) they failed to take advantage of this unique situation in any meaningful sense. In the view of Professor Denis Lawton, it was, in fact, 'the Golden Age of teacher control (or non-control) of the curriculum' (Lawton, 1980: 22).

Under Section 23 of the 1944 Act, dates of terms, length of the school day and secular instruction in all except voluntary-aided secondary schools became the responsibility of the local education authority although, as we have already noted, the really important decisions about curriculum content and teaching methods were to be taken in both primary and secondary schools by the headteacher and his or her staff under the general oversight of governors and managers.

Despite the absence of clear curriculum directions (or guidelines) from the central authority, there were, of course, a number of important factors influencing the shape of school curricula, and particularly at the secondary level. These included: examination syllabuses; university and other entrance requirements; the subject choices of parents and pupils; the availability of teachers and teaching materials; and the advice of local and government inspectors. And in addition to these practical, day-to-day considerations, there were other, more subtle, constraints which meant that there was no real necessity for the post-war Ministry to contemplate further interference from the centre. According to philosopher and historian John White (White, 1975), the proposals outlined in the Ministry's pamphlet *The Nation's Schools,* published in May 1945 (shortly before the election of a Labour government), can be viewed as a form of 'indirect control' over school curricula, since the authors enjoined local education authorities to organize secondary education on tripartite lines, thereby endorsing the view upheld in the 1943 Norwood Report (Secondary Schools Examinations Council, 1943) that there were, in fact, three 'rough groupings' of children with correspondingly three different 'types of mind'. A system of grammar, technical and modern schools would ensure that these three 'types of mind' were suitably recognized and nourished, with all children being prepared to take up the occupations 'best suited for them'. In White's view, despite the absence of specific parliamentary regulations, this process of 'indirect control' enabled the post-war Ministry to exert a powerful influence on the content of education for children in state schools.

The system envisaged by the Norwood Report also had a profound effect on the organization and curriculum of the country's post-war primary schools. With their reputation among parents largely dependent on the acquisition of an impressive number of grammar-school places each academic year, many of the larger primary schools began to 'stream' their pupils from the age of seven, with only the supposedly 'brightest' children in the 'top' stream being specially 'groomed' for success in the 11-plus selection examination, so that selection at 11 became, in effect, selection at 7. As many teachers and parents observed at the time, such a process was always bound to be arbitrary and unfair. Describing his experience of working with 10-year-old boys in a streamed (A, B, C) primary school, Brian Jackson wrote in 1961 that the more he had got to know these boys ('of the grammar-school type'; 'of the C type', and so on), the more he had become convinced that 'they had not been "given" to us in these neat categories: *we had manufactured them*'. In Jackson's view: 'they were the product of the educational society that we had established . . . That society demanded that they be selected or rejected at the age of eleven; therefore we pre-selected at ten, nine, eight, seven, even six' (Jackson, 1961: 6, 8). All this began to change, of course, in the late 1950s and 1960s as local authorities in various parts of the country began the process of abolishing the 11-plus and then reorganizing their secondary schools along comprehensive lines.

The first indication that the Government might one day regard the school curriculum as too important to be left in the hands of local education authorities and teachers came in March 1960 in a much-quoted House of Commons debate on the 1959 Crowther Report (on the future education of 15–18-year-olds: see Ministry of Education, 1959). It was on this famous occasion that Sir David Eccles (Conservative Minister of Education from 1959 to 1962) expressed his regret that so many parliamentary education debates had been devoted to 'bricks and mortar' and to 'the organization of the system' and then talked about the possibility of entering 'the secret garden of the curriculum':

> I regret that we hardly ever discuss what is taught to the seven million boys and girls in the maintained schools. We treat the curriculum as though it were a subject . . . about which it is not done for us to make remarks. I should like the House to agree that this reticence has been overdone. Of course, Parliament would never attempt to dictate the curriculum, but, from time to time, we could, with advantage, express our views on what is taught in schools and in training colleges. As for the Ministry of Education itself, my Department has the unique advantage of the countrywide experience of Her Majesty's Inspectorate. Nowhere in the kingdom is there such a rich source of information or such a constant exchange of ideas on all that goes on in the schools. I shall, therefore, try in the future to make the Ministry's own voice heard rather more often, more positively, and, no doubt, sometimes more controversially. For this purpose, we shall need to undertake inside the Department more educational research and also to strengthen our statistical services . . . In the meantime, the section in the Crowther Report on the Sixth Form is an irresistible invitation for a sally into the secret garden of the curriculum. (*Hansard,* House of Commons, Vol. 620, Cols 51–2, 21 March 1960)

Two years later, in 1962, David Eccles established the Curriculum Study Group, without any form of prior consultation with organized educational interests. This Group was to comprise HMIs, administrators and experts co-opted from the outside. It would provide a nucleus of full-time staff to organize and co-ordinate research studies. Its work would be linked with that of the universities, practising classroom teachers, local authorities, research organizations, professional institutes and others concerned with the content of the curriculum and examinations. According to a study of the role of the National Union of Teachers in the making of national educational policy between 1944 and the end of the 1960s, 'Eccles envisaged the Group as a relatively small "commando-like unit", making raids into the curriculum.' He recognized that the educational system was expected to service a rapidly changing society, and the Group could be seen as marking 'a definite departure in the Ministry's conception of its role in the formulation of an important area of educational policy' (Manzer, 1970: 91–2). While accepting that curriculum programming was not self-evidently the exclusive concern of teachers, the initial reaction of the teaching unions and professional educators was pretty hostile, and it was obvious that they viewed the Ministry's intentions with great suspicion; so much so, in fact, that in 1963 the new Minister of Education, Sir Edward Boyle, decided that the Group would have to be replaced by a less threatening organization. Accordingly the Lockwood Committee was set up to draw up the guidelines for a new Schools Council for the Curriculum and Examinations.

The new Council, which met for the first time in October 1964 with Sir John Maud as Chairperson, was certainly very different from the sort of body which David Eccles had had in mind. It was an independent organization with a majority of teacher members. Its declared purpose was to undertake research and development work in all aspects of curriculum and examinations in primary and secondary schools. In the words of Maurice Plaskow, who joined the headquarters staff of the Council in 1970, it was conceived as 'a hopeful act of reconciliation between central and local government and teachers' (Plaskow, 1985: 1). In all its work, it aimed to adhere to the general principle, expressed in its constitution, that each school should have the fullest possible measure of responsibility for its own curriculum and teaching methods based on the needs of its own pupils and evolved by its own staff. In, for example, Working Paper 53, *The Whole Curriculum 13–16,* published in 1975, it was argued that the aims of a school should be stated in a 'covenant' to which parents, pupils, teachers and society at large could subscribe. At the same time, the Paper was anxious to defend the principle of teacher autonomy in all matters relating to the curriculum, in this case the secondary-school curriculum:

British schools have for long been jealous of their independence in curricular matters. However much they may turn to outside bodies for resources, information and advice, they insist that the curriculum must be of their own making. We strongly affirm our support for this position for . . . we believe the surest hope for the improvement of the secondary-school curriculum lies in the continuing professional growth of the teacher, which, in turn, implies that teachers take even greater responsibility for the development of schools curriculum policies. Moreover, we have stressed the distinctive nature of the curriculum policies appropriate to particular schools, and it would be a denial of this to attempt to prescribe the sort of policies they should adopt. (Schools Council, 1975: 30)

From partnership to accountability

As we have already seen in Chapters 3, 4 and 6, it was in the 1970s that there was a powerful shift in the dominant metaphor of educational policy-making: from 'partnership' to 'accountability'. The economic crisis of 1971–3 was arguably the most cataclysmic event of the post-war world, coinciding as it did with demographic change and with a growing disillusionment with the underlying assumptions of the social democratic project. The social reforms which characterized the era of the welfare capitalist consensus were no longer on the agenda and were to be replaced by new sets of priorities which to a large extent represented the philosophical and political discourses of the New Right. During the period of the 1974–9 Wilson/Callaghan Government, the ground was being prepared for the reversal of what Sir Keith Joseph described in a speech to the Oxford Union in December 1975 as 'the left-wing ideological and policy ratchet' (Joseph, 1976: 21). In all areas of social policy, the culture of co-operation and public service was to be replaced by one of competition and enterprise. Educational reform was central to the New Right project for destroying the cosy networks which allowed professionals and local authorities to operate in an almost autonomous fashion. As Professor Stephen Ball has observed: 'the educational policies of Thatcherism involved a total re-working of the ideological terrain of educational politics and the orientation of policy-making was now towards the consumers of education – parents and industrialists; the producer lobbies were almost totally excluded' (Ball, 1990: 8).

Central control of the school curriculum was to become an important feature of the new-found desire to make schools and teachers more accountable to the public, though the early moves towards that goal were piecemeal and hesitant. As we have seen, both the confidential Yellow

Book and the Ruskin College speech of 1976 talked about establishing the case for a so-called 'core curriculum' of 'basic knowledge'; but it was not made really clear what this would amount to in practice. Matters were further complicated by the fact that a number of different groups had their own distinct views as to how a 'core' or 'common' curriculum should be defined.

Towards central control of the curriculum

As I argued back in 1988 (Chitty, 1988: 34), much of the problem of discussing curriculum issues in Britain centres on the question of definitions. In the 1970s and 1980s, politicians, civil servants, educationists and teachers were talking about a variety of curriculum models: an integrated curriculum, a compulsory curriculum, a common curriculum, a common culture individualized curriculum, a core curriculum, a common-core curriculum and, finally, a national curriculum. The impression was often created that these all amounted to the same thing in practice, which was in fact very far from the truth.

Of all the above concepts, two, in particular, are worthy of detailed consideration: the professional common-curriculum model put forward by, among others, a powerful group of Her Majesty's Inspectors; and the bureaucratic core-curriculum model advocated from the mid-1970s onwards by the civil servants of the DES and later expanded into the National Curriculum itself.

The professional common-curriculum approach was clearly outlined in the three HMI Red Books published between 1977 and 1983 and concerned chiefly with the secondary-school curriculum (DES, 1977b; 1981b; 1983). This approach reflected a genuine concern with the quality of the teaching process in schools and with the needs of individual students. It sought to transcend traditional subject boundaries, and saw the use of a subject-based timetable as simply a short-hand method of working towards 'higher-level' aims. It presupposed that the vast majority of teachers were well-trained, well-motivated and generally skilled in identifying specific learning problems. It was concerned with all students as developing individuals and wary of any system of assessment geared to 'writing off' large sections of the school population as failures.

It seems clear that a group within the Inspectorate had been giving serious consideration to the nature and purposes of the secondary curriculum since the late 1960s. Schools Council Working Paper 33,

Choosing a Curriculum for the Young School Leaver, published in 1971, provides a revealing account of a conference held in Scarborough in June 1969 where at least one of the curriculum discussion groups (which included an HMI representative) was willing to question the Schools Council's cautious and piecemeal approach to curriculum planning:

> A major problem to be faced was whether we were giving so much freedom to each individual school that continuity for our pupils in a mobile society was ignored. In fact do we not have so many *general* curricular questions to answer that there ought to be a project on the curriculum *as a whole?* Are we right to be juggling with the pieces in order to find new ways of putting them back together? Is there not a need to look at the whole conception of secondary education, and would this help headteachers to make their choices? . . . One group at this Conference, in seeking to define the school curriculum, was moving towards considerations of this kind, while an HMI representative pointed out that there was a group in the Inspectorate already giving it serious thought. He defined the essentials of a good common curriculum as giving importance to personal development, aesthetic experience, experience of the material world and of society, and 'transcendentalism' – ideals and inspiration. (Schools Council, 1971: 26)

The timing here is significant. The late 1960s marked the end of a period of ten or more years which has been described by Lawton and Gordon (1987: 24) as 'probably . . . the lowest period of HMI influence and morale'. For one thing, there was the continuing problem of overlap between HMI and local authority inspectors. At the same time, the Inspectorate itself felt that its professional expertise was not making itself felt. In an interview with Maurice Kogan published in 1971, Edward Boyle, who had served at the Ministry of Education in 1957–9 and again in 1962–4, conceded that civil servants had not always made effective use of the professional knowledge of the Inspectorate:

> Looking back over the period we're thinking of, about fifteen years, the Inspectorate has played less of a part in policy making than I for one would have liked to see . . . I don't think there was a sufficiently strong tradition that when you had a major discussion, the Senior Chief Inspector should normally be invited in . . . I think, there may have been personal reasons over the years why this tended not to happen. But, for whatever reason, he [sic] didn't play a big enough part in the policy making of the Department, whoever he was. (Boyle and Crosland, 1971: 130–1)

The findings of the 1967–8 Parliamentary Select Committee which scrutinized the work of HMI made it clear that there was a very real need for the Inspectorate to find a new role and one, moreover, which did not merely *duplicate* the work of LEA advisory services. With this in mind, it is possible to view the 1970 document *HMI Today and Tomorrow* (DES, 1970) as an attempt by the Inspectorate to justify its very existence: an attempt, in other words, at self-promotion. That justification was to be provided by the pursuit of a number of new strategies, foremost among them being the planning of a 'common culture' curriculum. By the time of the Yellow Book and the Ruskin College speech, this work was taking place alongside DES attempts to construct a 'core curriculum' of basic knowledge (which will be discussed later in this section).

At the end of 1977, the Inspectorate felt able to make its ideas available to a wider audience with the publication of a collection of papers which became known as Red Book One (DES, 1977b). Yet this was also the time when the advocacy of a 'common' or 'common-core' curriculum was seen by many teachers as part of the Government's obvious desire to exert greater control over the education service. Accordingly, the authors of the Red Book felt it necessary to assert right at the outset that their ideas should be judged on their merits as *curriculum* proposals:

> These pages have been overtaken by events, and it is important that neither their content nor their purpose should be misunderstood . . . There is no intention anywhere in the papers which follow of advocating a centrally controlled or dictated curriculum . . . The group of HM Inspectors who wrote these papers felt that the case for a common curriculum, as it is presented here, deserves careful attention and that such a curriculum, worked out in the ways suggested, would help to ameliorate the inconsistencies and irrationalities which at present exist, without entailing any kind of centralized control. (DES, 1977b: 1)

Without wishing to imply that there was only *one* model of 'good practice', the HMI approach recommended the adoption by secondary schools of a number of so-called 'areas of experience', to be used as the basis of curriculum construction or of reshaping and refining existing curricula. In Red Book One (DES, 1977b), eight such areas were recommended:

- the aesthetic and creative
- the ethical
- the linguistic
- the mathematical
- the physical
- the scientific
- the social and political
- the spiritual.

These 'areas of experience' were deliberately listed as above in alphabetical order so that no particular order of importance could be inferred: in the view of the Inspectorate, they were all to be considered equally important. Then, in a later HMI publication, *The Curriculum from 5 to 16*, which appeared in March 1985 (DES, 1985a), the HMI approach was broadened to encompass the primary years and the 1977 checklist was expanded to nine areas of learning and experience. The ethical became the moral; the linguistic became the linguistic and literary; the social and political became the human and social; and the additional area of experience was the technological.

Red Book Three, *Curriculum 11–16: Towards a Statement of Entitlement,* published in 1983 (DES, 1983), provided the Inspectorate with an opportunity to highlight the principles that had governed its view of the curriculum for more than a decade and to lay special emphasis on the concept of 'pupil entitlement':

> It seems essential to us that all pupils should be guaranteed a curriculum of a distinctive breadth and depth to which they should be entitled, irrespective of the type of school they attend or their level of ability or their social circumstances – and that the failure to provide such a curriculum is unacceptable . . . The conviction has grown that all pupils are entitled to a broad compulsory common curriculum to the age of sixteen which introduces them to a range of experiences, makes them aware of the kind of society in which they are going to live and gives them the skills that are necessary to live in it. Any curriculum which fails to provide this balance and is over-weighted in any particular direction, whether vocational, technical or academic, is to be seriously questioned. Any measures which restrict the access of all pupils to a wide-ranging curriculum or which focus too narrowly on specific skills are in direct conflict with the entitlement curriculum envisaged by us. (DES, 1983: 25, 26)

This idea that a unified curriculum appropriate to an age of comprehensive secondary schools should take the form of a broad synthesis of the vocational, the technical and the academic found favour with a growing number of teachers and educationists (see, for example, Holt, 1976; 1978; Chitty, 1979), but carried little weight with the civil servants of the DES who had their own separate agenda.

Unlike the HMI 'common-curriculum' model outlined above, organized around key areas of learning and experience and emphasizing the principle of 'pupil entitlement', the framework promoted by DES bureaucrats in a number of influential documents (see, for example, DES, 1977a; 1980; 1981a) envisaged a curriculum that allowed considerable scope for variation and flexibility but which had as its 'core' a limited number of traditional subjects. This seemed principally suited to conditions prevailing in the secondary school; but, by the end of the 1980s, the concept had been broadened to embrace the primary school as well.

The bureaucratic 'core-curriculum' approach was principally concerned with the 'efficiency' of the state education system and with the need to obtain accurate and precise information to *demonstrate* that efficiency. It was increasingly concerned with the process of *controlling* what was taught in schools, particularly secondary schools, and with making teachers generally more accountable for their work in the class-room. For this reason, testing and assessment were just as important as curriculum content itself. Whereas the professional HMI approach was concerned with individual differences and the nature of the learning process, the bureaucratic approach was associated with norms and benchmarks, with norm-related criteria and judgements based on the expectations of how a 'statistically normal' child should perform. Whereas the professional viewpoint saw the secondary-school curricu-lum as a carefully constructed synthesis of the vocational, the practical and the academic, DES civil servants were anxious to vocationalize the curriculum, particularly for students of 'average' and 'below-average' ability.

For the bureaucrats, there were normally five subjects that had a right to be included in the 'protected' or 'core' element of the secondary curriculum right through to the end of the fifth year (now Year 11): English, mathematics, science, a modern foreign language and religious education. A 1980 DES document, *A Framework for the School Curriculum* (DES, 1980), even went so far as to specify what proportion of the timetable should be spent on each of these core subjects, but this degree of government interference came in for wide criticism. A year later this proposal was withdrawn; and the 1981 document, *The School Curriculum* (DES, 1981a), made it clear that while the Government was still committed to the idea of a compulsory core, precise details concern-ing its implementation should be left to the discretion of local education authorities and teachers:

> English, mathematics, science and modern languages are generally treated as separate items in school timetables . . . It is important that every school should ensure that each pupil's programme includes a substantial and well-distributed time allocation for English, mathematics and science up to the age of sixteen, and that those pupils who do take a modern language should devote sufficient time to it to make the study worthwhile. The two Secretaries of State do not suggest minimum times which should be devoted to these

subjects. Any suggested minima might too easily become norms, or be interpreted too rigidly. It is for the local education authorities to consider, in consultation with the teachers in their areas, whether to suggest minimum time allocations in these subjects, simply as broad guidance for schools. (DES, 1981a: 14)

When *The School Curriculum* was published in 1981, there seemed little prospect of a Thatcher government introducing a fully-fledged national curriculum. Indeed, as late as March 1985, Keith Joseph's DES was still anxious to deny any intention of changing the terms of the ongoing curriculum debate to initiate legislation to control the school curriculum. The White Paper *Better Schools* (published in that month) included a strong reiteration of the traditional statutory position regarding curriculum control:

It would not in the view of the Government be right for the Secretaries of State's policy for the range and pattern of the 5–16 curriculum to amount to the determination of national syllabuses for that period. It would, however, be appropriate for the curricular policy of the LEA, on the basis of broadly agreed principles about range and pattern, to be more precise about, for example, the balance between curricular elements and the age and pace at which pupils are introduced to particular subject areas (e.g. a foreign language) . . . The establishment of broadly agreed objectives would not mean that the curricular policies of the Secretaries of State, the LEA and the school should relate to each other in a nationally uniform way . . . The Government does not propose to introduce legislation affecting the powers of the Secretaries of State in relation to the curriculum. (DES, 1985b: 11–12)

In the light of these unequivocal statements, it is surely fair to point out that the curriculum clauses in the legislation of 1988 represented a severe rupture in government policy.

The National Curriculum and its aftermath

Arrangements for a national curriculum and its assessment took up the first 25 sections of the 1988 Education Reform Act. This was clearly an innovation of unprecedented significance, and one might have expected it to have the full backing of the political establishment. Yet, as we saw in Chapters 3 and 6, the very idea of a centrally imposed curriculum was the subject of bitter argument between various sections of the New Right; and there were many among Mrs Thatcher's closest advisers and supporters who felt that such a rigid programme of study should have no place in a market system of state schools.

The broad concept of a subject-based national curriculum had the strong support of Kenneth Baker, who had replaced Sir Keith Joseph as Education Secretary in May 1986, and of the newly-formed Hillgate Group of right-wing political philosophers and activists (comprising Caroline Cox, Jessica Douglas-Home, John Marks, Lawrence Norcross and Roger Scruton), which saw it primarily as a useful form of 'social control' and as a means of ensuring greater teacher accountability. In the view of the Hillgate collective, a national curriculum should uphold the values of traditional subjects and instil respect for all the institutions of a bourgeois state. At the same time, it should accept the realities of life in a capitalist society and preach the moral virtue of free enterprise and the pursuit of profit (Hillgate Group, 1986; 1987).

Mrs Thatcher herself was among those who thought that anything more ambitious than a strictly limited 'core' curriculum was frankly incompatible with the provision of greater variety and choice in state education, and she made several attempts in 1987 to defeat her Secretary of State's proposals. In his 1993 autobiography, *The Turbulent Years: My Life in Politics,* Kenneth Baker made the surprising revelation that as late as October 1987 – just *three* weeks before the introduction of the Education Reform Bill into the House of Commons – he had felt obliged to use the threat of his own resignation to prevent his broad-based curriculum being radically amended by the Prime Minister:

> I saw the Prime Minister privately. I said to her: 'if you want me to continue as your Education Secretary, then we will have to stick to the Curriculum that I set out in the July Consultation Paper. I and my ministerial colleagues have advocated and stoutly defended the broad curriculum. We have listed the ten subjects, and I set them out before the Select Committee in April. You will recall, Prime Minister, that I specifically cleared my statement with you' . . . This was a tough meeting, but I was simply not prepared to give in to a last-minute rearguard action, even when waged by the Prime Minister herself. The broad-based curriculum was saved – for the time being. (Baker, 1993: 197)

Kenneth Baker got his own way on this occasion, but the Prime Minister continued to throw her weight behind the undermining tactics of the neo-Liberal wing of the New Right.

Section 3 of the 1988 Act listed the 'core' and 'foundation' subjects that were to constitute the new National Curriculum for England and Wales:

The 'core' subjects were to be:

(a) mathematics, English and science; and
(b) in relation to schools in Wales which were Welsh-speaking schools, Welsh.

The 'foundation' subjects were to be:

(a) history, geography, technology, music, art and physical education;
(b) in relation to the third and fourth key stages, a modern foreign language; and
(c) in relation to schools in Wales which were not Welsh-speaking schools, Welsh.

In addition, a further subject, religious education (the only compulsory school subject between 1944 and 1988, but overlooked in the original draft proposals), was to continue to be compulsory for all pupils as the one and only *basic* subject. It was anticipated that the majority of curriculum time at primary-school level in England would be spent on the three subjects making up the 'core' of the curriculum. Themes such as health education and information technology would have to be taught through foundation subjects.

According to Section 14 of the Act, three bodies were to be established to keep under review all aspects of the new curriculum and all aspects of examinations and assessment: the National Curriculum Council, the Curriculum Council for Wales and the School Examinations and Assessment Council. As part of the elaborate machinery deemed necessary for implementing the Government's plans, subject working groups, appointed by the Secretary of State, were to devise the programmes of study and attainment targets for each subject; and pupils were to be set Standard Assessment Tasks (SATs) in four key stages at 7, 11, 14 and 16. The ten levels of performance drawn up by the Task Group on Assessment and Testing (TGAT, 1987) were intended to cover the range of progress by individual children; and although the Group had deliberately given as much weight to *teacher* assessment as to any tests, these teacher assessments were soon to have very little significance. In the years following the 1988 Act, primary and secondary schools were subjected to an avalanche of curriculum documentation, guidance, regulations and circulars, so that teacher frustration grew and 'death by a thousand ring-binders', as one headteacher described it (quoted in Graham and Tytler, 1993: 102), became an accepted fact of life. Although it seems clear that the vast majority of classroom teachers worked hard to implement the new curriculum and its assessment, they soon came to realize that it was *schools* and *teachers* who were being assessed, and that schools with large numbers of pupils with learning difficulties would be in danger of occupying a low position on the published league tables of performance and of thereby forfeiting public esteem.

Some have argued (see, for example, Tomlinson, 2001: 56) that the National Curriculum had an unfortunate title at a time when 'globalization' and 'internationalism' were becoming 'key words' in the economy. There are also two particular respects in which the very term 'national' can be called into question: those of geography and social class. It was not intended in 1988 that the National Curriculum should be applied to Scotland or to Northern Ireland. At the same time, it was not intended that the new programmes of study and testing arrangements should be applied to the independent sector, although Kenneth Baker apparently believed that large numbers of independent schools would wish to follow the line required of LEA maintained and grant-maintained schools. Historian Richard Aldrich has asked some pertinent questions about the likely assumptions underpinning the Thatcher Government's policy towards independent foundations:

> What concept of a national curriculum and of a national education, indeed what concept of a *nation,* underlies this legislation? Is it that teachers in independent schools can be trusted to provide a balanced curriculum and appropriate standards of education, whilst teachers in state schools cannot? Is it that pupils in independent schools can be trusted to make the right choice of subjects and to work hard, whilst those in state schools cannot? . . . Is the real purpose of this legislation to promote a widening of those curricular and broader educational differences which have been such a recurring feature of education in this country since the nineteenth century? Are independent schools to be above the law? Apparently so, for we learn from the DES that the Government believe it would not be right to impose the national curriculum on independent foundations. (Aldrich, 1988: 29)

Professor Aldrich has also pointed out that one of the most striking features of the 1988 National Curriculum lies in its close resemblance to the list of subjects prescribed in the Regulations of 1904. State secondary schools were established by the 1902 Education Act, and two years later the Board of Education issued Regulations which prescribed the syllabus for pupils up to the age of 16 or 17 educated in such schools: 'The Course should provide for instruction in the English Language and Literature, at least one language other than English, geography, history, mathematics, science and drawing, with due provision for manual work and physical exercises, and, in a girls' school, for housewifery' (Gordon and Lawton, 1978: 22–3).

It is certainly instructive to compare the course of study prescribed in 1904 with the list of compulsory subjects in the 1988 National Curriculum, and this is shown in Table 7.1.

We can, of course, detect a few minor differences: the term '*modern foreign language*' in the 1988 list excluded Latin, which had featured prominently in the secondary-school curriculum of 1904; 'manual work/housewifery' from the 1904 Regulations became 'technology' in 1988; and music, which appeared in the 1988 list, had not been a compulsory subject at the beginning of the century. Nevertheless, despite these slight modifications, there is still much truth in Professor Aldrich's assertion that the 1988 National Curriculum, in so far as it was expressed in terms of 'core' and 'foundation' subjects, appeared as 'a simple reassertion of the basic grammar-school curriculum devised at the very beginning of the twentieth century' (Aldrich, 1988: 23). And it does seem rather extraordinary that this academic grammar-school curriculum was now to be extended to all state primary and comprehensive secondary schools in England and Wales.

The National Curriculum came in for heavy criticism on account of its almost exclusive reliance on traditional subject disciplines. This DES model was considered particularly ill-suited to the style of learning in the primary school. In a speech delivered to a conference, organized by the campaigning journal *Forum* and held in London in March 1988, Michael Armstrong, headteacher of a primary school in Oxfordshire, argued that primary teachers' philosophical objection to a subject-based

Table 7.1   A comparison of curricula, 1904 and 1988

1904	*1988*
English	English
Mathematics	Mathematics
Science	Science
History	History
Geography	Geography
Foreign Language	*Modern* Foreign Language
Drawing	Art
Physical Exercise	Physical Education
Manual Work/Housewifery	Technology
	Music

curriculum was not simply a matter of the need to find room for the ubiquitous primary-school 'topic':

> It is rather that most of the really fruitful classroom inquiries, whether on the part of an individual child, a small group of children, or an entire class, have a way of moving in and out of subjects, conflating traditions, confusing boundaries, eliminating distinctions and creating new ones. So a study of the life of a frog becomes an exercise in philosophical speculation, scientific observation, literary fantasy and artistic method. So designing a set of earrings turns into an investigation of the psychology of faces. So an examination of mathematical powers embraces the geography of the universe and the mythical origins of the game of chess . . . In learning . . . all the significant insights tend to come to those, teachers and pupils alike, who refuse to be bounded by subjects, who are prepared to move freely *between* traditions and *beyond* traditions – from science to philosophy to art to some new field of enquiry – without embarrassment. For every significant curriculum rewrites to some degree the history of knowledge. (Armstrong, 1988: 75)

For others, the whole National Curriculum framework lacked any sound philosophical underpinnings; and its shortcomings resulted from the failure of Mrs Thatcher's education ministers to treat the process of curriculum construction with the seriousness and sense of purpose it surely deserved. Delivering the Raymond Priestley Lecture at the University of Birmingham on 14 November 1991, Peter Watkins, the former Deputy Chief Executive of the National Curriculum Council, identified what he saw as the fundamental weakness of the Government's curriculum project:

> There is . . . one fundamental problem from which all others stem. The National Curriculum had no architect, only builders. Many people were surprised at the lack of sophistication in the original model: ten subjects, attainment targets and programmes of study defined in a few words in the 1987 Bill and 1988 Act, that was all. (Watkins, 1993: 73)

What the Government did *not* anticipate in 1988 was that each of the subject working groups would attempt to include everything that it considered important and relevant in its own particular curriculum. Neither the subject groups nor the ministers to whom they were responsible took very much account of whether or not all the various syllabuses, when added together, constituted a workable or coherent whole. Over the next five years, it became increasingly obvious to both civil servants and headteachers that the school curriculum was seriously overloaded at all levels, leading to low teacher morale and unprecedented levels of stress and illness.

At the same time, the Government faced a very real problem in trying to secure *professional* support for the structure and implementation of the testing programme. In his exhausting battles with the Prime Minister and her allies on the neo-liberal wing of the New Right, Kenneth Baker defended his broad-based Curriculum on the grounds that it would justify a massive programme of national testing at 7, 11, 14 and 16. In this respect, according to Baker's line of reasoning, a centrally-imposed curriculum was *not* incompatible with the principles of the free market. Standardized tests would yield results that could be published in the form of simple league tables, thereby providing parents with crucial evidence as to the desirability or otherwise of individual schools. Yet this was not, of course, the line that could be adopted with schools and teachers where it was necessary to stress that the chief purpose of the new testing programme was to monitor and enhance pupil progress and achievement. As things turned out, the TGAT proposals referred to earlier in this chapter proved an uneasy and ultimately ineffectual compromise between the various purposes of pupil assessment: talking the language of 'formative assessment' and 'professional expertise', but also making it possible for published results to be used in the interests of accountability, control and the intensification of market competition between schools. The TGAT Report certainly failed to find favour with the Prime Minister who liked the idea of batteries of standardized, 'pencil-and-paper', 'objective' tests for each subject and could see no reason why teachers had to be involved in the new assessment process.

By the spring of 1993, and with Education Secretary John Patten finding it very difficult to earn the respect of the teaching profession, the testing programme was in danger of being sabotaged by opponents. Speaking at a seminar organized by the Centre for Policy Studies and held in London in March, the right-wing historian, Robert Skidelsky, argued that the TGAT tests *deserved* to fail since they were essentially 'a fudge between the professional educator's doctrine that testing should diagnose individual strengths and weaknesses and the Government's wish to evaluate the effectiveness of teaching and schools' (reported in *The Guardian*, 18 March 1993). Then teacher disquiet concerning the nature of the English and technology tests for 14-year-olds developed very quickly into a decision by the three biggest teaching unions – the National Union of Teachers, the National Association of Schoolmasters/Union of Women Teachers (NASUWT) and the Association of Teachers and Lecturers – to ballot their members on staging a boycott of *all* National Curriculum tests. There was, admittedly, less unanimity of view than appeared on the surface: the NASUWT under the leadership of Nigel de Gruchy was largely concerned with the issue of *workload*; while the NUT maintained that it was opposed to Standard Assessment Tasks because they entailed 'an excessive teacher workload' and to simple 'pencil-and-paper' tests because they were 'educationally unsound'.

In desperation, the Major Government asked Sir Ron Dearing, a former Head of the Post Office and Chairperson-designate of the new SCAA (School Curriculum and Assessment Authority), to carry out a full-scale review of the National Curriculum and its assessment. Much of his time was spent on the unwieldy structure of Key Stage Four, and this will be dealt with in the next Chapter. Among the main proposals in the Final Report (SCAA, 1993), the detailed prescription of the content of lessons was to be reduced to allow more scope for professional judgement. The National Curriculum at Key Stage Three would be cut back to no more than 80 per cent of taught time, leaving the equivalent of at least a day a week for schools to use at their own discretion. At the same time, the old ten-level scale of knowledge and ability, covering all youngsters from ages of 5–16, would be replaced by an eight-level scale for 5–14-year-olds, with GCSEs (and, where appropriate, other qualifications) used to assess students at the end of the compulsory period of schooling. In accepting the recommendations in the Final Report, Education Secretary Gillian Shephard emphasized in November 1994 that this was to be 'the final peace offering to the teachers' (reported in *The Guardian,* 11 November 1994).

Curriculum developments since 1997

The process of simplifying and, in places, dismantling the National Curriculum has continued under New Labour. It was made clear as early as the summer of 1997 (see DfEE, 1997) that government education policy, at least during its first term in office, would concentrate on raising standards in the primary school, and that this would involve laying particular emphasis on securing improvements in literacy and numeracy. Where possible and appropriate, primary schools should consider reintroducing setting to facilitate accurately pitched 'whole-class' teaching and allow pupils of 'high ability' to proceed at a faster rate.

In January 1998, the Government announced that pupils under the age of 11 would no longer be required to follow the detailed national syllabuses in history, geography, design and technology, art, music and physical education. Primary schools that participated in one of the new

Education Action Zones would also be granted powers to modify or abandon parts of the National Curriculum.

All this caused unease even among those appointed to monitor progress in primary schools. Speaking on the BBC Radio Four programme *The World Tonight* on 16 May 2002, Mike Tomlinson, the former Chief Inspector of Schools, conceded that the National Curriculum in primary schools was being steadily 'whittled away' to facilitate concentration on issues of literacy and numeracy. He expressed concern that the Literacy Hour and the Numeracy Hour, with their accompanying national tests, represented a genuine threat to the provision of a broad and balanced primary curriculum. There was a real danger that the emphasis on core skills amounted, in Mr Tomlinson's phrase, to 'a silent revolution', whereby little time was now available for such important subjects as history, geography, art and music. Moreover, it would be most unfortunate if this dire situation were now to extend upwards to embrace curriculum provision for older pupils.

Meanwhile, the Government's testing programme, with the associated publication of results, continued to lack the support of the majority of primary-school teachers. A survey carried out for *The Times Educational Supplement* in the spring of 2002 found that 80 per cent of the teachers questioned wanted to see an end to the tests for all 7-year-olds. More than half wanted the Key Stage Two tests to be dropped as well. The poll also revealed widespread pessimism about achieving the Government's new targets for 11-year-olds whereby 85 per cent of pupils would be expected to achieve at least Level Four in maths and English by the year 2004. It looked as though England was in danger of ploughing a lonely furrow where testing was concerned. Wales was in the process of abolishing Key Stage One tests, while Northern Ireland was proposing to replace key stage assessments with annual reports. Scotland had already decided to test pupils when they were ready and had no league tables. According to John Bangs, Assistant Secretary of the National Union of Teachers: 'It is crystal clear from the findings of the *TES* [*Times Educational Supplement*] poll that the Key Stage One Test in England is simply duplicating teacher assessment and is a thundering waste of time. They can get rid of it in Scotland, Wales and Northern Ireland; so who is beginning to look like the isolated country?' (reported in *The Times Educational Supplement,* 19 April 2002).

Figures released on 26 September 2002 showed that the Government had, in fact, already failed to meet its original literacy and numeracy targets for 11-year-olds. As we saw in Chapter 4, the 1997 White Paper *Excellence in Schools* announced that there would be challenging national targets for the performance of 11-year-olds in English and maths. By the year 2002, the targets set were that 80 per cent would be reaching the standard expected for their age in English and 75 per cent the standard expected in maths. (The 'standard expected' referred to National Curriculum Level Four.) The figures released in September showed that 75 per cent had reached the standard expected in English and 73 per cent the standard expected in maths. On the day the new figures were released a government spokesperson said: 'These are our best set of results yet. Teachers and schools should be rightly proud of this historic achievement. However, we are not complacent, and we will be targetting those authorities and schools that continue to under-perform with extra support' (reported in *The Times Educational Supplement,* 27 September 2002). As we have already seen, the Government's failure to meet its well-publicized targets was to be put forward in the media as one of the reasons for Estelle Morris's unexpected resignation on 23 October.

An Ofsted report published on 26 November claimed that more than 200,000 7-year-olds were not able to read properly because the Government's literacy strategy had left many teachers 'confused' about how to teach reading. Speaking at the publication of the Report, Chief Inspector David Bell called for 'a critical review' of the national strategy for teaching reading and writing after test results in English for 11-year-olds had remained static at 75 per cent for three years. At the heart of the problem, according to Mr Bell, lay the strategy's 'ambiguous guidance' on phonics, a controversial teaching method where children learn how the sounds of words are written instead of trying to memorize their shape. It was Mr Bell's contention that although teachers had dropped their 'ideological objection' to phonics, many of them were not giving enough emphasis to the systemic teaching of phonics at the earliest stages of learning to read, and they still did not understand its importance for pupils aged 8 and 9. The Chief Inspector argued that these were 'urgent issues' which demanded 'better and more challenging teaching across the board' (reported in *The Daily Telegraph,* 27 November 2002).

In May 2003, there was a clear indication that the Government was aware of the widespread hostility towards the regime of targets at the primary level. Launching an 80-page document on primary education called *Excellence and Enjoyment: A Strategy for Primary Schools* (DfES, 2003c) on 20 May, Charles Clarke accepted that there was a need for greater flexibility and more teacher autonomy, but insisted that the new policy was *not* the first step towards dismantling the whole system of targets in the primary school. It was no longer essential for 85 per cent of pupils to achieve at least Level Four in maths and English by the year 2004, but the Government would like to retain the aspiration, and work towards 2006 as the new target date. Tests for all 7-year-olds would be downgraded to form only a minor part of an overall 'teacher judgement' about children's progress throughout the year. League tables of test results at 11 could also be modified to include judgements from Ofsted inspectors about the overall quality of education at individual schools.

The 2003 Primary Strategy generally met with a positive response from primary school headteachers; but some commentators pointed out that it was somewhat typical of the 'mixed messages' being delivered to primary schools about the future direction of government policy. For example: Professor Maurice Galton has noted that even the title of the 2003 Document was ambivalent, with the term 'Excellence' emphasizing the Government's success in raising standards in primary schools and the second half of the title appearing to recognize that there was 'an attitude problem' for both teachers and pupils. In Galton's view, there was little point in issuing a revised version of the Primary Strategy to take account of the need for greater pupil motivation and enjoyment unless this could be accompanied by a genuine reappraisal of the continuing emphasis on accountability and testing (Galton, 2007: 173). Professor Robin Alexander has been even more outspoken about the 2003 Revised Stragegy. In a paper published in 2004, he argued that the Strategy was 'ambiguous to a point of dishonesty about the Government's intentions towards primary education'. He further contended that, despite the rhetoric of 'enjoyment' and 'enrichment', the Strategy continued to foster 'a crude instrumentalism of purpose' that had characterized New Labour's time in office since 1997. Charles Clarke might talk about the need for 'greater flexibility' and 'more teacher autonomy', but the central dilemma of how teachers could take advantage of this 'flexibility' and 'autonomy' in a regime of targets and performance tables was left unresolved (Alexander, 2004: 28). Both Alexander and Galton have also accused Ofsted of sending out conflicting messages in its willingness to follow the government line on standards and accountability. In his 2003 Annual Report, Chief Inspector David Bell had argued that pressure on primary schools to improve literacy and numeracy was producing a two-tier curriculum, while, at the same time, he had seen fit to add to that pressure by expressing concern that the test scores at Key Stage Two were now at a standstill (Ofsted, 2004).

Reviewing the evidence concerning performance and progress in the primary school over the ten-year period of New Labour's tenure in government between 1997 and 2007, Professor Galton concluded in a paper published in 2007 that policies had been less successful in raising overall standards than the Government and its spokespersons often suggested. Gains, if any, had been limited to the first few years; and it seemed clear that, by the end of 2001, the upward trend in scores on the National Curriculum tests in English and mathematics at Key Stage Two had already begun to reach a plateau and that this trend had continued until at least 2005. There had been a serious deterioration in pupils' attitudes to school in general and to subjects such as English, mathematics and science in particular. Motivation appeared to have changed in ways that meant pupils felt no incentive to take up new challenges or to express themselves creatively. Teachers were arguing that they now worked excessive hours in an attempt to deliver a broad curriculum and attributed their feelings of stress to the fact that the Government no longer seemed to trust their judgements in curricular matters. Most seriously of all, in Galton's words, 'primary classroom practice now seemed more akin to stereotyped secondary school lessons, dominated by a fast pace, with restricted questioning and a tendency for teachers to control the discourse such that transmission rather than exploration dominated' (Galton, 2007: 173).

At a time when many educationists were preparing to celebrate the 40th anniversary of the publication of the 1967 Plowden Report (discussed in Chapter 3), a new enquiry was launched – the 2006–8 Review of Primary Education in England (usually shortened to the Primary Review) – to investigate the condition and future of primary education in England. Supported by the Esmée Fairbairn Foundation, based at Cambridge University's Faculty of Education and led by Professor Robin Alexander, the Review aimed to construct 'an accurate and illuminating account of the strengths and weaknesses of contemporary English primary education' and, upon that basis, to formulate a vision for the future which would lift educational horizons 'far above the need to comply with current government initiatives' (see Alexander, 2007a: 198).

At the time of writing, the academics responsible for carrying out the Primary Review have published 23 interim reports (available at http://www.primaryreview.org.uk). All have been measured, well-informed and convincing accounts of the effects of government education policy over the past ten years. They suggest that the Government's micro-management of primary classrooms and its attempt to determine the precise scope and content of the primary curriculum have had a devastating effect on schools. Teachers have lost much of their autonomy and discretion and are frequently obliged to follow pre-prescribed lesson plans laid down by Whitehall, rather than being free to engage creatively with the children in front of them. So-called 'high-achieving' pupils are invariably bored and frustrated, while the introduction of SATs has made the 'low-achieving' ones considerably more anxious and more afraid of being exposed as 'failures'. There has been a marked decrease in the overall quality of primary education because of the narrowing of the curriculum and the intensity of test preparation. Many children across the whole spectrum of 'ability' appear to be 'in flight' from an experience of learning that they find 'unsatisfactory, unmotivating and uncomfortable'. Inevitably, the authors of these reports raise a number of important questions: about whether the billion-pound Literacy, Numeracy and Primary Strategies and the elaborate apparatus of key stage tests have actually given value for money; about the reliability of the test evidence on which claims about 'national standards' and 'world class performance' are based; about the imbalance of summative and formative assessment – which may militate against further improvement – and about the extreme narrowness of the received definition of 'standards' (see Alexander, 2007b; Russell, 2008).

Not surprisingly, all this has not made comfortable reading for ministers; and each report has been routinely dismissed as containing material that is 'recycled', 'partial' or simply 'out-of-date'. In particular, the evidence-based conclusion that 'high-stakes testing' does not *of itself* 'drive up standards' constitutes a direct challenge to official thinking and has been vigorously challenged by the DCSF. Yet, whatever the Government may claim in defence of its policies, it is interesting to note that the reports' findings about the distorting effects of national SATs tests have recently been endorsed by the House of Commons Children, Schools and Families Select Committee which has argued that too many primary-school children are being fed 'a limited educational diet focused on getting them through the tests rather than improving their knowledge and understanding' (reported in *The Guardian*, 13 May 2008). It remains to be seen how the Government will respond to the Final Report of the Primary Review when it is published at the end of 2008.

The curriculum at Key Stage Three attracted comparatively little attention from ministers during the period of the Blair Government, although Education Secretary Estelle Morris did make a half-hearted attempt at intervention in 2002. Addressing teachers and educationists at an event in London hosted by the think-tank Demos on 21 March 2002, Ms Morris outlined her determination to tackle the quality of the learning experience for students aged 11–14 which she described as 'one of the long-neglected and toughest challenges facing schools' (Morris, 2002a: 3). It was a cause of some concern to the Education Secretary that, while large numbers of children were leaving their primary school with 'a great sense of confidence, excitement and anticipation', there was far too often 'a fall off in their attitude to learning' in the first year at secondary school. In her words:

> The majority of 11-year-olds arrive in their new school proud of their achievements at primary level and keen to build on those and play more of an active role in their own learning, with an appetite to learn new skills and extend their horizons. . . Yet in the past, we have too often failed to capitalize on that enthusiasm and not done enough to fire their imagination and stretch their ambitions. Most secondary schools have tended to focus their efforts on later examination classes; and teaching in the middle years has sometimes lacked pace and focus. (Morris, 2002a: 4–5)

In Ms Morris's view, the secondary school system was too uniform in structure and too inflexible in its approach to change. The answer was to provide a greater variety of schools and to lay a stronger emphasis on raising the expectations of all pupils through stretching 'the more able' and providing additional help for those who were 'struggling'. Building a more secure platform of achievement, motivation and engagement with learning by the end of Key Stage Three would then provide schools with the springboard needed for 'the greater choice and range of opportunities envisaged for 14–19-year-olds'. Among the measures designed to raise standards, national test results for 14-year-olds were to be published in the autumn of 2002 for the first time.

More recently, on 12 July 2007, the Government has revealed details of a new plan for the curriculum for 11- to 14-year-olds in England, to be introduced from September 2008, which is designed to 'free-up' 25 per cent of the school timetable. This 'slimmed-down' curriculum has been devised to liberate more time to help pupils either 'catch up on the basics' or 'play to their strengths'. The changes, in line with the Government's 'personalized learning agenda', reflect current anxieties both about the continuing 'tail of underachievement' in schools and about the growing number of children who are not being 'pushed hard enough, early enough'. Speaking at the launch of the new curriculum at Lord's Cricket Ground in London, Schools Minister Lord Adonis said: 'there will be a reduction in prescription from the Centre and a modernization of the Key Stage Three Curriculum to make it more relevant to the needs of young people in this world in the future'. He went on to argue that teachers would be encouraged to use the new time at their disposal either to arrange 'extra catch-up lessons in the three Rs for those pupils who were struggling in English and maths' or to devise 'exciting new lessons to stretch the more able pupils' (reported in *The Independent*, 13 July 2007). According to Ken Boston, Chief Executive of the Qualifications and Curriculum Authority (QCA), teachers would now have greater freedom to break free from the traditional subject-based National Curriculum and introduce topics to prepare youngsters of all abilities for adult life. These would range from lessons on Britain's place in the global economy to lessons on individual economic and general well-being – which could include such topics as how to avoid debt and buy a house, how to show respect for other cultures and how to develop healthy eating habits. In the words of Ken Boston: 'the development of such a customized or child-centred approach to teaching and learning is not some new-age obsession with making students feel good, or any rejection of the importance of formal teaching, or indeed a drift away from a discipline-based curriculum. . . It means implementing the internationally proven research-based strategy for improving learning and raising attainment at 'individual, school and national level' (quoted in *The Guardian*, 13 July 2007).

8

The 14–19 Continuum: Issues and Policies for Education and Training

In an article published in 1992 (Chitty, 1992), I argued that, on the face of it, the 1988 Education Reform Act, and particularly the clauses relating to the National Curriculum, appeared to represent a 'defeat' for the thinking of two major groups: Her Majesty's Inspectorate and a powerful faction within the Conservative Party of the 1980s often referred to as either the 'Industrial Trainers' or the 'Conservative Modernizers'. As we saw in the last chapter, the HMI model of a common 'entitlement' curriculum was based on the idea of eight or nine 'areas of learning and experience'; the curriculum programme for older students put forward by the so-called Modernizers (referred to briefly in Chapter 3) emphasized the concept of a 14–19 continuum or framework, with the status of vocational education and training radically enhanced. It has to be conceded that there were few among the decision-making class of the early 1990s who wished to resurrect the HMI model of curriculum planning; but the views of the Modernizers were not to be dismissed so lightly, and even in 1992 it was already becoming clear to many teachers that Key Stage Four of the National Curriculum would be heavily overloaded and that it could not be implemented in the form envisaged by Kenneth Baker and the civil servants of the DES. As we shall see later in this chapter, the idea of a 14–19 curriculum embracing both 'academic' and 'vocational' pathways steadily gained ground as the 1990s progressed and was to find expression in major modifications to the statutory Curriculum proposed by Sir Ron Dearing.

Before we look in some detail at the impact of the National Curriculum framework on the HMI model of curriculum planning for older students and on the concept of a 14–19 continuum, it is important to say something about changing attitudes towards provision for those above the age of 14 in the period from 1944 to 1988.

Before the raising of the school-leaving age

In the years before the raising of the school-leaving age (ROSLA) to 16 in 1972–3, it was possible for students to leave school without embarking on a fifth year of secondary schooling. (This would be a fourth year in Scotland, where secondary schooling began at the age of 12.) Indeed, large numbers of youngsters with the 'appropriate' dates of birth were able to leave school after completing only *two* terms in the fourth year, the situation being that if students were 15 by 2 February in the relevant year, they could leave school at the end of the spring term; whereas, if they were 15 *after* 2 February, they had to stay on until the end of the summer term and complete four full years of secondary schooling. In the case of Leicestershire, with its two-tier system of secondary schools, students could not even move from the high school to the upper school at the age of 14 unless they were prepared to commit themselves formally to at least two more years of full-time schooling. Moreover, there was early evidence that such a two-tier scheme, though regarded as 'acceptable' for 'a transitional period' by Circular 10/65, tended, in fact, to discriminate against the children of working-class parents who were less likely than were their middle-class counterparts to make the important life-enhancing transition from the high school to the upper school. It is significant that in Leicestershire, the 1964 staying-on (transfer) rate was 85 per cent in middle-class Oadby and only 39 per cent in the old industrial town of Hinckley (see Eggleston, 1965: 17). In 1966, the Leicestershire Education Committee reached the important decision that when the school-leaving age was eventually raised to 16, all students would automatically transfer from the high school to the upper school at the age of 14 (see Elliott, 1970).

A survey of British comprehensive schools carried out by Caroline Benn and Brian Simon at the end of the 1960s (see Benn and Simon, 1970; 1972) found that the overall staying-on rate in the participating schools (including those in Scotland) was 51 per cent, which meant that, in the typical comprehensive school of the period, just under half the students left school shortly after reaching the age of 15 (1970: 166).

In the early days of the comprehensive school reform – and regardless of how many youngsters stayed on for a full five years of secondary schooling – very few schools offered a common curriculum to all their students in all five years; and to do so in the upper school (which would now constitute Key Stage Four) was thought by most teachers and educationists to be neither practicable nor desirable. The fourth year (age 14 to 15) was the key point at which, according to Benn and Simon

(1970: 166–7): 'the differentiation of young people, already under way in some schools through such techniques as streaming and setting, becomes actual and recognised in terms of differences in courses and direction'.

Many of the early champions of the comprehensive school argued in favour of really large secondary schools on the grounds that they could offer a vast array of courses and options to their 14-year-old students. In his influential Pelican Original, *The Comprehensive School*, first published in 1963, Robin Pedley (who had created the two-tier Leicestershire Plan) cited with evident approval the diversity of subjects and courses available to fourth-year (Year 10) students at a large mixed comprehensive school in South London, with its 18 forms ranging from 4S and 4K for the scientists, down through 4N for the engineers and 4R with the emphasis on catering, to 4X for the Christmas leavers and 4Y for the Easter leavers. 'Such provision', argued Pedley (1963: 90) 'exceeds in diversity anything a normal grammar or "modern" school can offer.'

The 1966 ILEA survey of London comprehensive schools (published in 1967) came to the conclusion that 'a great deal of care is taken in most schools to ensure that the courses and variety of subjects on offer in the fourth and fifth years will, within the resources of the school, meet the needs of *all* the pupils and give each one the choice his [sic] interests and abilities require'. It was further claimed that many London schools could offer such a wide variety of courses and such a large number of possible combinations of subjects that 'no two pupils need necessarily be following the same timetable' (ILEA, 1967: 65).

A complicating factor in all these upper-school option arrangements was the co-existence of two parallel school examinations: the Ordinary Level GCE, which had been introduced in 1951, and the CSE (Certificate of Secondary Education), for which candidates were entered for the first time in 1965. Despite official recognition of a Grade One pass at CSE being equivalent to a GCE pass, the two examinations did not enjoy equal status among parents and employers; and it was not often thought feasible or desirable for GCE and CSE students to be taught together in the same class. Subjects which appeared in option columns on the fourth-year timetable could be offered in some cases only at GCE level and in others only at CSE.

The school-leaving age was finally raised to 16 in 1972–3 during Margaret Thatcher's four-year period as Conservative Education Secretary in the troubled 1970–4 Heath administration. What became known as ROSLA might have encouraged secondary schools to plan a common, unified five-year curriculum for *all* their students, but this did not immediately happen, and many schools simply viewed the change in terms of the problems posed by their 'below average' and potentially recalcitrant students. One-year outward-looking, life-adjustment' courses, of the type recommended for 'non-academic' fourth-year youngsters by the 1963 Newsom Report, were extended to fill the extra year (see Lawton, 1970). As we saw in Chapter 7, it was not until the second half of the decade that politicians and teachers began to talk seriously about a 'common' or 'core' five-year curriculum for *all* secondary-school students.

In the meantime, the first half of the 1970s could accurately be described as a period of missed opportunities. In *Framework for the Curriculum,* the Report of a National Foundation for Educational Research (NFER) study of the third-year curriculum in a number of West Midlands secondary schools carried out in the mid-1970s, Penelope Weston suggested that a common curriculum was sometimes seen as the one desirable goal which 'like virtue, all must be seen to be pursuing, whatever the context and circumstances of the school' (Weston, 1977: 46). But, in reality, as she discovered in the course of her research, the unified approach survived for barely two years; and the third year in most schools was a sort of 'bridge', when the pretence of a common course was finally dropped and preparations were made for the examination-dominated curriculum of the fourth and fifth years. In Weston's view, the raising of the school-leaving age to 16 could indeed have been viewed as a marvellous opportunity to plan a unified five-year curriculum embracing *all* students; instead, it had the adverse effect of turning the third year into a stressful time of decision-making and forward planning for all those very students. The pressure was obviously there for schools to promote differentiation in a number of key areas. In the words of one headteacher quoted in the study: 'the third-year curriculum is inevitably something of a compromise. Conflict between a common curriculum with stable primary groups and increased specialisation with the flexibility required is most acute in the third year' (Weston, 1977: 82).

An HMI survey of secondary education in England, carried out between 1975 and 1978 and published in 1979 (DES, 1979), showed that most comprehensive schools viewed an extension of the common curriculum into the fourth and fifth years as a quite unworkable proposition. Headteachers might talk in terms of promoting a 'core curriculum' for their older students, but this normally consisted of just four subjects (English, mathematics, religious education and physical education, with the addition of careers) and accounted for no more than about two-fifths of each student's timetable. The work in the rest of the timetable would then be organized in one or other of a number of different ways.

Some comprehensive schools ran completely segregated courses or 'bands', each with its own specific examination objectives. Students might be asked to choose a given number of subjects within their particular course or 'band': but the system had obvious in-built inequalities, and for those taking CSEs only or no examinations at all, the choice could often be very restricted and heavily weighted towards the practical and the vocational. Subjects which were limited to particular 'bands' were additional foreign languages (almost always reserved for students in the 'top' band) and the separate sciences. The 'bottom' band would often be following a programme reminiscent of the Newsom-type courses devised by schools for their early leavers in the years prior to the raising of the school-leaving age. A system of 'free choice', on the other hand, enabled students to choose from a wide selection of subjects ostensibly open to all; and a rigid banding structure gave way to more flexible grouping arrangements geared to the different examinations. A third less common possibility – which came closest to the idea of a common curriculum in years 4 and 5 – was the 'required option' system, where students were expected to obtain a 'balanced diet' by choosing at least one subject or course of study from each of the four major disciplines: science, humanities, languages and design.

The Inspectors concluded that the upper-school curriculum often involved a loss of breadth and balance:

> The organisation of options and courses in the fourth and fifth years is almost always complex, and frequently necessitates compromise on the part of both pupils and school. The 'less able' pupils are given, in effect, less real choice than are other pupils. The examination courses they take are sometimes inappropriate, and were not always designed for the levels of ability for which they are now used. The 'more able' pupils may be given opportunities to take additional languages and separate sciences, but may suffer from the loss of practical, aesthetic or humanities subjects and those courses devoted to aspects of personal and social education . . . It seems clear to us that the introduction of options in the fourth and fifth years leads to the abandonment of some important subjects for some pupils and to insufficient breadth in some individual pupils' programmes. (DES, 1979: 37)

It was just this lack of breadth and balance that led the Inspectorate to lay special emphasis on the concept of 'pupil entitlement' in the third of their three Red Books referred to in the last chapter (DES, 1983). There it was argued that 'any measures which restrict the access of all pupils to a wide-ranging curriculum or which focus too narrowly on specific skills are in direct conflict with the entitlement curriculum envisaged by us' (p. 26). For HMI, an 'entitlement' secondary-school curriculum always had to be balanced, coherent and inclusive.

A 14–19 continuum

Then just as secondary schools were becoming accustomed to receiving DES and HMI documents urging the need for whole-school 11–16 curriculum planning, something curious and unexpected happened which altered the whole context of the national curriculum debate.

As we saw in Chapter 3, Sir Keith Joseph, who was Margaret Thatcher's Education Secretary from September 1981 to May 1986, disappointed and shocked his supporters on the Far Right of the Conservative Party by abandoning the campaign for the education voucher and allowing himself to be influenced by a powerful group of politicians and industrialists, the Conservative Modernizers (see Jones, 1989).

This group stressed the idea of a 14–19 continuum or framework and wanted to see technical and vocational subjects assume a more prominent role in the secondary-school curriculum. While recognizing the need for selection, at 14 if not earlier, it had no time for the grammar-school tradition. It was highly critical of what it saw as the 'anti-industrial' values of a 'liberal' education; and it blamed comprehensive schools for maintaining a rigid distinction between 'high-status' academic knowledge and 'low-status' practical training. While accepting that vocational learning was often associated with youngsters of 'below-average' ability, it wanted to see 'able' and 'well-motivated' students pursue technical and practical courses. It presented its curriculum programme for older students as a means not only of serving the needs of industry but, by demolishing the old academic/practical barrier, of 'democratising' knowledge and of enabling students to demonstrate those kinds of achievement which the British education system, imbued with the outdated values of the public schools, had never fostered or recognized.

The group was particularly influential while David (now Lord) Young headed the MSC between 1982 and 1984 (see Benn and Fairley, 1986); and it was in this period that it succeeded in giving the Conservative Government a new set of priorities. Its main achievement in the area of curriculum reform was the TVEI, introduced in the autumn of 1983 in 14 local authorities deemed worthy of launching the programme on a pilot-scheme basis. The Initiative involved the selection of special groups of fourth-year students thought capable of benefiting from a curriculum emphasizing technical and vocational courses, and was therefore seen by some critics as a subtle means of undermining the comprehensive principle. Yet, despite the reservations, within three years, 95 local education authorities were taking part in the MSC programme.

The Modernizers clearly disliked the prestige attached to the academic curriculum offered in public and grammar schools; but it is still important to stress that their approach to educational provision was strictly hierarchical and not in any sense egalitarian. Their vision of the ideal system of education and training was, in fact, neatly summarized by Lord Young in an article published in *The Times* in September 1985:

> My idea is that there will be a world in which 15 per cent of our young go into some form of higher education . . . roughly the same proportion as now. Another 30 to 35 per cent will stay on after the age of 16 doing the TVEI, along with other suitable courses, and then ending up with a mixture of vocational and academic qualifications and skills. The remainder, about half, will simply go on to a two-year YTS (Youth Training Scheme). (*The Times*, 4 September 1985)

As stated at the beginning of this chapter, the curriculum provisions of the 1988 Education Reform Act took no account of the views of either the Inspectorate or the Conservative 'modernizing tendency'. The framework of the National Curriculum meant that the Government was now embracing the idea of a subject-based eleven-year 5–16 curriculum.

As an example of the rejection of the MSC approach, it is interesting to see how the TVEI Scheme fared in plans for the new National Curriculum overseen by Kenneth Baker and his allies within the DES bureaucracy. This Initiative had been awarded many column inches in the DES White Paper *Better Schools,* published in March 1985:

> The TVEI embodies the Government's policy that education should better equip young people for working life. The courses are designed to cater equally for boys and girls across the whole ability range and with technical or vocational aspirations, and to offer in the compulsory years a broad general education with a strong technical element followed, post-sixteen, by increasing vocational specialisation. The course content and teaching methods adopted are intended to develop personal qualities and positive attitudes towards work, as well as a wide range of competence, and more generally to develop a practical approach throughout the curriculum. The projects are innovative and break new ground in many ways, being designed to explore curriculum organization and development, teaching approaches and learning

styles, co-operation between the participating institutions, and enhanced careers guidance supported by work experience, in order to test the feasibility of sustaining a broad vocational commitment in full-time education for fourteen-to-eighteen year olds. (DES, 1985b: 16–17)

By way of contrast, the TVEI Scheme warranted only two brief mentions in the DES Consultation Document, *The National Curriculum 5–16,* published in July 1987:

The Government intends that the new legislation should leave full scope for professional judgment and for schools to organize how the curriculum is delivered in the way best suited to the ages, circumstances, needs and abilities of the children in each classroom. This will, for example, allow curriculum development programmes such as the Technical and Vocational Education Initiative (TVEI) to build on the framework offered by the National Curriculum and to take forward its objectives. (DES, 1987: 11)

Also:

For the final two years of compulsory schooling, the national extension of TVEI will help LEAs in the development and establishment of the National Curriculum, particularly in the areas of science and technology and in enhancing the secondary-school curriculum's relevance to adult and working life. (DES, 1987: 31).

Nowhere in the 1987 Consultation Document was there any mention of the many new subjects, such as hotel and food services, robotics, microelectronics or manufacturing technology, which teachers had been able to introduce – for at least some of their older students – as part of the MSC's TVEI Scheme.

Yet, as things turned out, while the HMI approach to curriculum planning found little favour with the Conservative Government, the ideas of the Modernizers were not to be dismissed so lightly. The National Curriculum was still in its infancy when it became obvious to the education ministers appointed by John Major that Key Stage Four could not be implemented in the form envisaged by the DES in 1987. Indeed, the last two years of compulsory schooling rapidly became the most problematic area of the Government's curriculum and assessment programme. There were practical problems involved in fitting so many subjects and cross-curricular themes into a finite amount of curriculum time. Many teachers complained that it was simply not possible to teach all ten foundation subjects (together with religious education) to students of all abilities, without risking considerable resentment and indiscipline. And as general economic prospects worsened, particularly after the General Election of 1992, there was renewed concern about the lack of qualified workers in Britain and renewed support for some of the underlying assumptions of the New Vocationalism. In other words, the battle for the high policy ground was about to be fought all over again in the changed conditions of the early 1990s.

As we saw in Chapter 7, the Major Government was soon turning to Sir Ron Dearing, a former Head of the Post Office and Chairperson-designate of the new SCAA, to help it out of its difficulties. Sir Ron Dearing believed that Key Stage Four of the National Curriculum was seriously overloaded, and that greater flexibility would allow schools to introduce either new vocational courses or alternative academic options. Interviewed for a 1996 Open University set text, *Generating a National Curriculum* (Chitty, 1996), he admitted that one of his aims in carrying out his 1993 Review was to resurrect, at least in a revised format, the MSC 14–19 agenda of the early 1980s (Dearing, 1995). Indeed, the Final Report of the Review argued that 'it will be a particular challenge to establish how a vocational pathway which maintains a broad educational component might be developed at Key Stage Four over the next few years *as part of a 14 to 19 continuum*' (SCAA, 1993: 47).

Media reports of the Dearing proposals stressed that, in response to teacher anxieties, the National Curriculum for Years 10 and 11 would now occupy students for only about 60 per cent of the normal school week, yet this assumed that the majority of students would choose no more than the *minimum* statutory requirement. As Table 8.1 shows, the National Curriculum at Key Stage Four could still, in fact, take up between 70 and 80 per cent of the school timetable if students opted to follow a double course in science and full courses in technology and a modern foreign language.

The Final Report of the Dearing Review identified *three* broad 'pathways' in post-16 education and training, with clear implications for the curriculum on offer at Key Stage Four:

- the 'craft' or 'occupational', linked to NVQs (National Vocational Qualifications)
- the 'vocational', linked to GNVQs
- the 'academic', leading to 'A' and 'AS' levels.

It recommended that the SCAA be asked to work 'closely and urgently' with the National Council for Vocational Qualifications (NCVQ) to identify whether 'various possibilities' concerning GNVQs for students aged 14–16 could now be developed (SCAA, 1993: 49).

Table 8.1 Two versions of the Dearing proposals at Key Stage Four

	Column 1 Minimum requirement proposal (%)	Column 2 Extended requirement proposal (%)
English	12.5	12.5
Mathematics	12.5	12.5
Science	12.5	20.0
Technology	5.0	10.0
Modern foreign language	5.0	10.0
Physical education	5.0	5.0
Religious education	5.0	5.0
Sex education and careers	2.5	5.0
Totals:	60.0	80.0

Column One would leave 40.0% of the timetable free for other options, Column Two only 20.0%

Source: *SCAA* 1993, p. 52.

In a speech to the Secondary Heads Association's (SHA) Annual Conference held in Bournemouth in March 1994, Sir Ron Dearing took this idea further by announcing that 14-year-old students would soon be able to study for national qualifications in one or other of five vocational areas (report in *The Financial Times*, 21 March 1994):

- manufacturing
- art and design
- health and social care
- leisure and tourism
- business and finance.

In December 1994, the Schools Minister, Eric Forth, announced the names of 118 schools that would be 'piloting' the new two-year GNVQ courses which could be offered as alternatives to GCSE courses from September 1995. The GNVQ Part One would be available at two levels (report in *The Guardian*, 22 December 1994):

- *foundation,* or the equivalent of two GCSEs below Grade C
- *intermediate,* or the equivalent of two GCSEs at Grade C or above.

In the new post-Dearing curriculum framework, a Part One GNVQ course at either *foundation* or *intermediate* level would be expected to take about the same time as *two* GCSE subjects and occupy a maximum of 20 per cent of curriculum time. It was not anticipated in the Dearing Report that any secondary school would be in a position to offer *full* GNVQs at Key Stage Four, because each of these would occupy at least 40 per cent of curriculum time and leave no room for other subject options, even if students opted for only the minimum National Curriculum requirement.

In the light of these interesting developments affecting the post-14 curriculum, and bearing in mind the need for improved progression across the age 16 barrier, it was, in the view of, among others, SHA General Secretary John Dunford (see Dunford, 2002), something of a mistake on the part of the Conservative Government of 1995 to invite Sir Ron Dearing to produce a report on the 16-19 curriculum.

The 2002 Green Paper

The concept of a 14–19 'continuum' received further powerful support in the Green Paper *14–19: Extending Opportunities, Raising Standards* which appeared in February 2002 (DfES, 2002). Indeed, the one clear message emerging from the Consultation Document was that the Blair Government was firmly committed to the idea of the 14–19 age range *as a single phase,* with all students enabled to develop at a pace best suited to their abilities and preferred ways of learning. The Green Paper claimed to present an evolving vision for far greater coherence in the 14–19 phase of education and training in England whereby the age of 16 would lose its traditional status as a major 'break-point' in the lives of young people.

In her foreword to the Document, Education and Skills Secretary Estelle Morris explained that the new Green Paper aimed to meet four challenges:

- to build an education system in which every young person and every parent has confidence
- to ensure that no young person is denied the chance of a decent education
- to reap the skills benefits of an education system that matches the needs of 'the knowledge economy'
- to promote education with 'character', meaning that while academic

achievement is essential, education must also be a basis for citizen-ship and inclusion.

According to Ms Morris, these were the four central challenges that had to be addressed in order to guarantee 'economic prosperity and social justice for all in this new century' (p. 4).

The Green Paper was refreshingly honest about the scale of the problem to be tackled. Only three out of four 16–18-year-olds in England were in full-time education and training at the end of 2000; and although this figure had been steadily rising, it was of serious concern that it remained well below European and OECD averages. In 2001, around 5 per cent of young people did not acquire any GCSE passes at all; and although the proportion of Year 11 students gaining five or more A* to C grades at GCSE had risen dramatically since the early 1990s, it still remained only 50 per cent of the cohort. Perhaps most worryingly of all, only 20 per cent of young people from the lower socio-economic groups went on to some form of higher education, against over 70 per cent from the highest. This dismal statistic was particularly significant given that one of New Labour's much-publicized targets was to increase and broaden participation in higher education so that, by the year 2010, some 50 per cent of young people aged between 18 and 30 would be going on to university, with access widened, in particular, for those whose families had no previous experience of any form of higher education.

In order to increase student motivation and widen participation in higher education, the Government was anxious to continue (and, indeed, *accelerate*) the process of dismantling Key Stage Four, the process begun under successive Conservative Education Secretaries and given the seal of approval in the Final Report of the Dearing Review, published at the end of 1993. The Green Paper argued that the existing framework for Key Stage Four was sometimes seen as 'a barrier to student motivation', rather than as 'a valued entitlement for all' (p. 21). Evidence of this was seen in the extent of disapplication'

Under existing arrangements, schools could 'disapply', for any one student, up to two National Curriculum subjects in order to:

- provide wider opportunities for 'work-related learning'
- allow students making significantly less progress than their peers to consolidate basic learning
- allow students with particular 'strengths' to emphasize a chosen curriculum area.

The monitoring of 'disapplication' procedures in 2000/1 by the QCA showed that around one-third of secondary schools were using the regulations in respect of a total of 5 per cent of students nationally. The most common reason given was the provision of an extended period of work-related learning, followed closely by the consolidation of other learning across the curriculum. The subject most frequently 'disapplied' was a modern foreign language, followed by design and technology, with science being 'disapplied' in just a small number of cases.

Proposals for 'slimming down' the Key Stage Four curriculum meant that it would now comprise: mathematics, English, science and ICT, alongside citizenship, religious education, careers education, sex education, physical education and work-related learning. Modern foreign languages and design and technology would no longer be 'required study' for *all* students; but they would join the arts and the humanities as subjects where, in the words of the Green Paper, there would be 'a new statutory entitlement of access' (p. 20). The Government's decision to make French, German and other modern European languages 'optional' at Key Stage Four would be offset by the introduction of a foreign language into the primary-school curriculum at Key Stage Two. As part of the plan to reduce the Curriculum for older students to a relatively small 'core', reviving memories of the situation that existed back in the 1970s, it was even seriously suggested by DfES civil servants (see the report in *The Times Educational Supplement,* 8 February 2002) that science should also become an 'optional' subject at Key Stage Four; but this rather extraordinary idea was removed from the Government's reform programme shortly before the Green Paper was published. All these new arrangements would not actually take effect until the academic year beginning in September 2004, when, or so it was assumed, existing disapplication procedures would become redundant and simply disappear.

The Government's concern to promote the idea of 'differentiated progress' meant that, henceforth, older students should be able to sit national examinations at times best suited to their individual needs: this point, as we shall see later in the chapter, became the leading item in a number of newspaper accounts of the contents of the Green Paper. In the words of the Consultation Document, young people should be allowed to progress at a pace 'consistent with their ability and potential', provided always that 'broader educational and pastoral needs would not be put at risk' (p. 49). There were a number of forms the new flexibility could take:

- capitalizing on accelerated learning in Key Stage Three and taking GCSE examinations early
- by-passing GCSE examinations in some subjects and beginning AS programmes early
- developing subject knowledge and understanding in greater breadth and in contexts beyond those defined by qualifications.

As part of a move away from the provision of GNVQs at Key Stage Four, the Green Paper extolled the virtues of the new range of GCSEs in vocational subjects. These were to be made available in some secondary schools in September 2002, with the prospect of wider availability from September 2003. The new 'vocational GCSEs' could initially be taken in: Applied Art and Design; Applied Business; Engineering; Health and Social Care; Applied ICT; Leisure and Tourism; Manufacturing; and Applied Science. Each would be a double award, equivalent to two GCSEs. It was expected that new subjects would shortly be added to the list, to be available for teaching from September 2004. It was also suggested that choice and genuine 'parity of esteem' would be better served by no longer attaching labels to signal that GCSEs were either 'general' or 'vocational', and by simply naming them all 'GCSEs' instead.

For similar reasons, it was also suggested that 'vocational' A Levels, the qualifications introduced to replace the GNVQ, could simply be known as 'A Levels'. This would help to end the academic snobbery that had always been attached to the traditional A Level programme. In his address to the Annual Conference of the Secondary Heads Association held in March 2001, reprinted in the educational journal *Forum,* General Secretary John Dunford pointed out that the designation of A Level Law as an 'academic', rather than as a 'vocational', subject was a good example of 'traditional academic snobbery' (Dunford, 2001: 132). And interviewed in *The Observer* in February 2002, just two days before the publication of the Green Paper, Estelle Morris emphasized that plans for new vocational GCSEs and for new vocational A Levels did *not* mean that education was 'getting easier' and was being 'dumbed down'. She went on to attack the academic snobbery that she claimed resided throughout the British educational system:

> There are many people in this country who every time a university launches a degree that has a vocational label, it is accused of 'dumbing down' and lowering standards. If only we viewed medicine, law and accountancy as *vocational* courses, maybe that academic snobbery would end. But, of course, these subjects are always regarded as straight intellectual academic qualifications. (*The Observer,* 10 February 2002)

Partly in an attempt to fend off this sort of criticism, the Green Paper announced plans for the launch of what was dubbed in the national press as a new 'super' A Level. This involved introducing, as soon as practicable, some 'more demanding' questions into the A2 papers which were taken at the end of A Level courses. In this way, the existing A Level papers would allow 'high achievers' to demonstrate a greater depth of knowledge, skill and understanding, without the need for separate examination papers. And with these harder questions incorporated into the A2 papers, it would be possible for some students to gain an A grade 'with distinction', as well as a simple 'A grade'. In order to ensure that A Level standards were maintained over time, the existing A to E grades would continue to be set at their existing levels. The new arrangements would, in the view of the Green Paper, produce a lean and simple A Level structure. They would address the concerns that A Level was 'too easy' for some students of very high ability. Unlike the simple addition of an A* grade, which was the solution adopted at GCSE level, 'able' students would, or so it was confidently hoped, be 'challenged' and 'stimulated' by the opportunity to tackle these harder and more demanding questions.

Yet the introduction of this new A grade 'with distinction' would appear to sideline or marginalize the new Advanced Extension Awards (AEAs) sat by students for the first time in June 2002. Taken separately from the main A Level papers but based on the same body of knowledge, AEA papers were introduced to 'stretch' the most able sixth-form students by requiring greater depth of understanding than A Level itself. Statistics show that one-third of the 7,000 students who sat these AEA papers for the first time were from the private sector (see Henry, 2002: 2). Of the 16 AEA subjects, English, maths and physics had the most entries. Papers in popular subjects such as psychology and sociology were not available; and there were no tests in vocational subjects. Although the AEA cost more than £1 million to develop, its long-term future would appear to be placed in jeopardy by the Green Paper's plans for the development of 'distinction' A Levels.

Finally, the Green Paper put forward proposals for a new Matriculation Diploma, a new overarching award to mark the completion of the 14–19 phase. Based around existing qualifications, it would, in the words of the Paper, 'inspire and motivate all young people to stay in learning beyond the age of sixteen' and 'offer all learners a common, challenging goal' (DfES, 2002: 40). The Diploma would not, of course, be a separate qualification, but would recognize significant levels of achievement in a range of different areas of learning and development. It would offer 'a means of recognising that genuine learning can take

Table 8.2   Main qualifications (three levels)

Higher Award
At least grades ABB at A Level,
plus an AS Level to show breadth, or NVQ Level 4

Advanced Award
2 A Levels and one AS (or equivalent),
or Advanced Modern Apprenticeship Diploma,
or NVQ Level 3 plus technical certificate

Intermediate Award
5 A*–C GCSE (or equivalent),
or Foundation Modern Apprenticeship Diploma

Source: DfES, 2002: 42:

place in a variety of ways – including general and academic programmes, mixed vocational and general study, vocational study at school and college, and achievements in modern apprenticeships in a work-based programme' (p. 41). It was suggested that the Diploma should be available at *three* levels: Intermediate, Advanced and Higher. The Intermediate Award would be at Level 2 (five or more good GCSEs or the equivalent); the Advanced at Level 3 (two A Levels or the equivalent); and the Higher would recognize greater achievement (very good and contrasting A Levels or NVQ Level 4) (see Table 8.2). All of these awards would include a guarantee of achievement in English, mathematics and ICT, and would also probably cover wider skills.

Initial reactions to the 2002 Green Paper

Initial newspaper coverage of the Green Paper tended to concentrate on the Government's concern to meet the needs of the 'able' and the 'gifted'. 'New super A-level aims at star pupils' was the headline of the story in *The Observer* (10 February 2002). *The Times* chose 'Bright pupils to bypass GCSE exams' for its front-page article on 12 February; while *The Guardian* had 'Top A-level pupils to have chance of distinction' for its story on the 11 February and 'Brightest children will be allowed to skip GCSEs' for the article on the day the Green Paper was published.

Considerable alarm greeted the Government's proposal to make foreign languages and design and technology 'optional' at Key Stage Four. Although it was intended that this should *not* take effect until September 2004, there was evidence to suggest that hundreds of secondary schools were prepared to break the law by dropping these subjects as part of the *compulsory* curriculum as soon as possible: for example, the figures from a survey carried out by the Association of Language Learning (ALL), reported in *The Times Educational Supplement* (24 May 2002), showed that nearly 30 per cent of the schools canvassed actually planned to abandon compulsory language lessons for their older students from September 2002. The veteran broadcaster Sir Trevor McDonald, who chaired the Nuffield Languages Inquiry, was reported in the same *TES* article as saying:

> If schools are contemplating making foreign languages optional from September 2002, as all the evidence suggests, then we should all be very concerned. Whichever career path children choose to follow, they are going to need the skills that will make them employable in a world where recruitment is increasingly global and where flexibility and mobility are at a premium.

Others expressed concern that, according to the available evidence, the majority of secondary schools planning to dispense with compulsory language lessons were those situated in deprived inner-city areas, raising fears that learning languages such as French and German to an advanced level could soon become an 'elitist' activity confined to largely middle-class areas. The decision to 'compensate' for all this by offering all primary-school pupils a new 'entitlement' to languages was dismissed by ALL President Terry Lamb as 'a half-hearted fudge', designed simply to 'deflect criticism from the post-14 proposal'.

The decision in the Green Paper to make the GCSE examination a 'staging-post' during the 14–19 phase, rather than, as at present, a publicly-recognized 'finishing-post', was welcomed by a number of teacher unions, including the Association of Teachers and Lecturers, the National Union of Teachers and the Secondary Heads Association; but there were others (see, for example, Chitty, 2000; 2002a; Berliner, 2002) who were arguing that the Government should go further and either abolish the GCSE altogether or, at the very least, end the publication of results. There was a case for saying that the exam was pointless for that growing proportion of young people who were moving on to advanced qualifications and then some form of higher education, and that it actually stood in the way of reaching that desirable goal where 18 was the effective school-leaving age. At the same time, there was convincing evidence (see Gillborn and Youdell, 1999; 2000) that because the performance tables based on GCSE results concentrated on the percentage of 16-year-old students achieving the 'top' A* to C grades, there was enormous pressure on schools to concentrate all their efforts on their 'average' students while neglecting those unfortunate youngsters thought incapable of gaining at least five of those all-important A* to C grades. In other words, schools were finding it necessary to 'ration' their attention and efforts in order to concentrate on those students at the 'borderline' between grades C and D.

Another criticism of the Government's new 14–19 strategy concerned the fading status of GNVQ and NVQ awards. Writing in *Education Guardian* in May 2002, Professor Alison Wolf attacked the Government's decision to more or less abandon GNVQs and place all its faith in vocational GCSEs:

> In the process of promoting the new vocational GCSEs, the Government has effectively destroyed the main strength of the old GNVQ system. For 14- and 15-year-olds who were doing poorly, GNVQs offered a clear progression route post-16, through three levels. Now, all that will be on offer if you do badly in your GCSEs – vocational and otherwise – are yet more GCSEs. So why bother? (Wolf, 2002)

There was also disquiet about the Green Paper's proposed structure for the new Matriculation Diploma. Both the Association of Teachers and Lecturers (ATL) and the SHA argued (see ATL, 2002; Dunford, 2002) that the absence of a 'foundation level' diploma *below* the 'intermediate level' sent out all the wrong signals to those students who were thought to be 'most difficult to motivate'.

The 2003 14–19 discussion document

The consultation on the 2002 Green Paper was one of the most extensive consultation exercises ever mounted by the Education Department. The DfES received almost 2,000 written responses to the document, and a series of informal events involving young students from schools and colleges resulted in the receipt of a further 4,000 individual written responses. During the summer of 2002, representatives of every secondary school and of every Further Education (FE) sector college in England, as well as a wide range of other interested parties, were invited to one or other of 58 regional 14–19 workshops where all the main themes of the Green Paper were discussed. The result of all this frenetic activity was the publication in January 2003 of a new discussion document, *14–19: Opportunity and Excellence* (DfES, 2003a).

This new document reiterated the Government's commitment to the idea of a 14–19 'continuum', that critical phase in young people's lives when, in the words of Charles Clarke's Introduction, they needed 'a coherent and motivating curriculum, delivered in a wide range of institutions, recognized by a coherent qualifications system' (p. 3). To all intents and purposes, the National Curriculum would effectively end at 14, followed by greater flexibility and a much clearer sense of continuity in the years spanning the age 16 barrier.

The document deliberately distinguished between *short-term* and *long-term* reforms, many of the former having been foreshadowed in the 2002 Green Paper.

Chief among the *short-term* reforms was that English, mathematics and science would become, from the 2004/5 academic year, the only academic survivors from the original 1988 framework, with the existing substantial programme of study for science having to be reviewed to arrive at a core content that was deemed suitable for all learners. All students would learn about work and enterprise; and ICT would remain compulsory for the time being, though with the understanding that the skills involved would increasingly be taught through other subjects in future years. Citizenship, religious education, careers education, sex education and physical education would remain compulsory to ensure, in the words of the document, that 'all students should continue to learn to be responsible and healthy adults'. At the same time, the Government had decided to reject the arguments of those campaigning for the inclusion of modern foreign languages and design and technology as *compulsory* elements in the new curriculum, and, as indicated in the earlier Green Paper, these subjects would join the arts and the humanities in no longer being 'required study' for all 14–16-year-olds.

The new document was anxious to highlight three initiatives designed to address the weakness and low status of vocational studies. It reminded readers that new GCSEs in eight vocational subjects had been introduced in September 2002, with the prospect of wider availability from September 2003. Now, to complement this development, there was to be a new system of 'hybrid' GCSEs, each with a common core but with optional 'vocational' or 'general' units. Second, modern apprenticeships would be improved and expanded, so that at least 28 per cent of young people could become apprentices by the year 2004. Third, GCSEs and A Levels would no longer be labelled as either 'academic' or 'vocational'. It was recognized that status mattered, and that engineering should enjoy equal status with mathematics or art and design.

There were a number of areas where the Government had had second thoughts since the publication of the 2002 Green Paper, and this was largely as a result of feedback from the 58 regional workshops. There would, for example, be no new A Level A grade 'with distinction', the Government preferring to persevere with the AEAs which, as we have seen, were introduced in the summer of 2002 to 'stretch' the most able students by requiring a greater depth of understanding than the A Level itself.

It was also decided to jettison proposals for a new Matriculation Diploma, an 'overarching award' designed to mark the completion of the 14–19 phase of learning. We have already noted that the idea was attacked by the ATL and the SHA for the lack of a foundation level diploma, and it is also true that universities and employers were not attracted to the whole idea; without such currency, it really stood little chance of being successful.

Where *long-term* measures were concerned, the most significant statement in the 2003 document related to the possible introduction of a new qualifications system for 18-year-olds (this is also discussed in Chapter 4). The Government would be appointing a new Working Group for 14 to 19 Reform, to be headed by former Chief Inspector Mike Tomlinson, which would be expected to look at ways of introducing an English Baccalaureate, designed to recognize vocational and academic achievements as well as activities outside the classroom, such as volunteering, and encompassing students across the so-called 'ability spectrum'. In the words of the document:

> Baccalaureate-style qualifications of this type work well in other countries, and we believe that this model, designed to suit English circumstances, could tackle long-standing English problems, giving greater emphasis to completing courses of study (and training as appropriate) through to the age of 18 or 19, without a heavier burden of examination and assessment. (DfES, 2003a: 13)

If such a reform were to mean far more than the Matriculation Diploma, already rejected, it could threaten the so-called 'gold standard' A Level, and this was recognized in a number of the newspaper accounts of the discussion document, the story in *The Guardian* (22 January 2003) being headed 'Broad-based "English Bac" could replace A Levels' and that in *The Times Educational Supplement* (24 January 2003) having the headline 'Future without A Levels is on the cards'.

Preliminary details of his proposals unveiled by Mike Tomlinson in July 2003 favoured the introduction of a broad 'baccalaureate-style' diploma comprising four levels of difficulty. The Entry Level would be equivalent to the standard expected at the age of fourteen; Foundation Level would be the same as the lower grades at the GCSE. The Intermediate Diploma would be roughly equal to five GCSE passes at Grace C or above; and the Advanced Level would be roughly equivalent to existing A Levels.

The Tomlinson plan did not explicitly call for the abolition of GCSEs and A Levels, but simply presented that as one of two options. Alternatively, the old examinations could survive as component parts of a single diploma, rather than as free-standing qualifications.

The Tomlinson Report

After an 18-month review of 14 to 19 qualifications, the Final Report of the Working Group headed by Mike Tomlinson, entitled *14–19 Curriculum and Qualifications Reform*, was finally published on 18 October 2004 (DfES, 2004b). In *The Observer* (17 October 2004), it was confidently asserted that acceptance of the Tomlinson proposals would represent 'the biggest shake-up of the examinations system in England in over half a century'. On the following day in *The Guardian* (18 October 2004), it was predicted that the main ideas in The Report would feature in New Labour's manifesto for the 2005 General Election.

The main reform advocated in the 116-page document was that the existing GCSE and A Levels would form part of a new diploma for all school leavers. This new Diploma would consist of four levels: two of them below GCSE, an intermediate diploma at GCSE pass level and an advanced diploma for A Level standard students. Most course-work would be scrapped, but a large proportion of assessment at intermediate level – the equivalent of GCSE – would be carried out internally by teachers. Along with less external testing for all students at 16, there would be more emphasis on work-related or vocational courses. Under the proposals, students could receive their diploma only after passing tests in three 'core' skills needed for the workplace: in literacy, numeracy and information and communications technology. Students would be able to choose from up to 20 'lines of learning' within the diploma framework – consisting of academic or vocational subjects or a mixture of the two. Core learning would entail completion of an extended project appropriate to the level of the Diploma. Each student's final Diploma would take account of work experience and extra-curricular activities. The highest level of Diploma – equivalent to existing A Levels, but in some ways even more demanding – would be assessed mainly by external exams. New A plus and A double plus grades would be introduced to 'stretch' the 'brightest' students. It was hoped that this reform would be welcomed by universities seeking to distinguish between youngsters with strings of A grades.

These, then, were the main reforms advocated in the 14–19 Report, designed, in the words of Mike Tomlinson's Letter to the Secretary of State, to set out 'a clear vision for a unified framework of 14–19 curriculum and qualifications'. One of the main aims of the Working Group was to bring back 'a passion for learning'; and it was also hoped that all learners would be enabled to achieve 'as highly as possible – and for all their achievements to be recognized'. The proposed reforms would ensure 'rigour', while, at the same time, equipping all young people with 'the knowledge, skills and attributes needed for Higher Education, employment and adult life' (DfES, 2004b: 1).

The Tomlinson proposals gained broad support from schools, union leaders and universities, but failed to convince many members of the business community that any long-term benefits would be worth the cost and disruption of reform. What was even more worrying was that Tony Blair and Education Secretary Charles Clarke appeared to undermine the spirit of the new diploma system by stopping far short of giving it their unequivocal endorsement. Mr Clarke presented the Tomlinson Report to the House of Commons on 18 October 2004 and gave it lukewarm praise. He said:

> I am determined that any evolution of the 14–19 system must increase public confidence in it. My approach will be to build on all that is good in the current system, including the real and great strengths of A Levels and GCSEs. They will stay as building blocks of any new system. (Reported in *The Guardian*, 19 October 2004)

The Prime Minister was not present for the debate, but in a speech that evening to the Confederation of British Industry at a meeting in Birmingham, he said:

> The purpose of reform will be to improve upon the existing system, *not* replace it . . . GCSEs and A Levels will stay, so will externally marked exams. Reform will serve to strengthen the existing system where it is inadequate, and there will be greater challenge at the top for those on track to Higher Education. There will also be a sharper focus on the basics of literacy and numeracy and ICT. And there will also be improved vocational provision. (*The Guardian*, 19 October 2004)

At a separate briefing in London, Mike Tomlinson argued that A Levels and GCSEs could form part of a new diploma framework as 'components', even if not as 'free-standing qualifications'. But he also said that he hoped that the names would 'eventually disappear' so that the Diploma would have 'full integrity': 'If you kept the names, it would clearly deny the fact that there is an integrity in the Diploma. This is a very subtle point, but it is also an important one' (*The Guardian*, 19 October 2004).

When the resulting White Paper on the 14 to 19 Curriculum, *14–19 Education and Skills*, was published by the new Education Secretary, Ruth Kelly, on 23 February 2005 (DfES, 2005a), it was obvious that the Government was scared of committing itself to a radical restructuring of the provision for older students shortly before a general election. In her Foreword to the White Paper, the Education Secretary claimed that it set out details of a reform programme 'building from the excellent work of Sir Mike Tomlinson and his Working Group on 14–19 Reform' (DfES, 2005a: 3), while the document itself rejected most of Tomlinson's key proposals. Specifically, it rejected the idea of a four-tier overarching diploma embracing all academic and vocational qualifications and opted instead to retain GCSEs and A Levels largely in their present form. Its main feature was to accept the need for a major rationalization of all vocational qualifications, with the replacement of the existing 'alphabet soup' of 3,500 separate qualifications by a three-tier system of 'specialized diplomas' in 14 occupational areas (DfES, 2005a: 53). The first four Diplomas, in information and communication technology, engineering, health and social care and creative studies and media, would be available in 2008. A further four would be available in 2010, and Diplomas would be made 'a national entitlement' by the year 2015 (DfES, 2005a: 50).

The contents of the White Paper and its rejection of the Tomlinson vision caused considerable alarm among large sections of the education community. Mike Tomlinson himself warned that the short-sighted decision to opt for a diploma only for vocational courses – while keeping the existing 'gold standard' exams – could 'backfire on the Government by prolonging and reinforcing the traditional snobbery towards work-related education'. He went on: 'What is being proposed risks emphasizing yet again the distinction between the vocational and the academic. It further fails fully to deal with the needs of those students for whom grade A* to C at GCSE is simply not attainable' (reported in *The Guardian*, 24 February 2005). A *Guardian* editorial noted that 'from every corner of the educational world has come expressions of deep disappointment', as 'heads, teachers, unions, private schools, universities and employers (as represented by the British Chamber of Commerce) are united in the view that this Blair Government has missed an opportunity to end an historic and crippling social divide dating back at least 150 years' (*The Guardian*, 24 February 2005). And education journalist Warwick Mansell, writing in *The Times Educational Supplement* on 25 February 2005, argued that 'all the attention given to the 14 to 19 age group, including the £1 million Tomlinson Inquiry, appears to have been rejected because the Government does not want to go into the 2005 Election being accused by the Tories and the media of scrapping A Levels' (Mansell, 2005: 13).

It was Schools Secretary Ed Balls, who had been given the post when Gordon Brown became Prime Minister in June 2007, who revisited the whole issue of 14 to 19 reform and appeared to signal a major change in government thinking in a speech delivered on 23 October 2007. Once again the proposals were hailed in the media as 'the biggest shake-up of the examinations system in over half a century' – and this time with some justification. Five diplomas would be introduced in September 2008 in about 900 schools and colleges, covering construction, media, engineering, IT and society, and health and development. This was clearly in line with the thinking of the 2005 White Paper; but Ed Balls went on to stress that in the future, new diplomas would no longer be confined to specifically work-related areas of the curriculum. Three new diplomas, in languages, sciences and humanities, would be launched in 2011, in a move designed to appeal to 'academic' students and the universities. As more 'academic' diplomas were introduced, they would compete with existing examinations and could well become the 'qualification of choice' for 14–19-year-olds. In the words of the Schools Secretary, diplomas could become 'the jewel in the crown' of the education system. A review of A Levels, expected in 2008, would be postponed to 2013 and would be expanded to cover all qualifications. Asked by members of the audience whether he could give a guarantee that GCSEs and A Levels would survive the Review, Ed Balls replied: 'It will be an open-minded review. Clearly, I'm not going to give you any guarantee about the precise outcome of the 2013 Review' (quoted in *The Times*, 24 October 2007).

The Government was very anxious that the new diplomas system should be a success, thereby ending the divide between vocational and academic learning. A clause in the new Education and Skills Bill introduced into Parliament on 14 January 2008 specified that schools would be forbidden from 'unduly promoting any particular options' to teenagers seeking advice on courses; and this was widely seen as a thinly-disguised attempt to prevent teachers from encouraging their students to study A Levels.

It is fair to point out that the new 14 to 19 proposals have caused real concern in certain quarters – and even among those who have *no* misgivings about the latest trend in government thinking. It was probably inevitable that Michael Gove, the Shadow Schools Secretary, should argue that the new diplomas in academic subject areas would 'undermine academic excellence' (quoted in *The Times*, 24 October 2007); but there have been many who are broadly supportive of the Government's long-term aims and who are nonetheless concerned about the *practical* difficulties involved in implementing the 14 to 19 plans. For example: John Dunford, General Secretary of the Association of School and College Leaders, has pointed out that adding three more diplomas to the 14 vocational ones already under construction by 2011, against the backdrop of continuing to provide GCSE and A Level courses, is 'a huge programme for an education system that is punch-drunk with change in recent years' (quoted in *The Times*, 24 October 2007). And many headteachers have argued that even if secondary schools were able to form partnerships with neighbours, providing all these courses was bound to prove 'a logistical nightmare'.

Writing in *Education Guardian* on 18 March 2008, education journalist Mike Baker pointed out that there was a major obstacle to the successful introduction of the new diplomas: their complexity. In Baker's view, it would be very difficult for individual schools to come to terms with all the pedagogical issues involved in teaching the new courses. And there were also 'genuine concerns about issues such as timetabling, the availability of work placements, and the movement of the diploma students between schools and colleges'. This was not just about transport problems in rural areas, but also about 'school uniform rules, tracking pupils' whereabouts, inter-school rivalries, and the accountability measures that promoted competition, not collaboration' (Baker, 2008).

Perhaps most worryingly of all, Jerry Jarvis, Managing Director of Edexcel, one of the UK's leading exam boards, gave an interview to *The Guardian* (17 April 2008) in which he claimed that the new diploma system 'risked failure' when it was introduced into schools. In this interview, which received a good deal of media publicity, Mr Jarvis listed a series of problems needing to be addressed, which included teachers not having adequate training; schools still not knowing how several features of the new diplomas should be taught; and fears being expressed that the new qualification would be too demanding for many pupils, leading inevitably to more young people leaving school with no qualification at all. Mr Jarvis said he fully supported the new diploma system, but that it was crucial for the Government and exam authorities to act quickly to ensure the qualification's success. In his words: 'we think it's going to be quite traumatic to get through this. The issue is about schools being able to cope'. He pointed out that the diplomas, which required the establishment of complex consortiums of schools and colleges for effective delivery, were coming into the system as new GCSEs and A Levels were also being introduced and as the Qualifications and Curriculum Authority, the government agency responsible for them, was being split into two separate organizations and relocating to Coventry. He concluded in apocalyptic terms:

> The pressure on the whole educational system is unprecedented. But for the sake of all our kids, this has got to work . . . If the Diploma doesn't earn its spurs as a qualification, and that means respect from employers, pupils, parents and Higher Education, we face a really serious problem. There is a huge educational risk to this country. (Curtis, 2008)

This interview which appeared in *The Guardian* on 17 April 2008 was accompanied by the results of a National Union of Teachers survey of teachers in secondary schools planning to deliver the diplomas, which revealed that 54 per cent had not received 'clear, unambiguous' information on how to teach the new courses and that only 38 per cent of staff who were expecting to teach part of the qualification felt 'confident about doing so' (reported in *The Guardian*, 17 April 2008).

As I write, it is not clear whether the new diploma system will indeed be a success. In his *Education Guardian* article referred to above, Mike Baker pointed out that 'the best chance in a generation to break out of the two-tier divide' was the publication of the Tomlinson proposals, which Tony Blair and his ministers rejected. England had failed to follow the example of Wales, which had already introduced the so-called Welsh BAC providing an integrated award for all young people incorporating academic and vocational pathways. Now, in Baker's view, the political timing was problematic to say the least. By the year 2013, when the review of A Levels is scheduled to take place, we will have had another general election. If the Conservatives win, A Levels will undoubtedly remain *outside* the diploma framework. Supporters of the Tomlinson Plan might hope that if the diplomas are well-entrenched by then, it will be hard for whoever is in power to continue to resist incorporating A Levels and GCSEs into a single system. But the reality is that by the time of the next election (probably May 2010), the diplomas will still be only half-formed. In which case, the supporters of the old regime will have benefited from New Labour's prevarication and lack of purpose.

9

Higher Education

At the time when the Robbins Report on the future of higher education was published in 1963 (Ministry of Education, 1963b), the proportion of young people able to go to university and other colleges of higher education was remarkably low, and these were predominantly students who had been educated in grammar and 'public' schools. As we saw in Chapter 6, Edward Boyle realized in the early 1960s (as the long period of Conservative administration was coming to an end) that pressure of numbers and the reorganization of secondary schooling would make it essential to expand rapidly both further education and higher education. The movement towards comprehensive education has been discussed in depth elsewhere in this book; in this chapter, we look at the major impact of post-war demographic factors on higher education and at the steady expansion of places in all forms of higher education since the 1960s.

The need for expansion in the 1950s and 1960s

The high level of births in 1947 and the relatively high figures of the following years had obvious long-term implications for the demand for places in higher education. There was also the trend for more and more students to stay on at school *beyond* the period of compulsory schooling and to then seek entry into one form or other of higher education. As Professor Roy Lowe has observed 'This reflected both the increased affluence of the 1950s and the growing realisation that the economic transformation towards the service industries and the professions demanded a more highly educated workforce' (Lowe, 1988: 152). The late 1950s saw a sharp up-turn in the number of sixth-formers gaining two or more A Levels: from 27,000 in 1956 to just over 60,000 by 1964. The immediate result was a sudden fall in the percentage of such sixth-formers able to take up available university places – from 80 per cent in

1956 to 65 per cent in 1964 – which prompted demands for a general expansion of facilities (Layard, King and Moser, 1969: 18–19).

At the same time, the post-war period saw significant and lasting changes in the catchment allocation of the main civic universities, which meant that they became more truly 'national' in character. Before and immediately after the Second World War, almost half of all university students lived at home. Of the rest, many were studying at their regional university. The greater availability of awards by the end of the 1950s meant that it became possible for growing numbers of 'first generation' university students to move away from their home environment. Before the War, only about 40 per cent of students in the universities of England and Wales had received financial assistance from public or private funds. By 1957–8, around 80 per cent of students in England and over 90 per cent in Wales were receiving some kind of financial support; and the proportion of students living at home had dropped to just over 25 per cent (Dent, 1961: 95). For a privileged group of young people – still predominantly middle-class, but also including a growing number of working-class grammar-school 'successes' – going to university now became associated with a fair degree of freedom and independence. But this was a 'luxury' shared to a lesser degree by students gaining admittance to the teacher training colleges and hardly at all by those in the technical sector (Lowe, 1988: 154).

The first phase of university expansion in the 1950s was largely confined to a number of existing institutions and was most marked in the most recent creations. Growth was particularly dramatic in the new university colleges, four of which – Exeter, Hull, Leicester and Southampton – had received their Charter by the end of the decade.

Yet none of this was sufficient to meet the needs of the expanding number of suitably qualified sixth-formers, particularly in southern and eastern England, with the result that in the late 1950s and early 1960s plans were drawn up for the establishment of seven new universities. These new institutions, situated at Norwich (East Anglia), Colchester (Essex), Canterbury (Kent), Lancaster, Brighton (Sussex), Coventry (Warwick) and York, found no difficulty in attracting applicants, and were soon able to prove that the number of young people able and anxious to benefit from higher education was certainly not fixed.

This was also the view taken by the Robbins Committee, which was appointed in 1961 and whose 1963 Report launched the most massive expansion of higher education ever seen in Britain. As three academics with either a close involvement with or a keen interest in the Robbins research have observed: 'Few official reports in British history, and certainly in educational history, have led to such immediate changes in government policy' (Layard, King and Moser, 1969: 22). Many of the main quantitative recommendations, with normally a 10-year time-scale, were accepted in a White Paper published within 24 hours of the Report's appearance. It is, of course, worth pointing out that 1963 was a good year for the Report to be published, with a general election in the offing; and this, rather than mere elitism or snobbery, may help to explain why it was acted upon so quickly. But, to quote Layard, King and Moser again: 'more important than all this was the imminence of the bulge and the Government's genuine belief in the importance of higher education on both social and economic grounds' (1969).

The Robbins Report anticipated that the number of home and over-seas students in full-time higher education would rise from 216,000 in 1962–3 to 558,000 in 1980–1. To meet this increased demand, it was proposed that there should be six more new universities in addition to those already in the process of being built. Furthermore, the Colleges of Advanced Technology (CATs) should be given full recognition as 'tech-nological universities'; and within the university sector there should be developed as soon as possible five Special Institutions for Scientific and Technological Education and Research. Underpinning all these specific proposals was the so-called Robbins principle that 'courses of higher education should be available for all those who are qualified by ability and attainment to pursue them and who wish to do so' (Ministry of Education, 1963b: 8).

To cope with the major issues raised by the Robbins Committee and, in particular, with the anticipated upsurge of entrants into universities and colleges, the Wilson Government of 1964–70 developed what is usually known as 'the binary policy' for higher education. This was articulated by Anthony Crosland (Education Secretary from 1965 to 1967) in speeches, first at Woolwich Polytechnic in April 1965, then at the University of Lancaster in January 1967. The new policy involved the development of higher education in two separate sectors: an 'autonomous' sector consisting mainly of old and new universities and colleges of advanced technology (which acquired university status in 1966–7); and a 'public' sector under local authority control and repre-sented by the leading technical colleges and the teacher-training colleges, to be known in future as colleges of education.

Brian Simon has described the Wilson Government's binary policy as 'a sledgehammer blow . . . aimed at the Robbins conception of a unitary system of higher education' (Simon, 1991: 247). The policy can certainly be seen as a deliberate repudiation of the basic Robbins principle that higher education provision was virtually synonymous with university education. The Robbins Committee had, after all, recommended the creation of a number of new universities and the virtual absorption of the teacher-training colleges (or colleges of education) into the university system. This part of the Robbins Report was rejected by the Labour Government which decided that there were to be no more new universities in the foreseeable future (apart from the renamed Colleges of Advanced Technology), and that the colleges of education for the training of teachers were to remain under local authority or voluntary body control. As David Elliott has pointed out: 'Robbins had gone in for university empire-building on a grand scale, and Crosland was preventing this from happening by developing the AFE (Advanced Further Education) sector as a respectable counterweight' (Elliott, 1985: 205). This objective was, in fact, largely accomplished, since the university sector was prevented from expanding: the statistics show that the proportion of full-time students studying in universities was 60 per cent in 1962–3 and 58 per cent in 1980–1 (Elliott, 1985).

Crosland clearly felt that the binary policy was infinitely preferable to the university-controlled system for higher education recommended by the Robbins Report. He claimed to be anxious to avoid a situation where the universities would be responsible for the vast majority of degree courses, with all other institutions left with 'sub-degree' or part-time work. Yet the Government's binary policy was still criticized for perpetuating an elitist and hierarchical system, falling far short of the undifferentiated comprehensive system of higher education advocated by such leading academics as Robin Pedley, Eric Robinson and Brian Simon. The polytechnics and other technical institutions were to be attacked for 'aping' the universities in much the same way that many secondary modern schools had once been criticized for seeking to emulate the grammar schools.

Developments under the Thatcher and Major administrations

By the time of the passing of the 1988 Education Reform Act, higher education in Britain had expanded considerably, with much of the growth foreseen by Robbins becoming a reality, though not necessarily in the form anticipated back in 1963. Universities had retained their relatively 'autonomous' status, funded by a university-dominated organization, the University Grants Committee (UGC). Polytechnics and higher education colleges were still the responsibility of local authorities, with their degrees awarded by a Council for National Academic Awards (CNAA). Students on both sides of what was often referred to as 'the binary line' were normally entitled to state grants covering fees and maintenance.

The 1988 Act removed some 30 polytechnics and 50 colleges from local authority control and set up a government-controlled Polytechnic and Colleges Funding Council; while the University Grants Committee was replaced by a new Universities Funding Council. It was also at this time that institutions of higher education were expected to develop a new 'entrepreneurial culture', incorporating the concepts of 'accountability' and 'value-for-money'. In the words of Professor Sally Tomlinson, writing in 2001:

> From 1989, universities found themselves pushed into adopting managerial methods, enhancing their role as entrepreneurs and measuring their performance on quantitative indicators. Vice-Chancellors became chief executives of their institutions, and senior academics became middle managers. Research and teaching output and quality were increasingly to be measured and funds distributed accordingly. (Tomlinson, 2001: 59)

In 1992 a Further and Higher Education Act ensured that funding for all higher education (HE) courses was unified and that all institutions of higher education would in future compete for funding for teaching and research. The 1992 Act removed more responsibility and financing from the local authorities, and set up a centrally controlled Higher Education Funding Council (HEFC) to distribute funds to all universities in England and Wales and hold them accountable for spending. Polytechnics and other HE institutions could now become degree-awarding bodies and assume the title of 'university' (subject to approval by the Privy Council); and the CNAA was to be abolished. Yet although (not surprisingly) the leading polytechnics were keen to take advantage of a perceived rise in 'status' by applying for the title of 'university' and joining the stiff competition for improved funding, they soon found that their traditional emphasis on teaching rather than research left them severely handicapped where the Research Assessment Exercise (RAE) that allocated research money to institutions was concerned, and it was almost impossible to catch up with the existing universities. At the same time, a new hierarchy was emerging among the 'old' universities as a group of leading vice-chancellors representing a number of wealthy, research-dominated universities and calling themselves 'the Russell Group' (after the hotel where they held their meetings in Bloomsbury in central London) claimed to be in charge of the 'elite' institutions where the Government should be allocating the bulk of its research funding.

Problems of access and inequality

The immediate impact of Robbins had been a rapid increase in the proportion of young people able to find a place in some form of higher education institution: from 4.7 per cent in 1963 to 6.3 per cent in 1967 in the case of students being admitted to universities and former CATS; and from 9.5 per cent in 1963 to 14.3 per cent in 1967 in the case of students entering all institutions offering higher education (Layard, King and Moser, 1969: 25). These figures are all the more remarkable when one considers that the proportion of 18-year-olds going to university had remained pretty static in the 1950s. Then, in the early 1970s, the Open University, one of the acknowledged 'success stories' of the Wilson Government, began providing part-time university first-degree courses for students over the age of 21 who might not otherwise have been able to benefit from the experience of tackling work at this level.

Did all this change and expansion have any marked effect on the *type* of student gaining advanced qualifications? In an article published in October 1983, Richard Hoggart, the then Warden of Goldsmiths College in south-east London, argued that the socially privileged character of higher education had hardly been challenged over the past 20 years: 'the great body of working-class people have been left almost untouched' (*The Times Higher Education Supplement,* 28 October 1983). Three weeks later, Gareth Williams of the Institute of Education in London reported on a research study which showed that the relative position of working-class and middle-class participation in higher education had hardly changed between 1960 and the end of the 1970s. In the words of Professor Williams: 'This suggests that unless there have been dramatic changes since 1960 in the distribution of intellectual ability among the social classes, the pool of "untapped ability" defined in Robbins' terms remains at least as large as it was then' (*The Times Higher Education Supplement,* 18 November 1983). Indeed, a Labour Party policy document published in 1982 used statistics to show that the proportion of children of manual workers among university students had actually *fallen* in the course of the 1970s: from 26 per cent in 1973 to 23 per cent in 1980 (Labour Party, 1982: 3). In an article published towards the end of the 1980s, Andy Green, an acknowledged expert on international trends in access and achievement at the post-16 level, could say of Britain that: 'We have the highest rate of early school leaving, the lowest rate of achievement in nationally recognised qualifications and the lowest rate of participation in higher education of almost any country in Europe, except Portugal and Spain' (Green, 1988: 25). Including both universities and polytechnics, Britain had around 15 per cent of the relevant age group in higher education, compared with the USA where around 30 per cent were studying at degree level, or with Japan where 37 per cent were in university or college education, or with West Germany where 20 per cent were in universities or polytechnics. Moreover, the proportion of working-class students studying for higher degrees in Britain was among the lowest in Europe (Green, 1988).

In a speech delivered at Lancaster University in January 1989, the then Education Secretary Kenneth Baker called for a doubling of the proportion of young people going on to universities or polytechnics, from 15 to around 30 per cent, over the next 25 years. But he also made it clear that the expansion he anticipated in higher education should ideally be based on American models of private funding, rather than on the Western European system of increased public finance (reported in *The Guardian,* 5 January 1989). In the same year, his immediate successor John MacGregor, in an interview with *The Guardian* (24 November 1989), abandoned the target of 30 per cent, adding that the Conservative Government was still committed to *some* expansion of student numbers, but 'only on a realistic and affordable basis, with the necessary funding coming from a variety of sources'. By the time the Conservatives left office in 1997, Kenneth Baker's 1989 target no longer appeared overoptimistic or unrealistic; but there was still little evidence of a real shift in the social composition of Britain's elite higher education institutions.

Higher education under New Labour

New Labour inherited a higher education situation in 1997 that was both full of exciting possibilities, but also fraught with very real difficulties. Over a period of 50 years, the overall participation rate had increased eleven-fold: from around 3 per cent in 1950 to around 33 per cent when David Blunkett became the new Education Secretary in Tony Blair's first administration (and with New Labour committed to a new participation rate of 50 per cent by the year 2010). Expansion had been particularly rapid since the 1988 Education Reform Act; but many would argue that this had been engineered 'on the cheap', with a tight squeeze on the 'unit of resource' for each student and university staff pay allowed to fall considerably below the rate of inflation. On this last point, it had been estimated by the CVCP (Committee of Vice-Chancellors and Principals) in 1996 that teachers working in universities would require a 37 per cent pay rise simply to bring them back to the pay levels they had enjoyed in 1981.

In July 1998, the Government passed the Teaching and Higher Education Act, which included new and expanded arrangements for student loans, the abolition of maintenance grants and the introduction of tuition fees for undergraduate students (this last being a move that Labour had strenuously opposed before coming into office). Among the chorus of disapproval and forebodings, the Universities and Colleges Admissions Service reported an immediate reduction in the numbers of members of 'under-represented' groups applying for admission to most type of universities: mature students, working-class students and students from minority ethnic communities (see Goddard, 1999). The 1998 Act also imposed fees on students attending Scottish universities; but one of the first Acts of the devolved Scottish Parliament in 1999 was to abandon this unpopular measure.

As the twentieth century neared its end, there was mounting concern among traditional Labour supporters about the imposition of under-graduate tuition fees and about the ongoing failure of working-class youngsters and of young people from 'socially deprived' areas of the country to achieve adequate representation within the university student population.

A report prepared by the Sutton Trust, *Entry to Leading Universities* (Sutton Trust, 2000), details of which were released to the press in April 2000, showed that 'thousands of bright youngsters from the state sector' who possessed 'the necessary grades' were not gaining access to 'our leading universities'. The Survey covered 13 universities in Britain: Oxford, Cambridge, Birmingham, Bristol, Durham, Edinburgh, Nottingham, St Andrews, Warwick, York, Imperial College (London), the London School of Economics and University College London. In carrying out its detailed research, the Trust made use of statistical information provided by the Higher Education Funding Council.

The Trust's research showed that, while accounting for only 7 per cent of the secondary-school population, students from the independent sector constituted 39 per cent of the entry to the 'top' universities. In fact, the probability of winning a place at one of the 13 universities surveyed was approximately 25 times greater for those from a private school than for those who came from 'a lower social class' or who lived in 'a poor area'. At Oxford and Cambridge, around half of the intake each year came from the independent sector, while only 10 per cent came from the three lowest socio-economic groups which together accounted for around 50 per cent of the population. The Trust argued that the marked imbalance of entry to the 'top' 13 universities was due to two main factors: a low proportion of applicants from 'suitably qualified less affluent students' and 'inadequacies in the universities' admissions systems'.

A month after the publicity accorded the Sutton Trust's research findings, Chancellor Gordon Brown provoked a good deal of criticism among Conservative politicians and sections of the media for daring to use a speech to a Trades Union Congress (TUC) audience in London to launch an outspoken attack on 'old school tie' elitism at Oxford and Cambridge (see the report in *The Guardian*, 26 May 2000). This was in the wake of the much-publicized case of Laura Spence, the Tyneside comprehensive-school sixth-former denied a place at Magdalen College, Oxford.

The February 2002 Green Paper, *14–19: Extending Opportunities, Raising Standards* reiterated the Government's determination that by the year 2010, some 50 per cent of those aged between 18 and 30 should be participating in higher education, with access widened for those whose families had no previous experience of higher education (DfES, 2002: 10). But it also emphasized the scale of the problem by pointing out that, currently, less than 20 per cent of young people under the age of 21 from the lower socio-economic groups went to university, compared with over 70 per cent from the highest (DfES, 2002).

In an interview with *The Guardian* in June 2002, the minister for higher education, Margaret Hodge, admitted that New Labour's objective of *widening* access to higher education had failed, particularly in England and Wales, 'so leaving untouched the major cause of inequality in the United Kingdom' . Indeed, far from closing the social divide in higher education, the Government had actually seen the gap widening over the past five years. Ms Hodge insisted that government targets must, in future, 'include a commitment to ensuring that proportionately more students came from low income group families'. Yet, like Estelle Morris, she denied that tuition fees, fully introduced in 1999, could well be preventing more students from impoverished backgrounds entering higher education. When it was pointed out to her that in Scotland, where there were no upfront tuition fees, participation in higher education had already reached the 50 per cent target, Ms Hodge replied that any attempt to make such a link was 'far too simplistic and misleading' (*The Guardian*, 24 June 2002).

An article in *The Times* in August 2002 reported that a long-awaited review of higher education finance would soon propose a new system of allowances designed to ease the financial fears that deterred many teenagers from going to university. According to the article, Tony Blair had personally ordered the review of the fees and loans system after Labour MPs reported intense hostility towards the Government on campuses across England and Wales at the time of the 2001 election (*The Times,* 8 August 2002).

The 2003 White Paper and the 2004 Higher Education Act

After 18 months of media speculation, four postponed launches and a number of well-informed 'leaked' stories about serious differences of opinion within Tony Blair's Cabinet, the new Education Secretary, Charles Clarke, finally announced the Government's plans for the future of higher education – and particularly the future funding of higher education – in a 105-page White Paper, *The Future of Higher Education,* published on 22 January 2003 (DfES, 2003b). This was in the same week that the DfES published a new consultation document on the related topic of 14 to 19 provision, *14–19: Opportunity and Excellence* (DIES, 2003a), already discussed in Chapter 8.

In his introduction to the White Paper, the Education Secretary felt able to make the proud claim that British universities were 'a great success story' where, over the past 30 years, 'some of the finest brains in the world' had 'pushed back the boundaries of knowledge, science and understanding'. Yet it would be wrong to be complacent about this and 'opt for a quiet life'. Universities were critical to Britain's national ability to 'master rather than be ground down by' the process of change in a fast-changing world. In the words of the introduction: 'Our future success depends upon mobilising even more effectively the imagination, creativity, skills and talents of all our people. And it depends on using all that knowledge and understanding to build economic strength and social harmony.'

The Education Secretary went on to identify three key areas where universities had to change and improve:

1 The expansion of higher education had to be extended to 'the talented and best from all backgrounds'.
2 Britain had to make better progress in harnessing knowledge to wealth creation.
3 The system for supporting students had to be made fairer. Having a university education brought huge benefits, and while the Government would continue to pay most of the cost involved in

studying for a degree, it was also reasonable to ask students to contribute to this.

Moving on to this third point, many of the more immediately controversial measures to be found in the White Paper were indeed concerned with funding. From 2006, universities in England would be able to charge 'top-up' tuition fees of up to £3,000 a year for their most popular and prestigious courses. Tuition fees would no longer be paid 'upfront'; and students would not have to pay their fees until they had graduated and were earning at least £15,000 a year (a repayment threshold that was higher than the previous one of £10,000). Payments after graduation would be made through the tax system, linked to the ability to pay. From 2004, poorer students with parents or families earning less than £10,000 a year would be eligible for a new grant of £1,000 a year, a measure designed to benefit around one-third of all students.

One of the stated aims of the White Paper's proposals was to see a broadening of access to institutions of higher education, with an acceptance of the premise that too many of those born into 'less advantaged families' still viewed a university place as being 'beyond their reach', whatever their ability. Statistics showed that the social class gap among those entering higher education was unacceptably wide and showing little sign of being ameliorated. Those from the 'top' three social classes were almost three times as likely to enter higher education as those from the 'bottom' three. Moreover, young people from professional backgrounds were over five times more likely to enter higher education than those from unskilled backgrounds.

The White Paper announced the appointment of an independent Access Regulator, whose main task would be to agree with universities on action to increase the take-up of students from 'disadvantaged groups' and who could then impose penalties or withdraw the right to charge variable fees, where appropriate, if universities failed to meet the targets they set for themselves. Those institutions that chose to charge 'top-up' tuition fees for *some* or *all* of their courses would, in fact, be required to have 'robust and challenging' Access Agreements in place setting out the action they would take in order to 'safeguard and promote access'.

The Government reiterated its intention of having at least 50 per cent of 18–30-year-olds in England entering some form of higher education by the end of the decade. Yet the White Paper made it clear that this ambitious target would largely be met by increasing the number of youngsters on new two-year vocational courses, many of these being offered at further education colleges. In the words of the document:

we do not believe that expansion should simply mean 'more of the same'. There is a danger of higher education becoming an automatic step in the chain of education – almost a third stage of compulsory schooling. We do not favour expansion on the single template of the traditional three-year honours degree. (p. 60)

Having devoted considerable and appropriate space to new funding arrangements and the widening of access, we need to emphasize in this chapter that the White Paper contained far-reaching implications for the future *structure* of higher education in England. The Government had been impressed by the achievements of universities in countries such as Germany, the Netherlands and the USA where research was concentrated in relatively few institutions. Three-quarters of research funding from the Higher Education Funding Council for England already went to just 25 institutions. Now it was being proposed that research money should be concentrated even more on 'top-performing' departments. The White Paper urged 'less research-intensive institutions' to all but forget about trying to make major breakthroughs in, say, science and technology and instead to concentrate their energies working closely with local businesses solving 'real world problems'.

Not surprisingly, much of the initial reaction to the White Paper tended to highlight the new funding arrangements. Around 150 Labour MPs signed motions opposing 'top-up' tuition fees, regarding the measure as a 'betrayal' of Labour's manifesto commitment *not* to contemplate such a change. It was estimated that many students could leave university with total debts amounting to at least £21,000, comprised of £9,000 in tuition fees and £12,000 in maintenance costs. Moreover, a group of accountancy experts calculated that the new charges could lead to graduates facing a higher rate of tax than that paid by millionaires, once they had reached the £15,000 threshold (report in *The Independent,* 23 February 2003). That being said, there were those whose chief worry about the White Paper concerned the proposed development or intensification of a hierarchy of institutions. A number of Labour MPs and some vice-chancellors warned that we could soon see a restoration of the two-tier university/polytechnic divide.

In November 2003, amidst fears that 'rebel' backbench Labour MPs might help to defeat the Government's plans to increase tuition fees, and just two days before these plans were due to form part of the Queen's Speech, the heads of five of Britain's 'elite' universities – Oxford, Cambridge, Imperial College, London, University College, London and the London School of Economics – wrote a letter to *The Times* demanding that there must be 'no retreat' over the issue of new fees. In this letter, they argued that Britain's top research universities would 'fall hopelessly behind' rivals in the United States unless the Prime Minister faced down opposition to 'top-up' tuition fees from within his own party. The signatories to the letter claimed that they had a commitment to 'equality of opportunity' and to 'ensuring access to higher education for any students capable of benefiting from it'; but they argued that this principle was at risk unless the nation's universities became 'sufficiently well-funded to be able to offer adequate bursaries and scholarships from an increase in fee income'. Unless the Government held its nerve, top universities could be forced to turn their backs on British undergraduates and recruit more foreign and postgraduate students who were expected to pay full fees. The vice-chancellors also urged the Education Secretary to abandon a recent pledge to freeze fees at £3,000 until 2010 or 2011, saying that charges would clearly have to rise again before then (Halpin, 2003).

In the event, the Government's Higher Education Bill got through its second reading in the House of Commons on 27 January 2004 with a majority of just five votes (316 to 311). Seventy-two Labour MPs rebelled and a further 19 abstained. With a paper majority of 161, the Government suffered the biggest revolt on a three-line whip in more than 50 years. At the third reading of the Bill held on 31 March an attempt to overturn the clauses relating to 'top-up' fees was defeated by 316 votes to 288, a government majority of 28; and this time victory for the Government was secured, somewhat ironically, by the support of 43 Scottish Labour MPs who stayed loyal on a bill that would not affect their own voters.

After many months of acrimonious discussion concerning issues of university funding in general and 'top-up' and variable fees in particular, the Government's higher education legislation finally reached the statute book on 1 July 2004. With their ability to charge higher fees, attract endowments and gain more funding for research, a limited number of research universities could now retain their top position in the diverse system of higher education. During the Bill's passage through Parliament, an official from the Higher Education Funding Council observed that 'there is now a clear perception of a hierarchy of universities. This is well-known to students and employers, and the institution attended makes a real difference to your life-chances' (House of Commons Education and Skills Committee, 2003: 56). Universities had certainly entered into what could be described as an era of total marketization in the business of attracting students; and the less 'research intensive' at the bottom of the hierarchy were expected to play a significant role in linking with business through Knowledge Exchanges and Knowledge Transfer Partnerships in order to promote local and regional economies.

Questions of access

Early statistics seemed to indicate that the new fees structure laid down in the 2004 Act was having an adverse effect on applications to higher education. According to figures released by UCAS (Universities and Colleges Admissions Service) on 15 February 2006, the number of students applying to university had fallen for the first time in six years, just months before the introduction of 'top-up' tuition fees. Almost 13,000 fewer young people had applied to university, although there were significant regional variations. Among English students applying to universities in England – the group most affected by the new tuition fees – applications were down by 4.5 per cent; whereas applications to Scottish and Welsh universities, which were not affected by the new funding system, showed a slight increase. Higher Education Minister Bill Rammell said he was confident we would soon see 'a return to a long-term upward trend, as happened after tuition fees were first introduced in 1998'. But Kat Fletcher, President of the National Union of Students, countered that the drop in applications was 'extremely worrying' and suggested that 'top-up' tuition fees and the debt they represented were 'deterring many potential students' (reported in *The Guardian*, 16 February 2006).

Figures released in January 2007 appeared to suggest that Bill Rammell's analysis was correct, in that the numbers of applications for England, Wales and Scotland were roughly back to 2004 levels. At the same time, student leaders claimed that there was anecdotal evidence that 'the fear of debt from increased fees was putting thousands of working-class students off higher education' (reported in *The Guardian*, 15 January 2007).

A front-page story in *The Independent*, published in the middle of August 2007 and headed 'A Generation in Debt', drew attention to some of the more alarming figures in the report of a survey of first-year undergraduates published on Push.co.uk, an organization providing a comprehensive guide for all new university students. It was found that, in the first year of the Government's new 'top-up' fees regime, first-year students had clocked up debts of nearly £6,000 – a 25.5 percentage point increase on the debts incurred by first-year students in the academic year

2005–6 – and that these new students faced leaving university owing more than £17,500 (Garner, 2007).

The most recent report on the impact of tuition fees on applications to higher education was published on 14 February 2008. It was the result of a study carried out for the Sutton Trust by researchers at Staffordshire University who interviewed more than 1,600 students aged 17 and 20 from 20 schools, both state and independent, across the country. It was found that teenagers from 'poorer families' were turning their backs on the prospect of a university education because of fears they would be saddled with thousands of pounds of debt. In fact, the study revealed that nearly two-thirds of students who had decided *not* to seek higher education cited anxieties about money as the main reason. It seemed that very few of the students from 'poorer backgrounds' knew about the bursaries or maintenance grants on offer. At the same time, a large number of relatively poor students from state schools were planning to study at universities close by so that they could live with their families – the overall percentage of such students having risen from 18 in 1998 to 56 in 2007. By comparison, students from independent schools were very happy about moving to a university in a different city, thereby opening up the option of Oxbridge and other 'leading institutions'. The Report concluded that 'students from disadvantaged backgrounds had very few options', while their contemporaries at independent schools could base their decisions 'on the reputation of the desired institutions, rather than the cost'. In the words of the Report: 'independent schools developed an ethos in which going away to university was perceived as being "the natural choice"'. Commenting on the Report, the President of the National Union of Students said: 'If this trend continues, the "prestigious universities" will be accessible only to the rich (reported in *The Guardian*, 14 February 2008).

Concern was also expressed at the beginning of 2008 about the large number of university 'drop-outs' each year – and, once again, it appeared to be the 'non-traditional' intake that was most 'at risk'. According to a report from a committee of MPs, published on 19 February 2008, an £800m drive to reduce the number of students 'dropping out' of university had had almost no effect. This Public Accounts Committee revealed that the proportion of students who failed to complete their course had remained steady at 22 per cent (nearly one in four students) for the past five years. Personal difficulties, dissatisfaction with courses and severe financial pressures were the most frequently cited reasons for giving up, with poorer, older and disabled undergraduates, and those with families, being the students most likely to 'drop out'. According to the Committee's Report, universities were getting larger, 'some could be impersonal' and many were often 'failing to provide experienced individual tutors to support students through their degrees'. Instead of improving support for their more vulnerable students, some universities were actually recruiting more and more students so that 'they did not end up out of pocket when those who "dropped out" took their funding with them' (reported in *The Guardian*, 20 February 2008).

The whole issue of student fees and their effect on access to higher education was the subject of a debate in the pages of *Education Guardian* in March 2008 between Eric Thomas, Vice-Chancellor of Bristol University, who had always supported the idea of 'top-up' fees, and John McDonnell, a leading left-wing Labour MP who said he was 'categorically opposed to any fees for education'.

It was Professor Thomas's view that while the introduction of £3,000 fees had been 'a step in the right direction', it was now time to go even further and lift the cap on fees imposed, albeit for a limited period, by the 2004 Higher Education Bill. In fact, the decision about whether to raise the existing cap on fees 'boiled down to simple mathematics'. British higher education needed additional income if it wished 'to continue to compete on the global stage and to provide all students with the quality of education they had a right to expect'. It had to be remembered that 'the lifetime return on a university degree' was 'phenomenal'. The average graduate earned £160,000 more over their lifetime simply as a result of gaining a degree. It was perfectly reasonable to expect that those who wished to profit from their university education should contribute more towards the cost of it. Politicians must now 'bite the bullet' and 'give universities the freedom to charge higher fees' – it was 'the only viable option'.

For John McDonnell, Labour MP for Hayes and Harlington, the whole debate about student fees was about more than university funding. It was about 'the nature of the society in which we want to live'. Education should *not* be viewed as a commodity. It was 'a public good, essential to any society with a claim to being civilized'. University should be 'an important rite of passage' for young people – 'an opportunity to establish independence, to study an area of interest, and hopefully to do so in a vibrant, stimulating environment, meeting new people and considering new ideas. There were already 'worrying indications' that the fees introduced in 2006 had had the effect of 'deterring many poorer school students from seeking a place at university'. And here John McDonnell was thinking of the Staffordshire University research carried out for the Sutton Trust, referred to earlier in this chapter. All the problems already highlighted would be exacerbated if the Government surrendered to the 'pro-market lobby' and allowed the imposition of 'top-up' fees of from £5,000 to £10,000. As the fifth richest country in the world, Britain was perfectly capable of meeting the cost of higher education if the Government 'addressed its own spending and taxation priorities, rather than forcing upon students the creation of a potentially dysfunctional education market' (*Education Guardian*, 4 March 2008).

The Government could not ignore the fact that there was a growing problem of young people from 'poor' and 'modest' backgrounds not getting through to one form or other of higher education. At the same time, it was clear that it was not going to meet its ambitious target of 50 per cent of all 18- to 30-year-olds going to university by the year 2010. Figures released in March 2008 appeared to show that progress in this area had stalled, with enrolments increasing by only 0.6 per cent in eight years, to 39.8 per cent in 2007. In an address to the Annual Conference of the Higher Education Funding Council for England, delivered on 8 April 2008, John Denham, the Universities Secretary, argued that there must be an attempt to achieve a wider 'social mix' at universities and that universities would have to become more 'transparent' about the process used to select students. In his words:

> Universities that try to take a student's background and the challenges that he or she has faced into account are liable to be accused of political correctness and social engineering. But it could be argued that the fact of a dispropor- tionate number of students from more privileged backgrounds at a particular university is *prima facie* evidence of snobbery and social bias on the part of admissions staff . . . Ultimately, the debate is corrosive of public confidence in the system. And the answer lies, as it so often does, in openness, trans- parency and accountability. It lies in each university having a published admissions policy. (Reported in *The Times*, 8 April 2008)

At the beginning of the previous month, the Government had announced plans for the creation of up to twenty new university towns across Britain, at a total cost of £150m (reported in *The Observer*, 2 March 2008). Yet the need for new campuses on such a large scale appeared to be contradicted by a report by the university umbrella group Universities UK, published on 10 July 2008 and warning its members that unless they addressed the looming shortage in students triggered by the fall in birth rates at the beginning of this century, they could face dire consequences. A drop in student numbers over the next ten years of nearly six per cent would obviously intensify competition between universities. Some could be forced to close or merge, others might have to lower standards to cut costs, and the split between the degrees from elite universities and those from further education colleges could become more marked. Echoing the findings from previous reports, the Universities UK document predicted that we could soon see a further intensification of the hierarchical nature of the universities sector. If universities were allowed to decide their own fees, with the Government lifting the cap on what they could change, we would be heading towards an American-style system, with, 'on the one hand, a small group of elite institutions charging high fees and, on the other, a number of local community colleges delivering degrees to the majority at lower prices' (reported in *The Guardian*, 10 July 2008).

10

Early Years and Childcare Strategies and the Concept of Lifelong Learning

This chapter involves discussion of a number of important educational and social issues: pre-school provision and childcare strategies and the concept of lifelong learning.

Pre-school education in Britain

Much attention has been paid in recent years to pre-school education in Britain. Indeed, many educationists have argued that quality pre-school education should be made universally available to all families with young children, regardless of their financial circumstances. New Labour responded to this argument in its 1997 White Paper *Excellence in Schools* by committing itself to securing 'high quality places' for all 4-year-olds whose parents wanted them and to setting ambitious targets for places for all 3-year-olds. At the same time, it announced the abolition of the Conservatives' recently introduced nursery voucher system which, it was claimed, had created an 'expensive bureaucracy', rather than 'effective co-operation'. The new Government's aim was 'a comprehensive and integrated approach to pre-school education and childcare' (DfEE, 1997: 16).

Categories of early childhood provision in Britain

There are three broad categories of provision for children under 5 in Britain:

- publicly funded services provided through local authorities
- voluntary services
- private services.

Local authority provision consists of two main sub-divisions: *education-based* services and *social (work)* services. As far as *education-based* services provided through local authorities are concerned, there are basically three broad types:

* nursery schools
* nursery classes attached to primary schools
* reception classes in primary schools (though this provision is not available in Scotland).

All these types of provision are staffed by both nursery teachers and nursery nurses.

In the *voluntary* sector (the second of our three broad categories of pre-school provision), playgroups, usually run by parents and especially mothers with the assistance of a playgroup leader, are the most common, although it should be noted that these are largely sessional, often opening for only two or three days a week and operating from premises which they share with other users. In the *private* sector, on the other hand, provision is likely to involve longer opening hours and a greater number of weeks, since this is the sector that caters largely for the needs of working parents. Provision varies significantly from child-minders who look after the children in their own homes, through private nurseries to nursery classes in independent schools.

As far as provision for *very young* children is concerned, J. Eric Wilkinson has pointed out that there is still in Britain a strongly entrenched view among both parents and many professionals that the 'under-threes' will be seriously disadvantaged unless they are reared almost exclusively by their mothers: in other words, 'mothering' is best for very young children and is a full-time occupation. There may be some signs of a recent change of attitude but, to quote Professor Wilkinson, 'the prevailing attitude in the UK means that there is very little educational provision for the under-threes, despite convincing psychological evidence that young children are able to form multiple attachments successfully and comparative evidence that many other European countries provide extensive and successful facilities for their under-threes' (Wilkinson, 1999: 44).

New Labour's early years and childcare strategy

While still in opposition but preparing for government, many leading members of the Labour Party attended a conference in 1996 with the title 'Transforming Nursery Education', at which two of the key speakers were Peter Moss and Helen Penn, authors of a book bearing the same name and published in the same year (Moss and Penn, 1996). At this important conference, Moss and Penn raised concerns about the fragmented nature of early years provision, the early starting-school age in Britain and the importance of addressing the needs of *all* working parents and not just those able and willing to pay for private provision. In their 1996 book, they argued that early childhood services were in a critical state and at a critical stage:

> These services are fragmented, inflexible, incoherent and full of inequalities, unable to meet the changing and varied needs of families. They rely on a workforce, most of whom are poorly paid and poorly trained. Like many other parts of the national infrastructure, early childhood services suffer the consequences of chronic under-resourcing. (Moss and Penn, 1996: vii)

The authors called for an early childhood service that was 'comprehensive, integrated and coherent, offering equal access to flexible, multifunctional and high quality services for all young children from 0 to 6 and their parents' (1996: 3).

At the time when New Labour came to power, the service was beginning to feel the effects of the Major Government's nursery voucher scheme which involved all 'settings' (as they were now called) receiving £1,100 per child, a sum considerably less than the £1,600 it cost to educate a child in a nursery class at the time. For a number of reasons, the scheme resulted in the unofficial lowering of the school-starting age to 4 as local education authorities sought to protect their funding by encouraging parents to send their children early to primary school reception classes and parents, in turn, felt under pressure to send their children to school at the age of 4 if they wanted to secure a place at the school of their choice a year later. Other forms of provision, and notably playgroups, suffered as a result.

The incoming Blair administration took note of many of the concerns raised by Peter Moss and Helen Penn, although ministers stopped short of raising the official school-starting age to 6. As well as announcing the abolition of the nursery voucher system, the 1997 White Paper indicated that each local authority would be required to set up, with local private and voluntary providers, 'an early years forum, representing the full range of providers and users of early years education in the area, as well as employers and others with an interest in early years services' (DfEE, 1997: 16). Although the 'mixed economy of provision' remained in most areas, an important part of the new Government's strategy was the funding of such provision through local authorities, now required to establish Early Years and Childcare Development Partnerships (EYCDPs).

It has been argued (see, for example, Tomlinson, 2005: 132) that whereas New Labour initiatives in other areas of education were often muddled and mutually contradictory, government policies on early years education and childcare, particularly during the first Blair administration, were remarkably coherent – with the additional benefit of being in some measure based on recent research. The Government's intentions were clear and well-articulated: to reduce the numbers of young children living in poverty, improve support for families with young children, and coordinate local services. Early years lecturer John Wadsworth pointed out in 2002 that while the early years picture was 'far from perfect', five years of a New Labour government had ensured that nursery provision had become 'more responsive to the needs of working parents' and was 'more readily accessible than in the past' (Wadsworth, 2002: 56).

What, then, was achieved in the early years of New Labour, and was the reforming zeal sustained during later administrations?

Firstly, the Government launched its National Childcare Strategy in May 1998, with the five-year goal of creating a million new childcare places, 20,000 after-school childcare projects, 60,000 new childcare jobs, along with the means for enabling 250,000 families to move off benefits. The Strategy brought with it additional funding, which was to be increased in the 2002 and 2004 Treasury Spending Reviews. It envisaged that the formation of partnerships with LEAs, with the Benefits Agency, with charities such as Education Extra and the Kids Club Network and with local Training and Enterprise Councils (see Tomlinson, 2005: 106).

Then came what was probably the most important anti-poverty intervention of the first Blair administration. This was the Sure Start Programme (see DfEE, 1999b), a £500 million project offering home visits and support from a wide range of health, education and social services personnel in order to improve the health, well-being and educational attainment of 0–3-year-olds living in disadvantaged areas. It was designed as a 10-year programme targeting areas of real deprivation, with the aim of lifting whole communities out of cycles of poverty. It was also, significantly, a government initiative that did *not* involve competitive bidding between local authorities and did *not* see the need for private funding. Sixty trailblazer programmes were launched in April 1999; and by 2003, around 500 Sure Start programmes were in operation in England, bring together midwives, health visitors and play workers to offer services and support to over 300,000 disadvantaged children (Ball, 2002). Parallel Sure Start plans were developed in Wales, Scotland and Northern Ireland.

The man normally looked upon as the 'architect' of the Sure Start intervention was the economist Norman Glass, a senior civil servant at the Treasury. He certainly took a very keen interest in the early development of the Sure Start Project and made sure that adequate funds were allocated to the Scheme. A Sure Start Unit was set up in the DfES in 2003 to oversee early years and childcare initiatives and the development of Childcare Centres. It is interesting to note that Norman Glass based his argument for Sure Start on compelling evidence from the USA. Randomized controlled trials of early interventions served to demonstrate the clear benefits for disadvantaged children of high-quality pre-school provision from birth to 5 years old. As Angela Anning and David Hall have pointed out (Anning and Hall, 2008: 9): 'the overall message from American research was that money spent on early preventative interventions was likely to save money on remedial services for children later in life; but that *only* sustained, high-quality interventions were truly effective'. As things turned out, Norman Glass was not to be able to sustain his early enthusiasm for the Sure Start Programme; and by early 2005, he had become concerned that his original aims for the Project had been subverted by government ministers, with the Programme becoming part of a new agenda to provide childcare places while poor mothers went out to work.

Yet, despite some initial setbacks and criticisms, there seems to be a widespread view that many aspects of the Sure Start initiative *have* proved a success. Local programmes have offered an opportunity for practitioners to learn from one another and this has happened on a number of levels. They have been able to learn from colleagues within multi-disciplinary teams, from practitioners from other agencies and organizations, and from all the families and communities with whom they have been associated. In a very real sense, Sure Start can be said to have offered a model of a learning community. In the words of Angela Anning and Mog Ball, editors of a recently published book evaluating the Sure Start Project and drawing on 'real-life' experiences gained through the intervention:

> Sure Start has always had a deeply serious moral purpose in addressing poverty and social exclusion. It was backed by a large-scale financial commitment from central government, and through the mechanism of local decision-making, it provided the flexibility to explore new ways of working. Although this left Sure Start open to the criticism that the intervention was

loose and unstructured, it enabled communities to conduct serious experiments in the improvement of services for families. (Anning and Ball, 2008: xvii)

Childcare policies with special implications for very young children were developed with a great sense of urgency following the death of Victoria Climbié, an 8-year-old child of West African origin who was murdered in February 2000, whilst supposedly being monitored by a number of separate agencies including health, social services and the police. This tragic case triggered a government enquiry led by Lord Laming and culminating in the publication of the 2003 Laming Report (Laming, 2003). Laming was highly critical of local authority departments' inability to work together, highlighting the poor coordination between social, health and educational services, and recommended that there should be a Directorate of Children's Services in each local authority. The recurring theme of the Report was that it was the responsibility of *all* professionals working with children to promote their health and development. It was largely as a response to the general feeling of unease that in June 2003 Tony Blair appointed Margaret Hodge to be the first Minister for Children, Young People and Families, based in the Department for Education and Skills and with responsibility for all education and social services for children, families and young people. The new Minister published a Green Paper *Every Child Matters* in September 2003 (HM Treasury, 2003), which provoked a huge debate about how best to integrate children's services to ensure that no child ever again slipped through the net. Proposals in the Green Paper included establishing a Director of Children's Services in each local authority to combine responsibility for education and for children's services, as recommended in the Laming Report. Then the Children Act of November 2004 gave legislative effect to many of the recommendations of the 2003 Green Paper, providing, among other things, for a Children's Commissioner, for a Director of Children's Services in each local authority and also for a Lead Local Council Member in each authority to oversee the integration of services. All local authorities were to be required to put in place a Children and Young People's Plan by 2006.

The 'Every Child Matters' agenda itself was really about delivering the *five* outcomes for children and young people in the 2004 Children Act. They were:

1 – be healthy
2 – stay safe

3 – enjoy and achieve
4 – make a positive contribution to society
5 – achieve economic well-being.

It was anticipated that, in future, every school would be inspected against the five 'Every Child Matters' outcomes and that Ofsted inspection reports would have to make reference to all five areas. It was not enough just to get good test results; schools had to look after the whole child. In this way, schools could make a valuable contribution to a situation where children like Victoria Climbié would be spotted in time and removed from danger.

In the light of the 'Every Child Matters' agenda, Sure Start began to change, and the plan now is for a network of Children's Centres, in a position to provide a universal offer of basic services to all families and utilizing many of the principles which informed the original Sure Start Project.

As far as education is concerned, all 3- and 4-year-olds have been entitled since April 2004 to a free, good-quality, part-time early education place (currently 12.5 hours per week for 38 weeks of the year). Parents have been able to access such places from a complex range of early education provision in the maintained, voluntary or private sectors. All providers, including childminders, have been required to deliver the *Birth to Three Matters* curriculum (DfES, 2002b) for 0–3-year-olds and *Foundation Stage* (QCA, 2000) for 3–5-year-olds. From September 2008, these two curricula will be combined into a single, coherent framework, the *Early Years Foundation Stage*, for the delivery of education and care. And it is to the history of these curriculum initiatives that we must now turn.

The pre-school curriculum

One area in the pre-school curriculum of continuing debate concerns the importance of 'play' which has been a central feature of nursery activities since the social reformer Robert Owen established an infant nursery as part of his model village in New Lanark, Scotland, almost 200 years ago in 1816. His workplace nursery offered places for children aged 12–18 months upwards, while their mothers and fathers were at work. Owen's emphasis was on the freedom of the child from any restraint, a stimulating 'child-centred' curriculum which included singing and dancing (he employed a small group of musicians to play to the children from a musicians' gallery) and methods which were based on the children's need to explore and create for themselves: 'the children were not to be annoyed with books, but were to be taught the uses or nature of common things around them by familiar conversation when the children's curiosity was excited so as to induce them to ask questions' (quoted in Silver, 1969: 65; see also Simon, 1960: 193–7).

Owen's infant nursery soon attracted visitors from all over the world; and his visionary view of nursery education and of the needs of the young child inspired generations of activists. The nursery was, however, discontinued after Owen left England in 1825 to establish New Harmony in America; and, as Harold Silver has pointed out (1969), it was difficult for his humane if somewhat naïve objectives to be sustained at a time of rapid and greedy industrialization. In the words of Peter Moss and Helen Penn: 'his vision faded from the public view, as did the idea of nursery education as a popular cause for the benefit of all and a distinct phase with its own relaxed methodologies and separate from formal schooling' (Moss and Penn, 1996: 59).

It is, of course, true that a number of educationists and philosophers, notably Margaret McMillan and Susan Isaacs, have written about the importance of nursery education since the pioneering work of Robert Owen; and the 1967 Plowden Report *Children and their Primary Schools* (DES, 1967), while adopting a somewhat cautious approach to nursery provision, did at least accept that it had an important role to play in 'areas of social deprivation'.

By the 1980s, a reaction had set in against the whole idea of 'child-centred' learning with 'play', structured or otherwise, forming an essential component of the curriculum. As we saw in Chapter 4, the case of the William Tyndale Junior and Infant schools, which hit the headlines in the mid-1970s, seemed to many parents and politicians to be indicative of the harm that could be done by 'progressive' individuals at all levels of the system. Interviewed by *The Times* in November 1991, Kenneth Clarke attacked what he saw as the rejection of formal structured learning in primary schools:

> What has been regarded as 'good practice' in our primary schools in recent years can't deliver because it is too play-centred, too child-centred . . . There is a great deal of this play-centred teaching . . . which means, at its weakest, there is a lot of the sticking together of egg boxes and playing in sand.

He made it clear that formalization of the curriculum should also apply to 4 year-olds in reception classes (*The Times*, 4 November 1991). Many educationists and practitioners were understandably alarmed later in the decade when participation in the Government's new nursery voucher scheme meant working towards a set of narrowly defined goals described as the Desirable Learning Outcomes (SCAA, 1996). As we have already seen, the scramble for 4-year-olds' vouchers led to a rapid increase in the number of young children experiencing 'nursery' or 'early years' education in the reception classes of primary schools. Naima Browne wrote in 1999 of the plight of reception class teachers having to ensure that their teaching was compliant with the requirements of the National Curriculum (for their older or 'more able' children), whilst simultaneously keeping in mind (for their younger children) the SCAA's Learning Outcomes (Browne, 1999: 74).

It has to be acknowledged that the 2000 *Curriculum Guidance for the Foundation Stage* (QCA, 2000), which was due to become the statutory curriculum framework for children of nursery and reception age in England when the Foundation Stage for early education was established by the 2002 Education Act, met with a very favourable response from many teachers and educationists. It was generally felt to be a vast improvement on the rigid and restrictive framework produced by the previous Conservative Government. There was now an emphasis on children learning through play, the importance of outdoor provision was emphasized, and the Conservatives' restrictive Desirable Learning Outcomes (DLOs) had been replaced by a more 'child-friendly' set of Early Learning Goals.

That being said, it was argued by a number of early years practitioners (see, for example, Wadsworth, 2002: 57) that the English *Guidance* could not be said to be as 'progressive' or 'enlightened' as the curriculum frameworks in place in Wales and Scotland. Neither the Welsh nor the Scottish curriculum documents placed the same emphasis on letter and number knowledge, the Welsh document making reference to children enjoying 'marking and basic writing experiences – using pencils, crayons, etc' (ACCAC, 2000: 56) and the Scottish *Framework* talking in terms of 'developing an awareness of letter names and sounds in the context of play experiences' (SCCC, 1999: 57). Significantly, the Scottish document contained no separate section on mathematics, as this was deemed to be part of 'communication and language'. Unlike the English framework with its 'Stepping Stones', there were no implied learning objectives in the Welsh and Scottish documents, the Welsh *Guidance* referring only to 'areas of experience' and the Scottish *Framework* including a useful introductory section outlining the differing learning needs of young children. Neither document went so far as to provide illustrative examples of what an average child might be able to achieve at a given age.

The Early Years Foundation Stage (EYFS) was not to retain its liberal curriculum framework; and in the years following 2005, when it became part of the National Curriculum, it took on a far more restrictive character. Under new regulations to come into force in the Autumn of 2008, children aged 3 to 5 would be continually assessed on 13 learning scales, including writing, problem solving and numeracy. They would be expected to use mathematics to solve practical problems, retell stories in the correct sequence, understand 'right' from 'wrong', read simple sentences on their own, sit quietly, be able to use a computer and understand that other people had their own views, culture and beliefs which had to be respected (Woolcock, 2008).

During 2007 a growing body of academics argued that the EYFS Framework would induce needless anxiety and dent young children's enthusiasm for learning. Then, at the end of July 2008, a powerful lobby of leading authors and educationists sent a letter to *The Times* accusing Beverley Hughes, the Children's Minister, of ignoring the recommendations of her own advisers and of setting children up for failure. The letter was signed by more than 80 campaigners, including psychologist Steve Biddulph, Professor Tim Brighouse of the Institute of Education in London, Professor Susie Orbach of the London School of Economics and children's authors Philip Pullman and Michael Morpurgo. It was pointed out in the letter that an authoritarian curriculum framework for young children had been 'resisted elsewhere in the UK' and it was argued that the 'compulsory learning requirements' proposed for England should be changed to 'voluntary guidance'. The one 'concession' that Beverley Hughes had made – a 34-page exemption process purporting to enable childcare providers to opt out of some of the 'learning requirements' – was described by the signatories as 'expertly camouflaged, labyrinthine and bureaucratically complex' as if it had been 'intentionally designed to deter anyone from applying'. The letter ended by saying that parents should have the right to choose how their preschool children were cared for and educated. Young children should also have the right to be 'protected from an imposed system which harnesses their development to prescribed targets, and which may well force them into inappropriate early learning' (letter to *The Times*, 24 July 2008).

Lifelong learning

After Tony Blair became Leader of the Labour Party in July 1994, it was repeatedly stressed in the Party's education policy documents that education and training were to be the means by which Britain would be transformed from a low-skill, low-wage economy into a high-skill, high-wage and technologically advanced economy. In other words, there was to be a virtual subservience of educational ends to economic and industrial priorities. This was not exactly something new, calling to mind one of the key themes running through the education documents of the Callaghan administration in the second half of the 1970s; but as a policy objective it was to be pursued with a new intensity. Sally Tomlinson has argued (Tomlinson, 2001: 82) that, while in opposition, New Labour actually used dubious evidence to support its contention that youngsters were leaving school without the skills necessary to survive in a modern economy. Shadow ministers repeatedly used a figure from a 1995 report on World Competitiveness compiled by a Swiss organization, the World Economic Forum, which put Britain in thirty-fifth place out of 48 countries for the adequacy and relevance of its state education system. The professor who compiled the report later admitted that the statistic actually represented the opinions of 500 business executives working in Britain, none of whom was necessarily knowledgeable about the British state school system.

This renewed emphasis on economic objectives in the years before New Labour came to power in 1997 had obvious implications for the Party's attitude towards lifelong learning and the learning society. At the same time, a commitment to lifelong learning and the concept of a learning age, where learning throughout life becomes the *norm* rather than the *exception,* was also used by New Labour as a strategic response to issues of equity and social cohesion. A 1996 paper on *Lifelong Learning* (Labour Party, 1996b) emphasized that continuous education was the key to economic success, social cohesion and national prosperity:

> Education is the key to economic success, social cohesion and active citizenship. Our future national prosperity depends on the skills and abilities of our people. In a rapidly changing, technologically advanced and increasingly competitive global economy, Britain needs a world-class system of education and training. The regular updating of skills and knowledge has become essential to maintaining and enhancing productivity and security in the workplace. (Labour Party, 1996b: 2)

Individuals were to be responsible for their own learning, and 'the young unemployed' had a responsibility to 'seek work, accept reasonable opportunities and upgrade their skills' (1996b: 7). In the same year, a paper with the title *Learn as You Earn: Labour's Plans for a Skills Revolution* (Labour Party, 1996a) stressed the importance of developing a portfolio of skills throughout working life, and promised the introduction of Individual Learning Accounts and the setting up of a University for Industry.

Differing views of a learning society

It has to be admitted that such terms as 'lifelong learning', 'the learning age' and 'the learning society' are capable of many differing interpretations. In his book *Towards the Learning Society*, published in 1994, Stewart Ranson argued that such a society should be one which encouraged the development of a new moral and political order, rather than one which merely prepared individuals to perform effectively and function efficiently in a modern capitalist economy. According to Ranson, only a new moral and political democratic order could, in turn, act as the foundation for sustaining the personal development of all. It would encourage all individuals to 'value their active role as citizens and thus their shared responsibility for the common wealth' (Ranson, 1994: 129). Critics – and these included politicians of all major parties – tended to argue that such a view was hopelessly naïve and idealistic, and that modern governments should promote a learning society which encouraged individuals to invest *in themselves* and accept responsibility for acquiring the skills needed to remain in regular paid employment. Only by shouldering this major responsibility could they avoid becoming a burden on the state.

Much of New Labour's attitude towards lifelong learning was indeed based on so-called human capital theory, which stressed the need for all individuals to 'learn as they earned' and 'invest in themselves': these ideas have a history going back at least as far as the early 1960s. It was, in fact, in 1960 that Theodore W. Schultz had argued in his Presidential Address to the American Economic Association (on the theme 'Investment in Human Capital') that the process of acquiring skills and knowledge through education was to be viewed not as a form of consumption, but rather as a productive investment. According to Schultz, 'by investing in themselves, people can enlarge the range of choice available to them. It is the one way free men [sic] can enhance their welfare' (Schultz, 1961: 2). According to this analysis, investment in human capital not only increased individual productivity but, in so doing, also laid the technical base of the type of labour force necessary for rapid and continuing economic growth.

Continuing the theme into the late 1990s, Anthony Giddens argued in his influential book, *The Third Way* (Giddens, 1998), that we should move away from the *negative* focus of the 1942 Beveridge Report with its famous declaration of war on Want, Disease, Ignorance, Squalor and Idleness and speak instead of *positive welfare,* to which individuals themselves and other agencies besides government contribute, and which is functional for wealth creation. The guiding ideology for governments should be 'investment in *human capital,* rather than the direct provision of economic maintenance. In place of the *welfare state,* we should put the *social investment state,* operating in the context of a *positive welfare society*' (Giddens, 1998: 117). In 1999, Hodgson and Spours pointed out that both Conservative and New Labour governments were fond of quoting comparisons with other developed countries to prove that those which had 'a more concerted and co-ordinated approach to investment in human capital' also had the more successful economies (Hodgson and Spours, 1999: 24).

All of this conveniently overlooks the fact that in any society, economically advanced or otherwise, there will be large numbers of individuals for whom human capital theory has little or no significance. For one thing, issues of gender, race and disability simply cannot be ignored. At the same time, there are many adults whose unhappy experiences at school will not have predisposed them to broadening their horizons beyond the age of 16.

Two important policy statements

The first Blair administration published two major policy papers with obvious implications for lifelong learning, *The Learning Age* in 1998 and *Learning to Succeed* in 1999, and it is important to deal with each of these in turn.

The first of these papers, *The Learning Age: A Renaissance for a New Britain* (DfEE, 1998) had been promised for the autumn of 1997 and had been billed as a White Paper, but finally appeared in February 1998 and was published as a Green Paper. Hodgson and Spours have pointed out (1999: 23) that 'it received a cautious welcome for its scope and some of its proposals, but disappointed many commentators because of its lowly status as a Green Paper'.

Blunkett's Foreword to the Paper argued that investment in human capital should be seen as 'the foundation of success in the knowledge-based global economy of the twenty-first century'. It went on to emphasize the role that lifelong learning could play in securing Britain's economic future:

To achieve stable and sustainable growth, we will need a well-educated, well-equipped and adaptable labour force. To cope with rapid change and the challenge of the information and communication age, we must ensure that people can return to learning throughout their lives . . . If we are to realise our ambition, we must all develop and sustain a regard for learning at whatever age. For many people, this will mean overcoming past experiences which have put them off learning. For others, it will mean taking the opportunity, perhaps for the first time, to recognise their own talent, to discover new ways of learning and to see new opportunities opening up. What was previously available only to the few can, in the century ahead, be something which is enjoyed and taken advantage of by the many. (DfEE, 1998: 7)

It is true that the 1998 Green Paper envisaged an *enabling* rather than a *regulatory* role for the state in supporting the development of lifelong learning; and it underlined the importance of a partnership approach, with due emphasis on the responsibilities of individuals, employers and trade unions in making the vision of a learning age a reality. It urged more co-operation and partnership between the Further Education Funding Council and local government, including the creation of local learning centres. Regional development agencies were to be set up and these were to have a central role to play in co-ordinating and planning an interrelated economic and education policy at the regional level. Two initiatives were said to exemplify the Government's approach to lifelong learning.

1 Individual Learning Accounts would enable men and women to take responsibility for their own learning, with support from both government and employers.
2 The University for Industry would offer access to a learning network to help people deepen their knowledge, update their existing skills and gain new ones (DfEE, 1998).

More details were provided about these two initiatives in the 1999 White Paper *Learning to Succeed: A New Framework for Post-16 Learning* (DfEE, 1999). Here Individual Learning Accounts were described as 'a major strand in the Government's programme for a lifelong learning revolution' (p. 56). People would be required to invest their own money in their Account, but the responsibility would *not* lie with the individual alone. The Government would give £150 to each individual in the first year of the Account, and there would be additional contributions from employers. There would be a discount on the cost of certain eligible courses, including computer literacy. To be launched nationally in the autumn of 2000, the University for Industry would promote lifelong learning by working with a wide range of partners to provide 'flexible access to high quality, relevant innovative learning opportunities'. It would offer a free, comprehensive information and advice service, and would 'broker a national learning network with learning materials which would allow people to learn at home, in the workplace or in learning centres based in their communities' (p. 57).

The White Paper seemed to envisage a key role for government in the funding, regulation and inspection of lifelong learning provision, but there was also a continuing emphasis on co-operation and partnership at all levels. Indeed the sharing of responsibility was included as one of the principles underpinning the Government's vision set out in the first chapter (DfEE, 1999: 13):

- investing in learning to benefit everyone
- lifting barriers to learning
- putting people first
- sharing responsibility with employers, employees and the community
- achieving world class standards and value for money
- working together as the key to success.

The key policy of the White Paper in establishing a new regulatory framework for post-16 education and training was the setting up of a national Learning and Skills Council (LSC) to replace the Further Education Funding Council and the Training and Enterprise Councils. This new body would assume responsibility for the funding, planning, management and quality assurance of all education and training for people over the age of 16, with the exception of higher education. The Secretary of State would appoint the Chair and members of the Council, with employers constituting the largest single group. The LSC would be expected to forge important links with the new University for Industry and other key partners at a local and national level. It would be responsible for the planned distribution of around £5 billion of public money and the welfare of over five million learners.

The ideas in the White Paper formed the basis for the measures outlined in the Learning and Skills Bill which was introduced into Parliament in December 1999 and had its second reading in the House of Lords by January 2000. Before it became law, the Bill was criticized by some on the grounds of the enormous power to be wielded by the new Learning and Skills Council (and indeed by a number of quangos and interrelated bodies).

The story of provision for adults and lifelong learning under New

Labour since 1997 has not been one of undiluted success. A press release issued by Estelle Morris in October 2001 announced that Individual Learning Accounts were to be suspended on account of growing concerns about fraud and with around 300 providers being under investigation by the police. Their figures published in *The Observer* in early June 2003 revealed that, despite the £663 million spent on adult education and skills initiatives between 1998 and 2002, with an additional £207 million earmarked for 2003, course enrolments had dropped significantly over a four-year period. Between 1998 and 2002, the number of those participating in adult education dropped by 73,000 (from 1,115,000 to 1,042,000). There was also a marked decline in the number of adult males opting for modern apprenticeships – from 188,300 to 151,400 – despite repeated calls from business that Britain needed more plumbers and skilled workers (*The Observer,* 8 June 2003).

In 2003, the Government published a Paper setting out the mode of delivery of a National Skills Strategy, and four months later, the DfES, the Department for Trade and Industry, HM Treasury and the Department for Work and Pensions published a joint Paper, *21st Century Skills: Realising Our Potential* (DfES, DTi, HM Treasury, DWP (2003) outlining the details of a new Skills Alliance, which would bring together government, employers and trade unions in a new social partnership. The Paper lamented the lower level of workforce skills in Britain than existed in France and Germany and promised to give employers greater choice and control over the sort of training they deemed necessary in order for Britain to survive in a competitive world.

11

Issues of Diversity, Equality and Citizenship

The purpose of this chapter is to examine the citizenship debate and to look at the ways in which schools are endeavouring to combat prejudice and discrimination in all their various forms.

At the end of a productive period of consultation and debate in the late 1990s, it was accepted by the DfEE that at the two primary key stages, a new citizenship programme should be integrated with personal, social and health education (PSHE) and that this should be *non-statutory* guidance; whereas, for the two key stages at the secondary level, time would have to be found for teaching citizenship as a new foundation subject and this would be a *statutory* requirement. The Secretary of State's proposals for the review of the National Curriculum, which were published in May 1999 (DfEE/QCA, 1999), placed considerable emphasis on citizenship education; and the Orders for Citizenship came into force in the autumn of 2002. As it became clear that at the two secondary key stages PSHE guidelines would remain *non-statutory,* there were concerns among some secondary teachers that PSHE programmes could lose their special character, in the process of being subsumed within the general framework of citizenship education.

A 1984 book on the concepts and content of personal and social education (Pring, 1984) emphasized that the personal, social and moral development of young people should be a major concern of all schools; and quoted in full a letter sent by an American high school principal to all his newly appointed teachers on the first day of each new academic year:

Dear Teacher
I am a survivor of a concentration camp. My eyes saw what no man should witness.
Gas chambers built by learned engineers.
Children poisoned by educated physicians.

Infants killed by trained nurses.
Women and babies shot and burned by high school and college graduates.
So, I am suspicious of education.
My request is: help your students to become human. Your efforts must never produce learned monsters, skilled psychopaths, educated Eichmans. Reading, writing, arithmetic are all important; but only if they serve to make our children more human. (Quoted in Pring, 1984: viii)

Many PSE teachers, and particularly those in secondary schools, will seek to ensure that citizenship education programmes do, in fact, address the fundamental issue outlined in this letter. Others will wish to emphasize the *interconnections* between PSE (or PSHE) and citizenship education. Before we move on to look at some of the topics which demand to be included in a modern citizenship programme and, in particular, at the main recommendations of the 1998 Crick Report, it will be useful to say something about the historical background to the current preoccupation with citizenship issues.

Historical background to the citizenship debate

Marsden (1989) and Phillips (1998) have argued that throughout the nineteenth century, geography and history lessons always had the intention of producing the 'good citizen' rooted in anti-papist Protestantism. Imperial developments in the 50 years or so prior to the First World War, as well as the impact of eugenicist ideas from the 1880s onwards, promoted narrow and often racist ideas about what it meant to be a decent patriotic British citizen.

The horrors of the First World War caused something of a reaction to jingoism and patriotic notions of heroism, and the interwar period saw the first attempts in school geography and history lessons to generate a concern for international understanding and citizenship. The fear of Fascism and other totalitarian doctrines and of the threat they posed to world peace even prompted a group of progressive educators to form, in 1934, the Association for Education in Citizenship which advocated *direct training* for citizenship, rather than the *indirect* method of using existing subjects to promote democratic attitudes and values.

Yet this concern to promote democratic ideals within the context of a sympathetic understanding of other people was not to have lasting appeal; and there was to be a comparative lack of interest in the League of Nations publication, *History Teaching and World Citizenship,* which came out in 1938. More popular and influential a year later was a short publication which advocated a 'line of development' or chronological approach to the teaching of British history which would, or so it was claimed, prove a sensible way of promoting 'good citizenship' (Jeffreys, 1939).

Denis Lawton (2000) has made the point that since 1945, there have been two main views of the nature and purpose of citizenship education: the *passive* citizen view, involving training for conformity and obedience; and the *active* citizen view, educating the future citizen for active participation in a modern democratic society. The passive citizen view would tend to encourage the teaching of facts about government institutions and about the (non-existent) British Constitution, as well as the duties and responsibilities associated with being a good citizen. Advocates of the active citizen view would want to concentrate on the understanding of political ideas and conflicts and, where appropriate, on developing independent and critical viewpoints (including a willingness to be critical of the status quo). As Professor Lawton tellingly observes (2000: 11): 'the first approach runs the risk of provoking boredom; the second the risk of facing accusations of subversion'.

A number of the secondary modern schools which grew up in the 1940s and 1950s experimented with basing their new curriculum on social studies as the dominating core to which everything else then had to be subservient. As Cannon has shown, such schemes failed for a number of reasons, not least the need for the new secondary modern schools to be seen to be achieving good examination results in a variety of subjects: 'Of all the reasons for the failure of this experimental approach to curriculum planning, most important probably were the social and economic pressures which led to an increasing concern for standards, and, in particular, to their expression in examination qualifications' (Cannon, 1964: 22).

Other non-selective schools emphasized the teaching of civics, which was often seen to be in the elementary-school tradition of imbuing working-class youngsters with an appropriate respect for authority and a clear sense of where they fitted into the social hierarchy. Here there was a clear risk of provoking that sense of boredom and alienation referred to earlier; and we know that the teaching of subjects such as civics, current affairs and even social studies, all of them concerned in some way or other with citizenship education, rarely conveyed that sense of excitement and relevance which was always an essential part of engaging the interest of secondary modern school pupils. The 1963 Newsom Report, concerned primarily with the education of older pupils of 'average or less than average ability', recognized the problems faced by schools in preparing young people for entry into the adult world:

Civics, current affairs, modern history, social studies, whether under those names or not, ought to feature in the secondary modern school programme. But they need sensitive handling if they are not to go sadly awry . . . Above all, they need lively presentation in terms of people and events, if they are not to seem arid and boring abstractions to most boys and girls. (Ministry of Education, 1963a: 73)

The arrival of comprehensive secondary schooling in the 1960s was not accompanied by a nationwide debate on the content and purpose of the curriculum which might have come up with some interesting ideas about suitable methods of preparing vulnerable youngsters to find their way in the modern world; and even when James Callaghan launched his Great Debate on Education in 1976, little attention was paid to the role of citizenship or political education. Then again, as we saw in Chapter 6, the National Curriculum which constituted such an important part of the 1988 Education Reform Act was based on a list of traditional subject disciplines, and it was confidently assumed that all cross-curricular themes could be 'delivered' through these all-important foundation subjects. It is true that a forward-looking 1990 National Curriculum Council (NCC) document, *Curriculum Guidance 3: The Whole Curriculum* (NCC, 1990), attempted to compensate for some of the shallow thinking underpinning the Thatcher Government's legislative proposals by identifying five cross-curricular themes that ought to appear in a curriculum claiming to be broad and balanced, and one of these was education for citizenship (the other four being economic and industrial understanding, careers education and guidance, health education, and environmental education). In the words of the NCC document (NCC, 1990: 5), the aims of education for citizenship were to:

• establish the importance of positive, participative citizenship and provide the motivation to join in
• help pupils to acquire and understand essential information on which to base the development of their skills, values and attitudes towards citizenship.

But laudable though these aims might have been, the NCC approach had the effect of reducing citizenship to a non-statutory, optional part of the school curriculum; and it was soon obvious that all cross-curricular themes would be marginalized as schools struggled valiantly to implement a seriously overloaded curriculum framework.

It was not until November 1997, after the election of a New Labour government in May, that Education Secretary David Blunkett set up an

Advisory Group on Citizenship, chaired by Professor Bernard Crick, charged with the task of 'providing advice on effective education for citizenship in schools', which then published its Report, *Education for Citizenship and the Teaching of Democracy in Schools,* in September 1998 (DfEE/QCA, 1998). It is to this Report we will now turn.

The Crick Report

The authors of the Crick Report described the aims of citizenship education in schools and colleges in the following terms:

> To make secure and to increase the knowledge, skills and values relevant to the nature and practices of participative democracy; also to enhance the awareness of rights and duties, and the sense of responsibilities needed for the development of pupils into active citizens; and, in so doing, to establish the value to individuals, schools and society of involvement in the local and wider community . . . It is clear that democratic institutions, practices and purposes must be understood, both local and national, including the work of parliaments, councils, parties, pressure groups and voluntary bodies, in order to show how formal political activity relates to civil society in the context of the United Kingdom and Europe, and to cultivate awareness and concern for world affairs and global issues. Some understanding of the realities of economic life is also needed, including how taxation and public expenditure work together. (DfEE/QCA, 1998: para. 6.6)

As far as the Crick Advisory Group were concerned, *three* components or strands had emerged in the course of debate to form a framework for school planning:

- social and moral responsibility
- community involvement
- political literacy.

Such general strands were relatively uncontroversial; but there followed a listing of the recommended learning outcomes for each key stage and, as Janet Harland (2000) has pointed out, these were considered problematic by all those educationists who were in favour of less prescriptive instructions to classroom teachers and who believed in a more 'humanistic' approach to the teaching–learning process.

The use of 'learning outcomes' was actually included by the Crick Committee within its 'Essential Recommendations' to be found at the beginning of the Report. In the words of the Committee:

we unanimously recommend that . . . the entitlement to citizenship education is established by setting out specific learning outcomes for each key stage, rather than detailed programmes of study. We advise substituting for the present input and output model of the existing National Curriculum subjects, an output model alone based on tightly defined learning outcomes. This will offer flexibility to schools in relation to local conditions and opportunities, and allow the possibility of different approaches to citizenship education, involving differing subject combinations and aspects of the curriculum based on existing good practice in each school . . . Moreover, the learning outcomes should be tightly enough defined so that standards and objectivity can be inspected by Ofsted. (DfEE/QCA, 1998: paras 4.2; 4.3)

The learning outcomes recommended by the Crick Advisory Group were founded on four essential elements:

- concepts
- values and dispositions
- skills and aptitudes
- knowledge and understanding.

In the words of the Report, 'the successful integration and progressive development of these essential elements across the key stages would ensure that schools achieved the learning outcomes and, in so doing, developed effective education for citizenship for all pupils' (DfEE/QCA, 1998: para. 6.8).

The key concepts were designed to provide a clear, overarching, conceptual core to citizenship education. It was anticipated that pupils would come to understand, as they progressed through the various key stages, how all these key concepts 'served collectively, though not exclusively, to underpin effective education for citizenship' (1998). They were listed on page 44 as follows:

- democracy and autocracy
- co-operation and conflict
- equality and diversity
- fairness, justice, the rule of law, rules, law and human rights
- freedom and order
- individual and community
- power and authority
- rights and responsibilities.

The idea of 'learning outcomes' was hotly debated when the Crick Report was published but, in the event, the 'outcomes' approach was somewhat toned down in the Secretary of State's Proposals of May 1999 which talked instead in terms of a 'learning framework' and placed a surprising and very welcome emphasis on teacher autonomy at all levels. It is not clear exactly why there was this change of heart, but Dr Harland (2000: 60) has argued that it may have been because the politicians and officials who drafted the 1999 Proposals decided not to risk laying yet further overt prescriptions on schools, especially in an area of the curriculum where it could be claimed that teachers had had little or no formal training, and where there were few acknowledged 'experts' able and willing to assume responsibility for seeing that the defined outcomes had, in fact, been reached.

The need to combat prejudice

It is well established that there are certain groups of people in British society who face prejudice and discrimination, and who suffer disproportionately in relation to others because they happen to be different from the majority. The classroom discussion of issues of unfairness and inequality has to be a useful step on the road to ensuring the eradication of prejudice and exploitation; and the creation of a just and civilized society is seen by many as a positive goal of lessons in PSE and citizenship.

It is, of course, true that this essentially 'reconstructionist' view of the purpose of education has not gone unchallenged. Over the last 20 or so years, a number of leading politicians and political pressure groups, particularly on the right, have argued against the explicit use of the school curriculum to combat prejudice.

In her triumphant address to the 1987 Conservative Party Conference (following a third massive electoral victory), Margaret Thatcher sought to ridicule and condemn all those who were said to be using education to tackle issues of diversity and social justice:

> Too often, our children don't get the education they need – the education they *deserve*. And in the inner cities – where youngsters must have a decent education if they are to have a better future – that opportunity is all too often snatched from them by hard-left education authorities and extremist teachers. Children who need to be able to count and multiply are learning anti-racist mathematics – whatever that may be. Children who need to be able to express themselves in clear English are being taught political slogans. Children who need to be taught to respect traditional moral values are being taught that they have an inalienable right to be gay. (Thatcher, 1987)

The year before, in 1986, one of the prominent right-wing pressure groups of the period, the Hillgate Group, had written an influential pamphlet, *Whose Schools? A Radical Manifesto,* in which it was argued that 'schoolchildren had to be rescued from indoctrination in all the fashionable causes of the Radical Left: "anti-racism", "anti-sexism", "peace education" (which usually means CND [Campaign for Nuclear Disarmament] propaganda) and "anti-heterosexism" (meaning the preaching of homosexuality, combined with an attack on the belief that heterosexuality is normal)'. To this end, all schools should be 'released from the control of local government', thereby 'depriving the politicised local education authorities of their standing ability to corrupt the minds and souls of the young' (Hillgate Group, 1986: 4, 13, 18).

Margaret Thatcher's successor as Prime Minister, John Major, appeared to share the right's contempt for 'fashionable causes' and 'politically correct' thinking. In his keynote address to the 1992 Conservative Party Conference, he was keen to emphasize his respect for traditional educational values and his rejection of the idea that schools should concern themselves with issues of equal opportunity:

> When it comes to education, my critics say I'm 'old-fashioned'. Old-fashioned? Reading and writing? Spelling and sums? Great literature – and standard English grammar? Old-fashioned? Tests and tables? British history? A proper grounding in science? Discipline and self-respect? Old-fashioned? Well, if I'm old-fashioned, so be it. So are the vast majority of Britain's parents . . . Because I'm old-fashioned, I want reform of teacher training in this country. Let us return to basic subject teaching and get rid of courses *in* the theory of education . . . Our primary teachers should learn how to teach children to read, not waste their time on the politics of gender, race and class. (Quoted in Chitty and Simon, 1993: 144)

As far as 'race' was concerned,[1] there was a marked change in the political climate following the murder of the teenager Stephen

---

[1]   It is now common for the term 'race' to be placed in quotation marks, and this is due to its problematic nature. It has been argued persuasively that the term is, in fact, 'socially constructed' and that it arises out of the 'pseudo-scientific' doctrines of the second half of the nineteenth century, which were chiefly concerned to promote the theory of 'white superiority'. It seems clear that 'race' is not a valid biological concept and that it lacks scientific underpinning as a means of categorizing people. It may sometimes be used to describe groups of people who share certain physical characteristics, such as skin colour, facial features or type of hair, but here the important point is the *social significance* that is placed upon these characteristics.

Lawrence. It was a cause of genuine public dismay when 18-year-old Stephen, who was the son of parents of Jamaican origin, sustained appalling and fatal injuries at the hands of five violent racists near his home in Eltham in south London on 22 April 1993. He was stabbed to a depth of about five inches on both sides of the front of his body, with both stab wounds severing axillary arteries, causing blood to pump out of his body until he finally collapsed. The public outcry over both the murder and the obvious shortcomings in the police investigation was so great that one national newspaper, *The Daily Mail,* was prepared to risk a libel action by actually printing the names of the five young men popularly thought to be the perpetrators of the crime. Three of the chief suspects were brought to trial in 1996 in a private prosecution, which failed because of the absence of any firm and sustainable evidence. Then, after a full hearing in the following year, the inquest jury returned the unanimous verdict that 'Stephen Lawrence was unlawfully killed in a completely unprovoked racist attack by five white youths'.

At the end of July 1997, the Labour Home Secretary, Jack Straw, asked Sir William Macpherson to head an inquiry into 'the matters arising from the death of Stephen Lawrence'; and after over a year of detailed information-gathering, the Macpherson Report was published in February 1999 (Macpherson, 1999). This lengthy document, running to 335 pages, contained a number of far-reaching implications and recommendations both for the future investigation and prosecution of racially motivated crimes and for the role of several institutions and agencies in the eradication of racism. In the words of the Report:

> Racism, institutional or otherwise, is not the prerogative of the Police Service. It is clear that other agencies, including, for example, those dealing with housing and education, also suffer from the disease. If racism is to be eradicated, there must be specific and co-ordinated action both within the agencies themselves and by society at large, particularly through the educational system, from pre-primary school upwards and onwards. (para. 6.54, p. 33)

The Report concluded by making a number of important recommendations under the heading 'Prevention and the Role of Education' (paras 67, 68, 69, 70, pp. 334–5):

- that consideration be given to amendment of the National Curriculum aimed at valuing cultural diversity and preventing racism, in order better to reflect the needs of a diverse society.

- that Local Education Authorities and School Governors have the duty to create and implement strategies in their schools to prevent and address racism. Such strategies should include:
  – that schools record all racist incidents;
  – that all recorded incidents are reported to the pupils' parents/guardians, School Governors and LEAs;
  – that the number of racist incidents are published annually on a school-by-school basis; and
  –   that the numbers and self-defined ethnic identity of 'excluded' pupils are published annually on a school-by-school basis.
- that Ofsted inspections include examination of the implementation of such strategies.
- that in creating strategies under the provisions of the Crime and Disorder Act or otherwise, Police Services, Local Government and relevant agencies should specifically consider implementing community and local initiatives aimed at promoting cultural diversity and addressing racism and the need for focused, consistent support for such initiatives.

Another obvious example of prejudice, both in schools and in society at large, relates to gay and lesbian young people and all those teenagers who are confused about their sexuality – one of the targets of Margaret Thatcher's 1987 Conference Speech quoted above. Here the key piece of recent legislation has been Section or Clause 28 of the Thatcher Government's 1988 Local Government Act.

The subject of a heated and often acrimonious debate that has lasted for over a decade, Section 28 laid down that a local authority should not:

- intentionally promote homosexuality or publish material with the intention of promoting homosexuality
- promote the teaching in any maintained school of the acceptability of homosexuality as a pretended family relationship.

This clause fulfilled one of its chief functions by causing considerable anxiety and apprehension among large numbers of teachers, particularly in the secondary sector; but, in reality, its impact on the teaching of sex education in schools *should* have been pretty negligible. What the sponsors of the measure had overlooked was the fact that, two years earlier, the 1986 Education Act had removed responsibility for school sex education from local education authorities and placed it in the hands of school governors. The new clause could not therefore prevent the informed discussion of homosexual relationships in the classroom, an important point which the Government was forced to concede in a rarely quoted Department of the Environment circular published in May 1988:

> Responsibility for school sex education continues to rest with school govern-ing bodies, by virtue of Section 18 of the Education (No. 2) Act of 1986. Section 28 of the 1988 Local Government Act does not affect the activities of school governors, nor of teachers. It will not prevent the objective discus-sion of homosexuality in the classroom, nor the counselling of students concerned about their sexuality. (Department of the Environment, 1988: 5)

That said, it is generally acknowledged that Section 28 *was* an impor-tant cultural and symbolic event in the recent history of sexual politics. It came at a time of increasing public awareness of child sexual abuse and of a moral panic surrounding the advent of HIV/AIDS; and it was to play a significant role in undermining the confidence and professional-ism of classroom teachers. As Rachel Thomson, a prominent worker in the area of HIV and sex education, observed in 1993:

> The phrase 'the promotion of homosexuality' had the insidious effect of constructing teachers as the potential corruptors of young people and of frightening teachers from saying what they thought was sensible and right out of fear of losing their jobs . . . The net effect . . . was to create a climate of paranoia around the teaching of sex education. (Thomson, 1993: 225)

It is clearly not the role of classroom teachers to 'promote' homosex-uality, or indeed any form of sexual orientation. The idea that certain gay and lesbian teachers are seriously concerned to put across the notion that homosexuality or bisexuality are somehow 'superior' forms of sexual orientation has always been a myth perpetuated by certain Conservative politicians and a number of right-wing national newspapers. What teach-ers *would* like to feel free to 'promote', without fear of being disci-plined, is the *acceptability* rather than the *superiority* of the homosexual lifestyle, although the use of the term 'lifestyle' in this context is some-what problematic, carrying with it subtle implications of something 'chosen', like a fashion accessory.

The real nature of the debate about Section 28 was articulated in an editorial in *The Observer* published in early 2000:

> Teachers have no wish to be in the business of 'promoting' any kind of sexu-ality, or family structure, over another. Section 28 was never about 'promo-tion' in this sense – it was all about stopping teachers from even talking about same-sex relationships as real, and serious, parts of the adult world for which

children were being prepared. The main reason for ditching Section 28 as soon as possible is to allow children to be taught about the real world, a world in which moral values such as commitment, fidelity, care and responsibility are more important than ever but are not attached exclusively to the marriage contract. (*The Observer*, 30 January 2000)

In July 2000, the Department for Education and Employment published *Sex and Relationship Education Guidance* (DfEE, 2000), a new framework for the provision of sex and relationship education in schools, designed to replace existing circulars and to take account of the revised National Curriculum, published in September 1999. This document began by arguing that school students should be taught about 'the nature and importance of marriage for family life and bringing up children', but it also recognized that there were strong and mutually supportive relationships outside marriage'. Students needed therefore 'to be given accurate information and to be helped to develop skills to enable them to understand difference and respect themselves and others – and for the purpose also of preventing and removing prejudice' (DfEE, 2000: 4). The section on 'Sexual Identity and Sexual Orientation' made it clear that school sex education programmes should aim to be relevant to *all* students, whatever their sexual orientation:

It is up to all schools to make sure that the needs of all students are met in their sex education programmes. Young people, whatever their developing sexuality, need to feel that sex and relationship education is relevant to them and sensitive to their needs. The Secretary of State for Education and Employment is clear that teachers should be able to deal honestly and sensitively with sexual orientation, answer appropriate questions and offer support. At the same time, there should be no direct promotion of sexual orientation. (DfEE, 2000: 12–13)

It is interesting to note that in the same month that this DfEE *Guidance* was published (July 2000), the Bill that would have repealed Section 28 was defeated for a second time in the House of Lords. Section 28 was finally repealed in November 2003.

Issues of gender and educational achievement

Concern relating to gender issues used to focus on the need to improve education facilities and job opportunities for girls: now all the attention, both in political debate and in well-publicized stories in the national media, appears to have switched to the so-called 'failing boys' phenomenon. Indeed, the current preoccupation with boys' 'underachievement' has acquired something of the status of 'a moral panic', with the former Chief Inspector of Schools, Chris Woodhead, arguing in March 1996 that 'the failure of boys, and, in particular, of while working-class boys, is one of the most disturbing problems we face within the whole education system' (quoted in *The Times Educational Supplement,* 15 March 1996).

It is clear that there is *some* justification for the recent change in emphasis; and a number of reasons have been put forward to explain why too many boys, and in particular working-class boys, perform badly in school and then find it difficult to carve out a role for themselves in modern society. A number of academic researchers have argued (see, for example, Arnot, David and Weiner, 1999) that boys in school are affected by insecurities in the adult job market. The decline of large manufacturing industries is said to have brought about the 'emasculation' of traditional working-class men, while the growth in service industries and increased full- and part-time female employment have signalled a marked change in working-class community lifestyles. These developments have strongly affected the nature of working-class men's and women's personal relationships, both in the domestic sphere and in the workplace. They also seem to have influenced the aspirations of many boys as they make their way through the school system.

At the same time, there is research evidence to suggest that boys who do work hard at school sometimes run the risk of having their 'masculinity' questioned by fellow students. Máirtín Mac an Ghaill (1994) and Tony Sewell (1997) have shown how different groups of boys learn to be men at school by actively policing their own and others' sexual identities.

A BBC Television *Panorama* programme 'The Future is Female', broadcast on 24 October 1994, contributed to the public alarm about boys' underachievement by using a wealth of material to convey the impression that girls were 'out-performing' boys at all stages of the schooling process and were then moving on to occupy some of the influential and lucrative jobs in society previously monopolized by men. Although much of the evidence presented was highly dubious and anecdotal, some of the boys and girls interviewed by presenter Mike Embley made observations that could not be easily dismissed: for example, when asked 'What would you think of a boy who worked hard at school?', one 6 year-old boy replied without hesitation: 'He's not a boy.' Such attitudes do persist into the secondary school; and the idea that 'real boys don't work' is often reflected in the bullying and harassment of high-achieving boys seen as 'sissies' or 'poofs' (see Epstein, 1998).

What much of the debate about school achievement ignores is the *class* dimension. In her book *Failing Working-Class Girls* (2000), Ofsted Inspector and educational consultant Gillian Plummer points out that while the greatest national concern at the present time is the under-achievement of boys, *class* differences in achievement are virtually ignored, and particularly where girls are concerned. In her words:

> The educational failure of working-class girls is normally hidden. First, by interpreting statistics recording the substantial rise in achievements of middle-class girls to represent 'all girls'. Second, by the persistence of seri-ous concerns about the deviant behaviour and particularly poor performance of many working-class boys. In ignoring the educational failure of working-class girls, we ignore the many problems that underlie their failure and which manifest themselves in harmful behaviour patterns: self-exclusion, with-drawal, depression, anorexia and early pregnancies. (Plummer, 2000: vii)

Segregation versus integration

The conflict between segregation and integration is one that permeates a number of the debates that come under the general umbrella of equal treatment and respect for diversity. There is space in this section to deal with only some of them.

With regard to the long-standing debate over the advantages and disadvantages of co-educational schooling, it used to be thought by some educationists that girls would benefit academically from the provi-sion of more girls' secondary schools where they could receive special encouragement in traditionally boys' subjects such as science and maths and would not find the use of the school computers monopolized by boys. Now the emphasis has shifted and, as we have already seen, it is boys' underachievement which receives all the attention, leading some to the conclusion that it is boys who need special help and encourage-ment in single-sex schools. The gender gap revealed in the 2002 GCSE results prompted new calls for boys to be taught separately, if not in single-sex schools then in special boys' streams or sets within co-educa-tional schools (see Woodward, 2002).

The debate about segregation and integration has assumed special significance in recent years with regard to those children deemed to have 'special educational needs'. This term clearly covers a very broad spec-trum of 'conditions', ranging from visual impairment to 'exceptional attainment', and is even used by some teachers to embrace those children with minor behavioural problems.

As we saw in Chapter 2, it was the leading eugenicist Cyril Burt who spent much of his early career devising tests for identifying those 'backward', 'feeble-minded' and 'handicapped' children who were thought to be incapable, by reason of their condition, of benefiting from the education provided in an ordinary state elementary school. This work was later broadened to provide the intellectual justification for allocating all children to different categories of secondary school at the age of 11. By the second half of the last century, Burt's work had been discredited on a broad front; and the term 'special educational needs' came into being as a genuine attempt to 'demedicalize' the labelling of children with disabilities: in other words, to replace offensive terms such as 'retarded', 'sub-normal', 'crippled' and 'handicapped' with what was hoped to be a less negative form of labelling based on real educational need.

'Special Educational Needs' was the title of the Report of the Warnock Committee which had been set up by the Education Secretary, Margaret Thatcher, to inquire into the education of 'handicapped children and young people'. This Report, published in 1978 (DES, 1978), estimated that around 20 per cent of children might at some time in their schooling have 'special educational needs' (rather than the 2 per cent already covered by the existing 'official' definition of 'special education'). It also argued that children formerly segregated by 'categories of handicap' into special schools should be progressively integrated into mainstream schools, and that all children with special educational needs should be integrated 'on a functional, social or locational basis' with other children. Mary Warnock herself wrote in *The Times Educational Supplement* at the end of September 1980 that 'ordinary schools must expect to cater for more children with special needs and the whole concept of provision for children with peculiar difficulties, or indeed peculiar talents, must become a natural part of the comprehensive ideal' (Warnock, 1980).

The 1978 Warnock Report formed the basis of the Education (Special Education) Act of 1981 which had four main provisions:

1 Categories of handicap should be replaced by the concept of special educational need, defined as present when a child has significantly greater difficulty in learning than the majority of children of his/her age, or has a disability which prevents or hinders the use of the educational facilities normally provided.
2 Local authorities should have the duty of identifying and assessing

children with special educational needs and of making and maintaining a statement of special educational needs for some children.

3 Parents should have the right to be consulted, to appeal against statements where appropriate and to request assessments.

4 Children with special needs should be educated in ordinary schools, providing that their needs could be met, that the education of other children would not be affected, and that there would be an efficient use of resources.

It has not always proved easy to implement all the major provisions of the 1981 Education Act, and Mary Warnock has herself acknowledged the difficulties involved in pursuing a policy of *complete* integration. In some parts of the country, the percentage of students being educated in a segregated setting has been reduced only minimally, while in others it has actually risen. Many classroom teachers at both the primary and the secondary level welcome *in principle* the idea of integrating as many 'special needs' children as possible into mainstream schooling, but fear the consequences of doing this without the necessary additional resources.

Another area of educational and social policy where the whole debate about segregation has aroused strong and partisan feelings centres on the related issues of 'race', ethnicity and religious affiliation. The existence of Jewish, Roman Catholic, Church of England and Methodist schools has caused other religious organizations and sects to demand the right to set up their own establishments. At the same time, there are those in the black community who argue that the well-publicized underachievement of black pupils – and especially boys – within Britain's education system can be tackled successfully only by the setting up of all-black schools, with exclusively black teachers, black headteachers and black boards of governors.

As long ago as 1981, Maureen Stone was arguing, in her controversial book *The Education of the Black Child in Britain* (Stone, 1981), that for far too many black children in state schools, steel band sessions and West Indian dialect classes had replaced the all-important instruction in basic skills. This, she argued, was leading to the setting up of community-run Saturday Schools where West Indian volunteers were attempting to compensate for the lack of discipline and 'standards' in mainstream schools.

Pupils of African Caribbean origin constitute the largest part of the intake of the Seventh Day Adventist John Loughborough School in Tottenham in north London, to which the Labour Government gave 'grant-maintained' status (along with two Muslim schools) in September 1998. The School does not actually classify itself as 'black' or 'African Caribbean', but in much of London members of the Seventh Day Adventist Church do tend to be of African Caribbean origin. Formerly a fee-paying independent school, John Loughborough attributes a large part of its success to the high expectation of its pupils by all the black teachers (see Jessel, 1999). In this respect, it represents the way forward for all those who argue that black children in multiracial schools will always be the victims of white prejudice and discrimination.

As we saw in Chapter 4, New Labour has been anxious to sponsor the creation of 'faith-based' schools; but this policy ran into difficulties at the beginning of 2002 when it was revealed in *The Guardian* (9 March 2002) that Emmanuel City Technology College in Gateshead, Tyne and Wear, was teaching 'creationism' (the biblical view of the creation of the world, as described in Genesis) as *scientific* fact (see Gillard, 2002). A number of leading scientists called on Ofsted to reinspect this state-funded College, but it was defended by the Prime Minister in the House of Commons on 13 March, arguing that it was an excellent school achieving 'very good academic results'. It now seems clear that a policy of promoting diversity in the education system could pose a number of awkward questions as to which groups should be allowed to sponsor and have a say in the running of state schools.

Conclusion

There are many educational issues raised by any discussion of diversity and equality, and this chapter has provided space to deal with only some of them. Others are discussed in some detail elsewhere in the book: for example, the whole question of enhancing working-class participation in post-16 education is discussed in Chapters 8 and 9. It would seem axiomatic that all primary and secondary schools have the twin functions of promoting the achievement of all their pupils and, at the same time, challenging prejudice and intolerance in all their various forms. The first aim involves the adoption of strict monitoring procedures to ensure that no pupil is disadvantaged or discriminated against in any area of the curriculum; the second is concerned with having whole-school policies related to bullying and unacceptable behaviour and with making adequate space on the timetable for lessons designed to enable all children to become active and caring citizens when they leave school.

12

Conclusion

Change and continuity since 1997

The General Election of May 1997 brought to a sudden end 18 years of right-wing Conservative administrations during which even 'collectivist' Wales and Scotland felt the effects of a succession of radical and far-reaching policies designed to destroy the educational culture which had developed between 1944 and 1979. It is fair to say that in many quarters, New Labour's astonishing electoral victory was, in fact, greeted with a heady mixture of hope, optimism and expectancy. As Phillips and Harper-Jones argued in 2003: 'The majority of professionals working in all spheres of education, from early years to higher education, looked forward to working under (or even *with*) a new government that was genuinely committed to progressive educational reform after nearly two decades of retrenchment, declining morale and confrontation (Phillips and Harper-Jones, 2003: 126). Yet the feeling of excitement and optimism was to prove short-lived, and it became difficult to argue that the arrival of New Labour marked a new beginning and a decisive break with the past. It was indeed soon being claimed by a number of commentators (see, for example, Chitty and Dunford, 1999; Docking, 2000; Tomlinson, 2001) that, for all the rhetoric, the Blair Government's policies for education were fundamentally those of the Conservatives under Margaret Thatcher and John Major, 'dressed up in New Labour clothes'.

There were admittedly a few early outright reversals of Conservative education policy: the abolition of nursery school vouchers; the ending of the Assisted Places Scheme; and the phasing out of grant-maintained schools operating outside local authority control. Yet these were to prove the exceptions to the rule. In virtually all other respects, both Conservative philosophy and Conservative measures were to remain intact.

The Teacher Training Agency and Ofsted were to remain in place, along with the policy of identifying 'failing' schools and making teachers more accountable for the progress of their pupils. Britain's need to compete successfully in world markets continued to be put forward as a prime motive for the general raising of educational standards and for the 'modernization' of the schools system. There was to be much talk of the promotion of social inclusion and social cohesion; but this laudable aim was to be seriously undermined by the continued emphasis on choice and diversity, particularly at the secondary level, where a policy of selection based on school status was to be increasingly replaced by one based on curricular specialization. The already steep pecking order of secondary schools was exacerbated by the creation of City Academies which were, in fact, a New Labour version of the Conservatives' City Technology Colleges.

In matters relating to the school curriculum, New Labour has continued the 1990s Conservative policy of amending and, where necessary, *jettisoning* whole areas of the National Curriculum. The new curriculum frameworks, to be introduced in September 2008, will simply continue the well-entrenched process of rethinking the curriculum agenda laid out in 1987. New Labour has also intervened, to a remarkable degree, in issues affecting school pedagogy and classroom practice. Previous Conservative governments made inroads into pedagogy and practice, issuing pronouncements on the teaching of such subjects as peace studies and sex education. But the Blair administrations have gone much further in their highly detailed and prescriptive interventions about how to organize classrooms and group students, thereby challenging the professional competence of teachers on an unprecedented scale. In addition to the introduction of the highly structured Literacy and Numeracy Hours in the primary school, teachers have been faced with clear pronouncements on the undesirability and impracticability of 'mixed-ability' teaching.

It is, of course, important to concede that, in areas which had nothing to do with ideology as such, New Labour has been prepared to compensate for years of low education expenditure and comparative neglect. After a period when it was felt necessary to keep *within* Conservative spending limits, the Blair Government was keen to find the money for the long-overdue refurbishment of many run-down school buildings; and New Labour's investment in technology meant that many school classrooms were to be strikingly well equipped, with computers, electronic whiteboards and the like. There was also an increase in the numbers of support staff in schools, which meant that many children were now able to get one-to-one help or benefit from small group provision on a scale largely unknown in the 1990s. The effects of all this should not be underestimated.

Globalization and education inequality

The Government blames current economic problems on global trends and some dismiss increasing income and social inequality in the same way. Indeed, it is often argued that increasing social inequality and the erosion of societal cohesion are the inevitable results of globalization. Yet it could be countered that it all depends on *how* globalization is managed. And some countries seem to manage it rather well, not least through their education policies.

Andy Green and Lorna Unwin have analysed the results of a 2006 survey of literacy and numeracy skills amongst 15-year-olds carried out by OECD (Organisation for Economic Co-operation and Development) which tell a remarkable story about the sheer scale of educational inequality in Britain, or, more accurately, in England. In this 2006 Survey, the UK had the third highest variation in tested scores amongst 29 OECD countries. But it is interesting to note that skills were more unequally distributed in England and Northern Ireland than in either Wales or Scotland. Perhaps more damning still is what this Survey reveals about how social background influences achievement. The impact of social origins on individuals' scores in the UK was greater than in all but four of the OECD countries. Most countries had either large differences in outcomes *between* schools (in countries with selective systems, like, for example, Germany) or *within* schools (in a number of the countries with comprehensive systems). England had both. For all the political rhetoric about raising educational standards and furthering opportunity, English schools do more to lock in intergenerational inequality than to promote social mobility.

It seems clear that educational (in)equality is closely correlated with measures of societal cohesion, such as trust in people and institutions, civic cooperation and low rates of crime. Countries with more equal outcomes in education and fairer distributions of adult skills, such as the Nordic and East Asian states, tend to have lower rates of crime and higher levels of trust and civic cooperation. English-speaking countries – with the exception of Canada – have higher skills inequalities and fare worse in terms of income distribution and social cohesion. The differences may be partly due to welfare and labour market policies, but the organization of schooling also appears to play a part. All the more 'egalitarian' states, including the Nordic states, Japan and South Korea, have highly egalitarian, non-selective and 'mixed ability' comprehensive education systems. The most unequal states have either selective education systems, as in the German-speaking countries, or, as in the English-speaking countries, 'quasi-comprehensive' systems with extensive school choice, a large degree of diversity at the secondary level and rigid ability grouping in schools (Green and Unwin, 2008).

Major themes of the last sixty years

A number of research studies indicate that Britain's comprehensive schools, and particularly where their populations have been socially mixed, have had a disproportionately beneficial effect on the educational attainment of working-class students and that the total numbers of working-class students achieving success in public examinations at 16 and 18 and then securing access to one form or other of higher education have increased enormously since 1945.

From substantial research on the effects of comprehensive reorganization in Scotland, Andrew McPherson and J. Douglas Willms concluded at the end of the 1980s that 'since the mid-1970s, the reorganization that was initiated in 1965 has contributed both to a rise in examination attainment and to a fall in the effect on attainment of social class' (McPherson and Willms, 1988: 39). They called these two trends respectively 'improvement' and 'equalization', and they further argued that while these trends were especially marked in Scotland, there was evidence of 'similar but weaker trends in England and Wales' (ibid.). In addition, a meticulous review of the impact of comprehensive reorganization in Britain led Howard Glennester and William Low to conclude in 1980 that comprehensive schools had been responsible for 'really major improvements in examination performance achieved mainly by "average-ability" students in the period since 1965' (Glennester and Low, 1990: 61). The Benn/Chitty Survey of comprehensive schools, carried out in the academic year 1993–4, compared the effectiveness of comprehensive and selective secondary school systems and the authors concluded that so-called 'bright' students did as well – and those labelled 'average' or below did much better – in areas which had abolished selection (Benn and Chitty, 1996: 465; see also Chitty, 2001: 39–40). That being said, however, it was also clear that except in Scotland, where attitudes to reorganization were far more positive and enthusiastic, comprehensive schools were largely failing to reduce social class inequalities in attainment (Benn and Chitty, 1996: 287). And this is a subject of continuing controversy.

Writing in 1987, Anthony Heath talked in terms of two major tendencies and of 'a striking contrast' in post-war education in Britain and particularly in England: on the one hand, rising levels of educational attainment; on the other, 'a remarkable resilience of class inequalities', in the face of which 'educational reforms seem powerless, whether for good or ill' (Heath, 1987: 186–7). Writing ten years later, and making use of research carried out in the 1990s, Ivan Reid concluded that the relationship between social class and educational achievement had remained remarkably constant over the years (Reid, 1998). And a study of participation in higher education by Gareth Rees and Dean Stroud, published in 2001, concluded that while working-class families had benefited considerably from a widening of access to universities, their *relative* position remained 'hugely disadvantaged' (Rees and Stroud, 2001: 80). It is, of course, fair to point out that comprehensive reorganization (especially in England) has never been completed and that independent and grammar schools have continued to enjoy enormous privileges where entry to universities and the higher professions is concerned.

The whole question of the relationship between educational success and social class origins is, of course, closely linked to the issue of social mobility and the extent to which Britain can be truly described as a 'meritocratic' society. In his Leader's Speech to the 2007 Labour Party Conference, Gordon Brown proudly proclaimed that 'this is the century when our country cannot afford to waste the talents of anyone'. He promised to work for 'a genuine meritocratic Britain – a Britain of all the talents' and went on to claim that 'whenever we see talent underdeveloped; wherever there are aspirations unfulfilled; wherever there is potential wasted and obstacles to be removed – this is where we, Labour, will be' (quoted in *The Guardian*, 25 September 2007). Yet it could be argued that these sentiments were being expressed at a time when the gap between rich and poor was wider than ever and true social mobility had all but ground to a halt.

Right-wing commentators seek an explanation for this phenomenon in the phasing out of large numbers of grammar schools in the 1960s and 1970s. The grammar school is seen as having been a significant engine of social mobility, enabling 'talented' but 'disadvantaged' working-class youngsters to 'escape from their backgrounds' and move up the social scale. An alternative viewpoint would accept that only a small percentage of working-class children were ever able to benefit from a grammar-school education and find a more plausible explanation in the slow decline in the number of middle-class jobs. It was simply no longer possible for 'able' working-class youngsters to take advantage of a huge expansion in 'white collar' employment.

It is the view of respected education journalist Peter Wilby that the issue of social mobility also highlights a major contradiction at the very heart of New Labour education policy. Despite all the rhetoric about promoting and sustaining a 'meritocratic' society, Tony Blair and his ministers were very wary of alienating the middle classes. They were well aware that it was the middle classes who would always benefit from the operation of a market in education (Wilby, 2006).

The education system in England has now reached the point where, if it is accepted that educational standards are still not high enough and that too many youngsters still leave school at 16 without decent qualifications, the only agenda being put forward is one of greater competition between schools, greater choice and diversity, particularly at the secondary level, and the increasing reliance on private sponsorship. There are other scenarios on offer, but they are not represented in the thinking of the leaders of the main political parties. Only in Wales and Scotland are alternative solutions being proposed, and it remains to be seen if their more 'communitarian' approach ever regains a foothold in the thinking of mainstream politicians at Westminster.

References

ACCAC (2000) *Desirable Outcomes for Children's Learning before Compulsory School Age* (Cardiff: Qualifications, Curriculum and Assessment Authority for Wales).

ACCAC (2004) *Assessment Arrangements for Key Stages Two and Three* (Cardiff: Qualifications, Curriculum and Assessment Authority for Wales).

Adonis, A. and Pollard, S. (1997) *A Class Act: The Myth of Britain's Classless Society* (London: Hamish Hamilton).

Ahmed, K. (2002) 'Labour's new network', *The Observer*, 2 June.

Aldrich, R. (1988) 'The National Curriculum: an historical perspective', in D. Lawton and C. Chitty (eds), *The National Curriculum*, Bedford Way Paper 33 (London: Institute of Education), pp. 21–33.

Aldrich, R. (1996) *Education for the Nation* (London: Cassell).

Alexander, R. (2004) 'Still no pedagogy? Principle, pragmatism and compliance in primary education', *Cambridge Journal of Education*, Vol. 34, No. 1, pp. 7–33.

Alexander, R. (2007a) 'Where there is no vision . . .', *Forum*, Vol. 49, Nos. 1 and 2 (Spring and Summer), pp. 187–99.

Alexander, R. (2007b) 'Three reports should prompt debate on primary education's future', *The Times Educational Supplement*, 2 November.

Anning, A. and Ball, M. (eds) (2008) *Improving Services for Young Children: From Sure Start to Children's Centres* (London: Sage Publications).

Anning, A. and Hall, D. (2008) 'What was Sure Start and why did it matter?' in A. Anning and M. Ball (eds) *Improving Services for Young Children: From Sure Start to Children's Centres* (London: Sage Publications), pp. 3–15.

Armstrong, M. (1988) 'Popular education and the National Curriculum', *Forum*, Vol. 30, No. 3 (Summer), pp. 74–76.

Arnot, M., David, M. and Weiner, G. (1999) *Closing the Gender Gap* (London: Polity Press).

ATL (2002) 'Update', *ATL Report*, Vol. 24, No. 5 (March/April), pp. 15–18.

Auld, R. (1976) *William Tyndale Junior and Infant Schools Public Inquiry: A Report of the Inner London Education Authority by Robin Auld, QC* (London: ILEA).

Baker, K. (1993) *The Turbulent Years: My Life in Politics* (London: Faber & Faber).

Baker, M. (2008) 'Bid for respect could kill off diplomas', *Education Guardian*, 18 March.

Ball, M. (2002) *Getting Sure Start Started* (London: DfES Publications).

Ball, S. J. (1990) *Politics and Policy Making in Education: Explorations in Policy Sociology* (London: Routledge).

Ball, S.J. (2007) *Education plc: Understanding Private Sector Participation in Public Sector Education* (London: Routledge).

Barber, M. (1994) *The Making of the 1944 Education Act* (London: Cassell).
Barber, M. (1996) *The Learning Game: Arguments for an Education Revolution* (London: Cassell).
Beckett, F. (2004) 'Business class', *The Guardian*, 9 July.
Beckett, F. (2007) *The Great City Academy Fraud* (London: Continuum).
Benn, C. (1990) 'The public price of private education and privatization', *Forum*, Vol. 32, No. 3 (Summer), pp. 68–73.
Benn, C. and Chitty, C. (1996) *Thirty Years On: Is Comprehensive Education Alive and Well or Struggling to Survive?* (1st edn) (London: David Fulton).
Benn, C. and Chitty, C. (1997) *Thirty Years On: Is Comprehensive Education Alive and Well or Struggling to Survive?* (2nd edn) (Harmondsworth: Penguin Books).
Benn, C. and Fairley J. (eds) (1986) *Challenging the MSC: On Jobs, Education and Training* (London: Pluto Press).
Benn, C. and Simon, B. (1970) *Half Way There: Report on the British Comprehensive School Reform* (1st edn) (London: McGraw-Hill).
Benn, C. and Simon, B. (1972) *Half Way There: Report on the British Comprehensive School Reform* (2nd edn) (Harmondsworth: Penguin).
Bennett, N. (1976) *Teaching Styles and Pupil Progress* (London: Open Books).
Berliner, W. (2002) 'Break for the border', *Education Guardian,* 19 March.
Berlins, M. (1988) 'The Power Brokers', *The Illustrated London News,* June, pp. 32–49.
Blair, T. (1994) *Socialism* (London: Fabian Society), July.
Board of Education (1943) *Educational Reconstruction* (White Paper) (London: HMSO).
Bogdanor, V. (1979) 'Power and participation', *Oxford Review of Education,* Vol. 5, No. 2 (June), pp. 157–68.
Bowles, S. and Gintis, H. (1976) *Schooling in Capitalist America: Educational Reform and the Contradictions of Economic Life* (London: Routledge & Kegan Paul).
Boyle, E. (1972) 'The politics of secondary school reorganisation: some reflections', *Journal of Educational Administration and History,* Vol. 4, No. 2 (June), pp. 28–38.
Boyle, E. and Crosland, A. (1971) *The Politics of Education* (Harmondsworth: Penguin).
Boyson, R. (1969), 'The essential conditions for the success of a comprehensive school', in C. B. Cox and A. E. Dyson (eds), *Black Paper Two: The Crisis in Education* (London: Critical Quarterly Society), pp. 57–62.
Briault, E. (1976) 'A distributed system of educational administration: an international viewpoint', *International Review of Education,* Vol. 22, No. 4, pp. 429–39.
Brittan, L. and St John-Stevas, N. (1975) *How to Save Your Schools* (London: Conservative Political Centre).
Brown, G. (2008) 'Time for the third act in public sector reform', *The Financial Times*, 10 March.
Browne, N. (1999) 'Don't bite the bullet in the early years!' *Forum,* Vol. 41, No. 2 (Summer), pp. 74–7.
Browne, S. (1986) Interview with the author, 24 July.
Burt, C. (1913) 'The inheritance of mental characters', *The Eugenics Review,* Vol. 4, pp. 1–16.

Burt, C. (1933) *How the Mind Works* (London: Allen & Unwin).

Burt, C. (1950) 'Testing intelligence', *The Listener,* 16 November.

Butler, R. A. (1971) *The Art of the Possible* (London: Hamish Hamilton).

Callaghan, J. (1987) *Time and Chance* (London: Collins).

Cannon, C. (1964) 'Social studies in secondary schools', *Educational Review,* Vol. 17, pp. 18–30.

Carvel, J. (1998) 'Barbed school report brings battle between advisors out into the open', *The Guardian,* 6 February.

CASE (1997) *Parents and Schools,* Bulletin No. 95.

CCCS (1981) *Unpopular Education: Schooling and Social Democracy in England since 1944* (London: Hutchinson).

Chitty, C. (1979) 'The common curriculum', *Forum,* Vol. 21, No. 2 (Spring), pp. 61–5.

Chitty, C. (1988) 'Two models of a national curriculum: origins and interpretation', in D. Lawton and C. Chitty (eds), *The National Curriculum,* Bedford Way Paper 33 (London: Institute of Education), pp. 34–48.

Chitty, C. (1989a) *Towards a New Education System: The Victory of the New Right?* (Lewes: Falmer Press).

Chitty, C. (1989b) 'City Technology Colleges: a strategy for elitism', *Forum,* Vol. 31, No. 2 (Spring), pp. 37–40.

Chitty, C. (1992) 'Key Stage Four: the National Curriculum abandoned?', *Forum,* Vol. 34, No. 2 (Spring), pp. 38–40.

Chitty, C. (1994) 'Consensus to conflict: the structure of educational decision-making transformed', in D. Scott (ed.), *Accountability and Control in Educational Settings* (London: Cassell), pp. 8–31.

Chitty, C. (1996) *Generating a National Curriculum* (Buckingham: Open University Press).

Chitty, C. (1997a) 'Interview with Keith Joseph', in P. Ribbins and B. Sherratt (eds), *Radical Educational Policies and Conservative Secretaries of State* (London: Cassell), pp. 78–86.

Chitty, C. (1997b) 'The White Paper: missed opportunities', *Forum,* Vol. 39, No. 3 (Autumn), pp. 71–2.

Chitty, C. (1997c) 'Privatization and marketization', *Oxford Review of Education,* Vol. 23, No. 1, pp. 45–62.

Chitty, C. (1998) 'Secondary education in the Wilson Years: the comprehensive school becomes national policy', *Revue Française de Civilisation Britannique,* Vol. 10, No. 1, pp. 131–41.

Chitty, C. (2000) 'Why the GCSE should be abolished', *Forum,* Vol. 42, No. 1 (Spring), pp. 28–30.

Chitty, C. (2001) 'Modernization spells destruction', *Education Review,* Vol. 15, No. 1 (Autumn), pp. 37–44.

Chitty, C. (2002a) 'The inclusive curriculum', *Forum,* Vol. 44, No. 3 (Autumn), p. 99–102.

Chitty, C. (2002b) 'The role and status of LEAs: post-war pride and *fin de siècle* uncertainty', *Oxford Review of Education,* Vol. 28, Nos 2 and 3 (June and September), pp. 261–73.

Chitty, C. (2002c) 'Why New Labour shouldn't be touched with a bargepole!', *Forum,* Vol. 44, No. 2 (Summer), p. 45.

Chitty, C. (2006) 'A bad White Paper and a bad Education Bill', *Forum,* Vol. 48, No. 1 (Spring), pp. 3–8.

Chitty, C. and Dunford, J. (eds) (1999) *State Schools: New Labour and the Conservative Legacy* (London: Woburn Press).

Chitty, C. and Simon, B. (eds) (1993) *Education Answers Back: Critical Responses to Government Policy* (London: Lawrence & Wishart).

Collins, T. (2005) 'Opinion', *Education Guardian*, 24 January.

Conservative Party (1979) *The Conservative Manifesto* (London: Conservative Central Office).

Conservative Party (2001) *Time for Common Sense* (2001 Conservative Party Election Manifesto) (London: Conservative Party).

Conservative Party (2004) *Right to Choose* (London: Conservative Party).

Corbett, A. (1969) 'The Tory educators', *New Society*, 22 May, pp. 785–7.

Cox, C. B. and Boyson, R. (eds) (1975) *Black Paper 1975: The Fight for Education* (London: Dent).

Cox, C. B. and Boyson, R. (eds) (1977) *Black Paper 1977* (London: Maurice Temple Smith).

Cox, C. B. and Dyson, A. E. (eds) (1969a) *Black Paper Two: The Crisis in Education* (London: Critical Quarterly Society).

Cox, C. B. and Dyson, A. E. (eds) (1969b) *Fight for Education: A Black Paper* (London: Critical Quarterly Society).

Cox, C. B. and Dyson, A. E. (eds) (1970) *Black Paper Three: Goodbye Mr Short* (London: Critical Quarterly Society).

Curtis, P. (2008) 'Exam chief: rival to A Level in disarray', *The Guardian*, 17 April.

Dale, R. (1983) 'Thatcherism and education', in J. Ahier and M. Elude (eds), *Contemporary Education Policy* (London: Croom Helm), pp. 223–55.

Davidson, J. (2004) 'Distinctive education policies in Wales', *Forum*, Vol. 46, No. 2 (Summer), pp. 46–51.

Dearing, R. (1995) Interview with the author, 12 December.

Dent, H. C. (1961) *Universities in Transition* (London: Cohen & West).

Department of the Environment (1988) *Local Government Act 1988* (Circular 12/88) (London: Department of the Environment).

DES (1965) *The Organisation of Secondary Education* (Circular 10/65) (London: HMSO).

DES (1967) *Children and their Primary Schools* (2 vols: The Plowden Report) (London: HMSO).

DES (1970) *HMI Today and Tomorrow* (London: DES).

DES (1972) *Education: A Framework for Expansion*, Cmnd 5174 (London: HMSO).

DES (1976) *School Education in England: Problems and Initiatives* (The Yellow Book) (London: DES), July.

DES (1977a) *Education in Schools: A Consultative Document*, Cmnd 6869 (London: HMSO), July.

DES (1977b) *Curriculum 11–16* (HMI Red Book One) (London: HMSO), December.

DES (1978) *Special Educational Needs* (The Warnock Report) (London: HMSO).

DES (1979) *Aspects of Secondary Education in England: A Survey by HM Inspectors of Schools* (London: HMSO).

DES (1980) *A Framework for the School Curriculum* (London: HMSO).

DES (1981a) *The School Curriculum* (London: HMSO), January.

DES (1981b) *Curriculum 11–16: A Review of Progress* (HMI Red Book Two) (London: HMSO), March.

DES (1983) *Curriculum 11–16: Towards a Statement of Entitlement: Curricular Reappraisal in Action* (HMI Red Book Three (London: HMSO).

DES (1985a) *The Curriculum from 5 to 16* (HMI Series: Curriculum Matters 2) (London: HMSO), January.

DES (1985b) *Better Schools,* Cmnd 9469 (London: HMSO), March.

DES (1986) *Report by Her Majesty's Inspectors on the Effects of Local Authority Expenditure Policies on Education Provision in England – 1985* (London: DES).

DES (1987) *The National Curriculum 5–16: A Consultation Document* (London: DES), July.

Dewey, J. (1916) *Democracy and Education* (New York: Macmillan).

DfE (1992) *Choice and Diversity: A New Framework for Schools,* Cmnd 2021 (London: HMSO).

DfEE (1996a) *Equipping Young People for Working Life* (London: DfEE).

DfEE (1996b) *Self-Government for Schools,* Cmnd 3315 (London: HMSO).

DfEE (1997) *Excellence in Schools,* Cmnd 3681 (London: HMSO).

DfEE (1998) *The Learning Age: A Renaissance for a New Britain,* Cmnd 3790 (London: HMSO).

DfEE (1999a) *Learning to Succeed: A New Framework for Post-16 Learning,* Cmnd 4392 (London: HMSO).

DfEE (1999b) *Sure Start: A Guide for Trailblazers* (London: TSO).

DfEE (2000) *Sex and Relationship Education Guidance* (London: DfEE).

DfEE (2001) *Schools: Building on Success: Raising Standards, Promoting Diversity, Achieving Results,* Cmnd 5050 (London: HMSO).

DfEE/QCA (1998) *Education for Citizenship and the Teaching of Democracy in Schools: Final Report of the Advisory Group on Citizenship* (The Crick Report) (London: QCA).

DfEE/QCA (1999) *The Review of the National Curriculum in England: The Secretary of State's Proposals* (London: QCA), May.

DfES (2001) *Schools Achieving Success,* Cmnd 5230 (London: HMSO).

DfES (2002a) *14–19: Extending Opportunities, Raising Standards* (Consultation Document), Cmnd 5342 (London: HMSO), February.

DfES (2002b) *Birth to Three Matters: A Framework for Supporting Children in their Earliest Years* (London: TSO).

DfES (2003a) *14–19: Opportunity and Excellence* (London: HMSO).

DfES (Department for Education and Skills) (2003b) *The Future of Higher Education,* Cmnd 5735 (London: HMSO).

DfES (2003c) *Excellence and Enjoyment: A Strategy for Primary Schools* (London: TSO).

DfES (2004a) *Five Year Strategy for Children and Learners: Putting People at the Heart of Public Services,* Cmnd 6272 (London: TSO), July.

DfES (2004b) *Curriculum and Qualifications Reform: Final Report of the Working Group on 14–19 Reform* (The Tomlinson Report) (Nottingham: DfES Publications), October.

DfES (2005a) *14–19 Education and Skills,* Cmnd 6746 (London: the Stationery Office), February.

DfES (2005b) *Higher Standards, Better Schools for All: More Choice for Parents and Pupils*, Cmnd 6677 (London: TSO), October.

DfES, DTi, HM Treasury, DWP (2003) *21st Century Skills: Realising Our Potential* (London: TSO).

Docking, J. (2000) 'What is the solution? An overview of national policies for schools, 1979–99', in J. Docking (ed.), *New Labour's Policies for Schools: Raising the Standard?* (London: David Fulton), pp. 21–42.

Donoughue, B. (1986) Interview with the author, 16 January.

Donoughue, B. (1987) *Prime Minister: The Conduct of Policy under Harold Wilson and James Callaghan* (London: Jonathan Cape).

Dunford, J. (2001) 'The future for secondary education', *Forum,* Vol. 43, No. 3 (Autumn), pp. 131–3.

Dunford, J. (2002) 'Perspective on the 2002 Green Paper', *Forum,* Vol. 44, No. 2 (Summer), pp. 89–91.

Dunford, J. (2006) 'The Grand March or Beating the Retreat?', *Forum,* Vol. 48, No. 1 (Spring), pp. 33–40.

Edwards, T., Fitz, J. and Whitty, G. (1989) *The State and Private Education: An Evaluation of the Assisted Places Scheme* (Lewes: Falmer Press).

Eggleston, J. (1965) 'How comprehensive is the Leicestershire Plan?', *New Society,* 25 March, p. 17.

Elliott, B. (1970) 'The implementation of the Leicestershire Plan', *Forum,* Vol. 12, No. 3 (Summer), pp. 76–8.

Elliott, D. (1985) 'Higher education: towards a trans-binary policy?' in M. Hughes, P. Ribbins and H. Thomas (eds), *Managing Education: The System and the Institution* (London: Cassell Education), pp. 198–220.

Epstein, D. (1998) 'Real boys don't work: "underachievement", masculinity and the harassment of "sissies"', in D. Epstein, J. Elwood, V. Hey and J. Maw (eds), *Failing Boys? Issues in Gender and Achievement* (Buckingham: Open University Press), pp. 96–108.

Finch, J. (1984) *Education as Social Policy* (London: Longman).

Finn, D. (1987) *Training Without Jobs: New Deals and Broken Promises* (London: Macmillan).

Galton, M. (2007) 'New Labour and education: an evidence-based analysis', *Forum,* Vol. 49, Nos 1 and 2 (Spring and Summer), pp. 157–77.

Galton, M., Simon, B. and Croll, P. (1980) *Inside the Primary Classroom* (London: Routledge & Kegan Paul).

Gamble, A. (1988) *The Free Economy and the Strong State: The Politics of Thatcherism* (London: Macmillan).

Garner, R. (2004) 'Should these people be running state schools?', *The Independent,* 8 July.

Garner, R. (2007) 'A generation in debt', *The Independent,* 14 August.

Giddens, A. (1998) *The Third Way: The Renewal of Social Democracy* (Cambridge: Polity Press).

Gillard, D. (2002) 'Creationism: bad science, bad religion, bad education', *Forum,* Vol. 44, No. 2 (Summer), pp. 46–52.

Gillborn, D. and Youdell, D. (1999) 'Weakest not at the table', *The Times Educational Supplement,* 26 November.

Gillborn, D. and Youdell, D. (2000) *Rationing Education: Policy, Practice, Reform and Equity* (Buckingham: Open University Press).

Glennester, H. and Low, W. (1990) 'Education and the Welfare State: does it add up?' in J. Hills (ed.) *The State of Welfare: The Welfare State in Britain since 1974* (Oxford: Clarendon Press), pp. 28–87.

Goddard, A. (1999) 'Costs thwart broader access', *The Times Higher Education Supplement,* 8 October.

Gordon, P. and Lawton, D. (1978) *Curriculum Change in the Nineteenth and Twentieth Centuries* (London: Hodder & Stoughton).

Gosden, P. (1976) *Education in the Second World War: A Study in Policy and Administration* (London: Methuen).

Gow, D. (1988) 'Why the test is far from child's play', *The Guardian,* 29 March.

Graham, D. and Tytler, D. (1993) *A Lesson for Us All: The Making of the National Curriculum* (London: Routledge).

Grant, L. (1994) 'Inside story', *Guardian Weekend,* 22 October.

Gray, J. and Satterly, D. (1976) *Two Statistical Problems in Classroom Research* (Bristol: University of Bristol).

Green, A. (1988) 'Lessons in standards', *Marxism Today,* January, pp. 24–30.

Green, A. (1990) *Education and State Formation: The Rise of Education Systems in England, France and the USA* (London: Macmillan).

Green, A. and Unwin, L. (2008) 'We won't get a fair and healthy society this way', *The Guardian,* 8 July.

Griggs, C. (1985) *Private Education in Britain* (Lewes: Falmer Press).

Griggs, C. (1989) 'The New Right and English secondary education', in R. Lowe (ed.), *The Changing Secondary School* (Lewes: Falmer Press), pp. 99–128.

Halpin, T. (2003) 'Colleges demand no retreat on fees', *The Times,* 24 November.

Halsey, A. H. (1965) 'Education and equality', *New Society,* 17 June, pp. 13–15.

Harland, J. (2000) 'A curriculum model for citizenship education', in D. Lawton, J. Cairns and R. Garden (eds), *Education for Citizenship* (London: Continuum), pp. 54–63.

Hatcher, R. (2001) 'Privatization and schooling', in C. Chitty and B. Simon (eds) *Promoting Comprehensive Education in the 21st Century* (Stoke-on-Trent: Trentham Books), pp. 63–73.

Hattersley, R. (1997) 'Read Blunkett's Lips – then read again', *The Guardian,* 26 November.

Hearnshaw, L. (1979) *Cyril Burt, Psychologist* (London: Hodder & Stoughton).

Heath, A. (1987) 'Class in the classroom', *New Society,* 17 July.

Hennessy, P. (1986) *Cabinet* (Oxford: Basil Blackwell).

Henry, J. (2002) 'Bright test is "magnet" for private pupils', *The Times Educational Supplement,* 28 June.

Hill, C. (1993) *The English Bible and the Seventeenth-Century Revolution* (Harmondsworth: Allen Lane, The Penguin Press).

Hillgate Group (1986) *Whose Schools? A Radical Manifesto* (London: Hillgate Group).

Hillgate Group (1987) *The Reform of British Education: From Principles to Practice* (London: Hillgate Group).

HM Treasury (2003) *Every Child Matters,* Cmnd 5860 (London: TSO).

Hobsbawm, E. (1984) *Worlds of Labour: Further Studies in the History of Labour* (London: Weidenfeld & Nicolson).

Hodgson, A. and Spours, K. (1999) *New Labour's Educational Agenda: Issues and Policies for Education and Training from 14+* (London: Kogan Page).

Holt, M. (1976) 'Non-streaming and the common curriculum', *Forum,* Vol. 18, No. 2 (Spring), pp. 55–7.

Holt, M. (1978) *The Common Curriculum: Its Structure and Style in the Comprehensive School* (London: Routledge & Kegan Paul).

House of Commons (1976) *Tenth Report of the Expenditure Committee, Session 1975–76 Policy Making in the DES* (The Fookes Report) (London: HMSO), September.

House of Commons Education and Skills Committee (2003) *Fifth Report: Higher Education* (London: TSO).

Howard, A. (1987) *RAB: The Life of R.A. Butler* (London: Jonathan Cape).

ILEA (1967) *London Comprehensive Schools 1966* (London: ILEA).

Jackson, B. (1961) 'Notes from two primary schools', *New Left Review,* No. 11 (September–October), pp. 4–8.

Jefferys, K. (1984) 'R.A. Butler, the Board of Education and the 1944 Education Act', *History,* Vol. 69, No. 227, pp. 415–31.

Jeffreys, M.V.O. (1939) *History in Schools: The Study of Development* (London: Pitman).

Jessel, S. (1999) 'High parental demand and academic performance in a separate school: some possible contributory factors', *Forum,* Vol. 41, No. 2 (Summer), pp. 65–8.

Johnson, R. B. (ed.) (1925) *The Letters of Hannah More* (London: The Bodley Head).

Jones, G. W. (1985) 'The Prime Minister's aides', in A. King (ed.), *The British Prime Minister* (2nd edn) (London: Macmillan), pp. 72–95.

Jones, K. (1989) *Right Turn: The Conservative Revolution in Education* (London: Hutchinson Radius).

Jones, K. (2003) *Education in Britain: 1944 to the Present* (Cambridge: Polity Press).

Joseph, K. (1976) *Stranded on the Middle Ground? Reflections on Circumstances and Policies* (London: CPS).

Joseph, K. (1981) Speech to the Conservative Party Conference.

Judd, J. (1996) 'Lessons with a logo "tainted by advertising"', *The Independent,* 24 May.

Kamin, L. (1974) *The Science and Politics of IQ* (New York: John Wiley & Sons).

Kerckhoff, A., Fogelman, K., Crook, D. and Reeder, D. (1996) *Going Comprehensive in England and Wales: A Study of Uneven Change* (London: Woburn Press).

King, A. (1985) 'Margaret Thatcher: the style of a prime minister', in A. King (ed.), *The British Prime Minister* (2nd edn) (London: Macmillan), pp. 96–140.

Knight, C. (1990) *The Making of Tory Education Policy in Post-War Britain, 1950–1986* (Lewes: Falmer Press).

Kogan, M. (1971) *The Politics of Education: Edward Boyle and Anthony Crosland in conversation with Maurice Kogan* (Harmondsworth: Penguin).

Labour Party (1982) *16–19: Learning for Life* (London: Labour Party).

Labour Party (1993) *Opening Doors to a Learning Society* (A Consultative Green Paper on Education) (London: Labour Party).

Labour Party (1995) *Diversity and Excellence: A New Partnership for Schools* (London: Labour Party).

Labour Party (1996a) *Learn as You Earn: Labour's Plans for a Skills Revolution* (London: Labour Party).

Labour Party (1996b) *Lifelong Learning at Work and in Training* (London: Labour Party).

Labour Party (1997) *Because Britain Deserves Better* (London: Labour Party).

Labour Party (2001) *Ambitions for Britain* (2001 Labour Party Election Manifesto) (London: Labour Party).

Labour Party (2005) *Britain Forward Not Back* (London: Labour Party).

Laming, H. (2003) *The Victoria Climbié Inquiry* (London : TSO).

Lawler, J. M. (1978) *IQ, Heritability and Racism: A Marxist Critique of Jensenism* (London: Lawrence & Wishart).

Lawlor, S. (1988) *Correct Core: Simple Curricula for English, Maths and Science* (London: CPS).

Lawton, D. (1970) 'Preparations for changes in the curriculum', in J. W. Tibble (ed.), *The Extra Year: The Raising of the School Leaving Age* (London: Routledge & Kegan Paul), pp. 97–116.

Lawton, D. (1980) *The Politics of the School Curriculum* (London: Routledge & Kegan Paul.

Lawton, D. (1984) *The Tightening Grip: Growth of Central Control of the School Curriculum,* Bedford Way Paper 21 (London: Institute of Education).

Lawton, D. (1989) *Education, Culture and the National Curriculum* (London: Hodder & Stoughton).

Lawton, D. (2000) 'Overview: citizenship education in context', in D. Lawton, J. Cairns and R. Gardner (eds), *Education for Citizenship* (London: Continuum), pp. 9–13.

Lawton, D. and Gordon, P. (1987) *HMI* (London: Routledge & Kegan Paul).

Layard, R., King, J. and Moser, C. (1969) *The Impact of Robbins* (Harmondsworth: Penguin Books).

Letwin, O. (1988) *Privatising the World* (London: Cassell).

Liberal Democrats (2001) *Freedom, Justice, Honesty* (2001 Liberal Democrat Election Manifesto) (London: Liberal Democrats).

Lowe, R. (1988) *Education in the Post-War Years: A Social History* (London: Routledge).

Mac an Ghaill, M. (1994) *The Making of Men: Masculinities, Sexualities and Schooling* (Buckingham: Open University Press).

MacLeod, D. (1997) 'Softly, softly on grammars', *The Guardian,* 28 January.

Maclure, S. (1988) *Education Re-formed: A Guide to the Education Reform Act 1988* (London: Hodder & Stoughton).

Macpherson, W. (1999) *The Stephen Lawrence Inquiry: Report of an Inquiry by Sir William Macpherson of Cluny* (London: HMSO).

Mandelson, P. and Liddle, R. (1996) *The Blair Revolution: Can New Labour Deliver?* (London: Faber & Faber).

Mandeville, B. (1970 edition) *The Fable of the Bees* (Harmondsworth: Penguin).

Mansell, W. (2002) 'Winning over teachers was the toughest job of all', *The Times Educational Supplement,* 26 April.

Mansell, W. (2005) 'Playing politics with our exams', *The Times Educational Supplement,* 25 February.

Mansell, W. (2007) *Education by Numbers: The Tyranny of Testing* (London: Politico's).

Manzer, R. A. (1970) *Teachers and Politics: The Role of the National Union of Teachers in the Making of National Educational Policy in England and Wales since 1944* (Manchester: Manchester University Press).

Marquand, D. (1988) *The Unprincipled Society: New Demands and Old Politics* (London: Jonathan Cape).

Marsden, W. (1989) "'All in a good cause": geography, history and the politicisation of the curriculum in 19th and 20th century England', *Journal of Curriculum Studies,* Vol. 21, No. 6, pp. 509–26.

Matheson, D. (2000) 'Scottish Education: myths and mists', in D. Phillips (ed.), *The Education Systems of the United Kingdom* (Wallingford: Symposium Books), pp. 63–84.

McPherson, A. and Raab, C. (1988) *Governing Education: A Sociology of Policy since 1945* (Edinburgh: Edinburgh University Press).

McPherson, A. and Willms, J. D. (1988) 'Comprehensive schooling is better and fairer', *Forum,* Vol. 30, No. 2 (Spring), pp. 39–41.

Ministry of Education (1944) *Education Act, 1944* (London: HMSO).

Ministry of Education (1951) *Education, 1900–1950,* Cmnd 8244 (London: HMSO).

Ministry of Education (1959) *Fifteen to Eighteen* (Report of the Central Advisory Council for Education: The Crowther Report) (London: HMSO).

Ministry of Education (1963a) *Half Our Future* (The Newsom Report) (London: HMSO).

Ministry of Education (1963b) *Higher Education: A Report of the Committee appointed by the Prime Minister under the Chairmanship of Lord Robbins, 1961–63,* Cmnd 2154 (London: HMSO).

Morgan, K.O. (1984) *Labour in Power, 1945–1951* (Oxford: Clarendon Press).

Morris, E. (2002a) *Transforming Secondary Education: The Middle Years* (London: DfES).

Morris, E. (2002b) 'Why comprehensives must change', *The Observer,* 23 June.

Mortimore, P. (1998) 'A big step backward', *Education Guardian,* 24 March.

Moss, P. and Penn, H. (1996) *Transforming Nursery Education* (London: Paul Chapman).

Mountfield, A. (1991) *State Schools: A Suitable Case for Charity?* (London: Directory of Social Change Publications).

Nash, I. (1988) 'CTCs forced to alter tack', *The Times Educational Supplement,* 17 June.

National Assembly for Wales (2001) *The Learning Country: A Paving Document: A Comprehensive Education and Lifelong Learning Programme to 2010 in Wales* (Cardiff: National Assembly for Wales).

NCC (1990) *Curriculum Guidance 3: The Whole Curriculum* (York: NCC).

NYEC (1974) *Unqualified, Untrained and Unemployed* (Report of a working party set up by the NYEC) (London: HMSO).

OECD (1975) *Review of National Policies for Education: Educational Development Strategy in England and Wales* (Paris: OECD).

Ofsted (Office for Standards in Education) (2004) *Annual Report of Her Majesty's Chief Inspector of Schools 2003–4* (London: TSO).

Ozga, J. (1999) 'Two nations? Education and social inclusion–exclusion in

Scotland and England', *Education and Social Justice*, Vol. 1, No 3 (Summer), pp. 44–64.

Passmore, B. (2001) 'Downing Street is watching you', *The Times Educational Supplement*, 28 September.

Paterson, L. (2002) 'Scotland' in L. Gearon (ed.), *Education in the United Kingdom* (London: David Fulton), pp. 29–39.

Patten, J. (1992) 'Who's afraid of the "S" word?', *New Statesman and Society*, 17 July, pp. 20–1.

Pedley, R. (1963) *The Comprehensive School* (Harmondsworth: Penguin Books).

Phillips, R. (1998) *History Teaching, Nationhood and the State: A Study in Educational Politics* (London: Cassell).

Phillips, R. and Harper-Jones, G. (2003) 'Whatever next? Education policy and New Labour: the first four years, 1997–2001', *British Educational Research Journal*, Vol. 29, No. 1 (February), pp. 125–32.

Plaskow, M. (1985) 'A long view from the inside', in M. Plaskow (ed.), *Life and Death of the Schools Council* (Lewes: Falmer Press), pp. 1–13.

Plummer, G. (2000) *Failing Working-Class Girls* (Stoke-on-Trent: Trentham Books).

Pring, R. (1983) *Privatization in Education* (London: RICE, Right to a Comprehensive Education).

Pring, R. (1984) *Personal and Social Education in the Curriculum: Concepts and Content* (London: Hodder & Stoughton).

Pring, R. (1986) 'Privatization of education', in R. Rogers (ed), *Education and Social Class* (Lewes: Falmer Press), pp. 65–82.

Pring, R. (1987) 'Privatization in education', *Journal of Education Policy*, No. 2, October–December, pp. 289–99.

QCA (2000) *Curriculum Guidance for the Foundation Stage* (London: QCA/DfES).

Raffe, D. (2000) 'Investigating the education systems of the United Kingdom', in D. Phillips (ed.), *The Education Systems of the United Kingdom* (Wallingford: Symposium Books), pp. 9–28.

Raggatt, P. and Evans, M. (eds) (1977) *Urban Education 3: The Political Context* (London: Ward Lock Educational, in association with The Open University Press).

Raison, T. (1976) *The Act and the Partnership: An Essay on Educational Administration in England* (Centre for Studies in Social Policy) (London: Bedford Square Press).

Ranson, S. (1984) 'Towards a tertiary tripartism: new codes of social control and the 17+', in P. Broadfoot (ed.), *Selection, Certification and Control: Social Issues in Educational Assessment* (Lewes: Falmer Press), pp. 221–44.

Ranson, S. (1994) *Towards the Learning Society* (London: Cassell).

Rees, G. and Stroud, D. (2001) 'Creating a mass system of higher education', in R. Phillips and J. Furlong (eds), *Education, Reform and the State: Twenty-Five Years of Politics, Policy and Practice* (London: Routledge Falmer), pp. 72–86.

Reid, I. (1998) *Class in Britain* (Cambridge: Polity).

Rogers, R. (1980) 'The myth of independent schools', *New Statesman*, 4 January.

Rogers, M. and Migniulo, F. (2007) *A New Direction: A Review of the School Academies Programme* (London: TUC).

Russell, J. (2008) 'The NUT has cried wolf too often, but this time it's right', *The Guardian*, 26 March.

Salter, B. and Tapper, T. (1981) *Education, Politics and the State: The Theory and Practice of Educational Change* (London: Grant McIntyre).

SCAA (1993) *The National Curriculum and its Assessment: Final Report* (London: SCAA).

SCAA (1996) *Nursery Education: Desirable Outcomes for Children's Learning on Entering Compulsory Education* (London: SCAA).

SCCC (1999) *A Curriculum Framework for Children 3 to 5* (Dundee: Scottish Consultative Council on the Curriculum).

Schools Council (1971) *Choosing a Curriculum for the Young School Leaver* (Working Paper No 33) (London: Evans/Methuen Educational).

Schools Council (1975) *The Whole Curriculum 13–16* (Working Paper No. 53) (London: Evans/Methuen Educational).

Schultz, T. (1961) 'Investment in human capital', *American Economic Review,* No. 51 (March), pp. 1–17.

Scott, K. (2001) 'Brave hearts', *Education Guardian,* 9 October.

Scruton, R. (1980) *The Meaning of Conservatism* (London: Macmillan).

Secondary School Examinations Council (1943) *Curriculum and Examinations in Secondary Schools* (The Norwood Report) (London: HMSO).

SED (1965) *Reorganisation of Secondary Education on Comprehensive Lines* (Circular 600) (Edinburgh: Scottish Education Department).

Seldon, A. (1986) *The Riddle of the Voucher: An Inquiry into the Obstacles to Introducing Choice and Competition in State Schools,* Hobart Paper No. 21 (London: IEA).

Sewell, T. (1997) *Black Masculinities and Schooling: How Black Boys Survive Modern Schooling* (Stoke-on-Trent: Trentham Books).

Sexton, S. (1987) *Our Schools – A Radical Policy* (London: IEA Education Unit).

Sexton, S. (1995) Interview with the author, 24 November.

Silver, H. (1969) *Robert Owen on Education* (Cambridge: Cambridge University Press).

Simon, B. (1955) *The Common Secondary School* (London: Lawrence & Wishart).

Simon, B. (1960) *The Two Nations and the Educational Structure, 1780–1870* (London: Lawrence & Wishart).

Simon, B. (1981) 'The primary school revolution: myth or reality?', in B. Simon and J. Willcocks (eds), *Research and Practice in the Primary Classroom* (London: Routledge & Kegan Paul), pp. 7–25.

Simon, B. (1991) *Education and the Social Order, 1940–1990* (London: Lawrence & Wishart).

Slater, J. (2001) 'Wales: a privatisation-free zone', *The Times Education Supplement,* 7 September.

Smithers, R. (2004) 'Capita's school deal under fire', *The Guardian*, 2 October.

Stone, M. (1981) *The Education of the Black Child in Britain: The Myth of Multiracial Education* (London: Fontana).

Sutton Trust (2000) *Entry to Leading Universities* (London: Sutton Trust).

Tawney, R.H. (1931) *Equality* (London: Unwin Books).

TGAT (1987) *Report of the Task Group on Assessment and Testing* (London: DES).

Thatcher, M. (1987) Speech to the 1987 Conservative Party Conference.

Thatcher, M. (1992) 'Don't undo my work', *Newsweek*, 27 April, pp. 14–15.

Thatcher, M. (1993) *The Downing Street Years* (London: HarperCollins).

Thomson, R. (1993) 'Unlikely alliances: the recent politics of sex education', in J. Bristo and A. R. Wilson (eds), *Activating Theory: Lesbian, Gay, Bisexual Politics* (London: Lawrence & Wishart), pp. 219–45.

Tomlinson, S. (2001) *Education in a Post-Welfare Society* (Buckingham: Open University Press).

Tomlinson, S. (2005) *Education in a Post-Welfare Society* (2nd edn) (Buckingham: Open University Press).

Tomlinson, S. (2006) 'Another day, another White Paper', *Forum*, Vol. 48, No. 1 (Spring), pp. 49–53.

Wadsworth, J. (2002) 'Nursery education: the current state of play', *Forum*, Vol. 44, No. 2 (Summer), pp. 55–8.

Walford, G. (1990) *Privatisation and Privilege in Education* (London: Routledge).

Wallace, R. G. (1981) 'The origins and authorship of the 1944 Education Act', *History of Education*, Vol. 10, No. 4, pp. 283–90.

Warnock, M. (1980) 'A flexible framework', *The Times Educational Supplement*, 26 September.

Watkins, P. (1993) 'The National Curriculum: an agenda for the nineties', in C. Chitty and B. Simon (eds), *Education Answers Back: Critical Responses to Government Policy* (London: Lawrence & Wishart), pp. 70–84.

Weston, P. (1977) *Framework for the Curriculum: A Study in Secondary Schooling* (Slough: NFER).

White, J. (1975) 'The end of the compulsory curriculum', in *The Curriculum* (The Doris Lee Lectures), Studies in Education (new series) 2, Institute of Education, University of London, pp. 22–39.

White, M. and Taylor, M. (2005) 'Shake-up will give schools independence', *The Guardian*, 26 October.

Wilby, P. (2006) 'A delay on the road to meritocracy', in G. Dench (ed.), *The Rise and Rise of Meritocracy* (Oxford: Blackwell Publishing), pp. 214–20.

Wilby, P. and Midgley, S. (1987) 'As the New Right wields its power', *The Independent*, 23 July.

Wilkinson, J.E. (1999), 'Pre-school education in the UK', in D. Matheson and I. Grosvenor (eds), *An Introduction to the Study of Education* (London: David Fulton), pp. 42–58.

Willetts, D. (1987) 'The role of the Prime Minister's Policy Unit', *Public Administration*, No. 65, pp. 443–54.

Wintour, P. (2002) 'Protect us from politicisation says top civil servant', *The Guardian*, 27 March.

Wolf, A. (2002) 'Will vocational GCSEs bring credibility to the alphabet soup of qualifications?', *Education Guardian*, 28 May.

Woodward, W. (2001) 'Great Wales', *Education Guardian*, 2 October.

Woodward, W. (2002) 'Boys' GCSE failures spark new "lads" row', *The Guardian*, 22 August.

Woolcock, N. (2008) 'Authors unite against early literacy, *The Times*, 24 July.
Wragg, T. (1976) 'The Lancaster Study: its implications for teacher training', *British Journal of Teacher Education*, Vol. 2, No. 3, pp. 281–90.
Young, H. (1989) *One of Us: A Biography of Margaret Thatcher* (London: Macmillan).
Young, H. (1993) 'Times long gone', *The Guardian*, 6 July.
Young, H. (2002) 'The Blairites have wrecked the best of the Civil Service', *The Guardian*, 28 February.

Index

Contents

List of Figures

Acknowledgements

It is impossible to do justice to all those who have contributed to this volume. In one sense it is a tribute to all who have worked in the Tourism and Recreation Research Unit and whose contributions are acknowledged in the various publications on page 240. Pride of place, however, must go to Mrs Sharyn Reilly for the part she has played in the production of this book. Mrs Reilly has done a vast amount of preparatory work in checking references and locating and abstracting publications; she has received, checked and made intelligible the authors' manuscripts; prepared and checked tables and illustrations; acted as intermediary between the authors and provided the spur that has brought the book from rough draft to finished manuscript.

Another major contribution has been made by Mrs Mona Robertson, the Unit's secretary, who has typed or co-ordinated the typing of many drafts and coped with typical academic scrawls. Mrs Robertson has had the capable assistance of Caroline Czoski and Monica Barry who have both helped with the typing. In addition, the authors are most grateful to those outside the Unit who have helped the book forward, notably the staff of the Regional Computing Centre, especially Mr W. Gordon, Assistant Service Manager, Mr Colin Davies, Mr Dave Sturgess and the operating staffs of the IBM 360/50 and ICL 4/75; the staff of the Department of Geography, especially Mrs S. Allan, Mrs P. Paterson and Mrs P. Robertson, secretaries, and Messrs A. Carson Clark, A. Bradley and R. Harris of the cartographic and reprographic unit; and the staff of the Research Centre for the Social Sciences, under Mr J. Nimmo. Essential, too, has been the work of others in this field, on whose publications the authors have drawn extensively, notably Professor H.B. Rodgers, Professor J. Allan Patmore, Mr K.K. Sillitoe, Dr M. Young and Professor P. Willmott, the North West Sports Council and the North Regional Planning Committee.

The authors also wish to acknowledge with gratitude the financial support provided by a number of bodies, for without this neither the book nor the studies on which it is based would have been possible: the Natural Environment and Social Science Research Councils; the Countryside Commission for Scotland; the Forestry Commission; the Highlands and Islands Development Board; the Scottish Tourist Board; the local authorities that participated in the studies; and the University of Edinburgh, which has provided a home for the Unit, much indirect support and access to a range of facilities. Many of the staffs of these different organisations have contributed in various ways and their help is gratefully acknowledged.

We would wish to record our appreciation of the work of our colleague Mike Owen, who has shared with us the joys and tribulations of the extensive research programme that the Unit has implemented over the last six years, and Steve Dowers, the Unit's Systems Analyst, who has undertaken most of the computing. Our sincere thanks are also due to Sheila Coppock who has contributed to the book in various ways, especially by casting a critical eye on professional jargon and ambiguity, so helping to make the text more readable and comprehensible. Lastly our thanks are due to our families for tolerating the neglect which that spare-time occupation, academic authorship, inevitably brings. No doubt they are all too well aware of the paradox that research in leisure and recreation leaves no time for recreation and leisure for the researchers.